Endorsements

MW00811614

"**I love this book.** Esther's story is amazing, her writing is captivating, and her deep faith and wisdom shine through each and every page. *Miracles Against the Wind* is definitely chicken soup for all of our souls!"

— **Jack Canfield,** co-author of the #1 New York Times bestselling *Chicken Soup for the Soul®* series and *The Success Principles™*

"Esther Kurniawan-Hauser, a Chinese-Indonesian, has written a fun read about growing from childhood to young adulthood in turbulent times. Her stories illustrate the clear hand of God's leading and intervening in the circumstances of an out-of-the-ordinary life. **I didn't put her manuscript down until I finished reading.**"

— **Bob Moffitt,** author of *Could Evangelism Lead to Sin,* co-author of *If Jesus were Mayor,* teacher, Founder and Director of Harvest Foundation, Phoenix, AZ

"**A very inspirational and engaging memoir.** As a young child, Esther Kurniawan-Hauser lived through tumultuous times in her native Indonesia. From an ethnic Chinese family, she describes the discrimination and difficulty during the postwar period and the struggle her country encountered after emancipation from the Dutch. Her deep beliefs in Divine intervention and her ever present faith provided her with the miracles she writes about in the book. Esther's life serves as a role model for young women by her commitment to family values and solid work ethic."

— **Dr. Marsha H. Lupi**, retired professor and former interim Dean at University of North Florida.

"This first in a series of autobiographical novels by author Esther Kurniawan-Hauser held my interest from beginning to end, in particular her vivid descriptions of the first years of her life in Indonesia. As the title suggests, her story is deeply faith-based, and that faith guided her through often perilous times. **I recommend this book to anyone with an interest in history and diverse cultures. And, yes, miracles abound!**"

— **Camille Cira**, author of 8 novels and Leader of the Carlsbad, CA Senior Center Writers' Group

"**Amazing faith journey. This awesome true life story is testimony that miracles are real and that prayers truly work.** Esther's great inspirational stories of her many encounters with the divine when God revealed himself through dreams and visions give hope to all who may at times have doubts. Her deep trust and belief in Him and the power of prayer guided her wherever her destiny took her, through sickness and downturns, yet she never wavered. I applaud her honesty in sharing her insights and encouraging and renewing her readers' faith through her personal experiences."

— **Marina Shakour Haber**, author of *Dream a Better Dream: Change your mind to Save the World*

"**A brave life journey that reveals the powers hidden in the miracles of life.** For many people, 'miracles' are something they read about in a fairy tale, but in this heart wrenching and mind illuminating life story beautifully told by Esther, the reader is taken on a journey that restores their faith in the power of belief and in the miracles of God."

— **Tony J. Selimi**, international speaker and author of the #1 international best-selling book *A Path to Wisdom*

"One can't help but be inspired by a God who is alive and actively pursues His creation. **Esther's story is a compelling journey of miracles, riveting suspense and joyous victory.** You will be touched and fall deeper in love with God's masterful craftsmanship. He not only seeks and saves the lost, but also fulfills dreams and destiny far better than we can imagine. This book is a reminder that the Lord is Good. He is faithful to complete what He has begun. I look forward to the movie version of this book."

— **Josiah Dela Torre**, Founder, Spark Digital Inc., Philippines

"**Refreshing, delightful, a story of miracles. This well-written tale is told with grace and style.** The story and adventures of a girl with Indonesian-Chinese origin, Esther grew and matured in a variety of south-Asian cultures. Told simply and directly, often in conversations, this book provides a realistic picture of her day-to-day encounters with ways of life that are rapidly disappearing except in the most remote areas. A valuable personal portrait of past times and family values— this is a unique and must read story."

— **Land Wayland**, Immigration attorney and visitor to more than 50 countries (including 45 trips to China) spanning over 40 years

"Reading Esther's story made me smile, and I feel happy. People will feel strongly her faith in God and God's presence in her. Meeting her husband was definitely the gift of God to her." **A must read.**

— **Edna Seckel**, Retired Sales Assistant for Cosmetics and Chanel in Hawaii, and Expo Design Center, Huntington Beach, CA

"**A page turner and inspiring memoir.** Esther's story is a delightful tale of an Indonesian-Chinese Christian girl, born and raised in the Muslim country of Indonesia. She lives with a God who answers prayers in detailed and miraculous ways. **If you want to be inspired and encouraged about the God who sees you, read this book!**"

— **Dr. Hal Seed**, Lead Pastor of New Song Church, Author of *The God Questions, The Bible Questions* and *I Love Sundays*

"**A marvelous tale of personal faith.** This book is filled with humor and conflict, which makes for an intriguing adventure and an enjoyable read. Esther's perseverance in writing her memoirs of early Indonesian life when the Japanese invaded her home country will inspire her readers. The struggle to put into words her experiences was not easy since English is not her native language. But with the help of our writing critique group, she advanced her writing skills to a remarkable degree."

— **Richard DellOrfano**, Leader of the Writers Critique Club, San Marcos, CA

"**Incredible faith, and a great read. Definitely a journey with God's grace.** God was there at every step of the way since Esther was a young girl. Her life seemed without concerns as her belief makes God close to her."

— **Veronica Hutapea**, Secretary, English Department Alumni, Christian University of Indonesia, Jakarta, Indonesia. Founder and Chairlady of Land and Nation Group, a foundation to assist 1000 students with scholarships.

"**Readers will be inspired and fascinated** by Esther Kurniawan-Hauser's journey. **A remarkable story of faith, courage, and a belief in miracles** brought her from Jakarta to Bali and, with God's help, to the United States. *Miracles against the Wind* is a vivid account of an ethnic Indonesian-Chinese girl's life growing up in Indonesia through turbulent times."

— **Wanda McLaughlin**, Member of the Writer's Critique Club, San Marcos, CA

"An inspiring and fascinating story for dreamers who look out into the stars to find a way to get there! I highly recommend reading this captivating journey of Esther Kurniawan-Hauser."

— **Miriam Day**, member of the Writers Critique Group, San Marcos, CA

"There is synergy to Esther's wisdom – and it comes alive in the pages of *Miracles Against the Wind*. It reminds us that we are not alone as we walk in the darkness. All writing is spiritual. Sometimes it can elevate a story into something beyond words and sentences. I have a love of inspirational memoirs, a natural bias, and this is a nice addition to my collection."

— **Richard Campbell**, co-author of *Writing Your Legacy: The Step-by-Step Guide to Crafting Your Life Story*

"This book is absolutely fascinating. It will take you on quite the journey. here are so many life's lessons to be learned. The biggest take away from this book, for me, was about faith, trust and relationship with Jesus. Esther captured it well.

—**Terri Williams Klapf**, Co-Owner of Out of the Box Coaching, a Real Estate Investment services company.

Miracles
Against the Wind

Esther Kurniawan-Hauser

Dedicated to My Parents

Khouw Eng Hoe
(a.k.a. Edward Hardja Kurniawan)

Who taught me dignity, honesty, pride in
our Chinese heritage, to never give up
and always stay focused.

Lena Tan
(a.k.a. Lena Jonathan)

From whom I learned to be creative, always singing, positive in my outlook
and to never waver in my faith. Her words of wisdom will be with me forever.

This story is their legacy.

Acknowledgments

A special thank you to:

Camille Cira, an author in her own right. My editor, my Good Samaritan, who helped me night and day to meet the deadline **Farah A. Hauser**, my daughter-in-law, who had patiently walked me through the creation of my website. **Phil G. Hauser**, my husband, who read my stories tirelessly and gave valuable contribution of ideas.

The San Marcos Writers Critique Club, who kept me focused and on track. **Miriam Day**, my sincere thanks for introducing me to the group and invaluable help to improve my writing. **Michael McLeod**, my greatest appreciation to my writing mentor for the first eight months, who guided me through the process of becoming the author I am today. **Richard DellOrfano**, who believed in me and my story, and said my book will create a splash in the spiritual world. **Marsha H. Lupi**, my special proofreader/editor, who left no stone unturned. **Clive Gill**, my thanks for introducing me to the Pro Writing Aid software program in order for me to write better. **Wanda McLaughlin**, **Della Arms**, **Devan Crable**, **Gary Wallace** and **Woodrow Wilson** (Woody) for their tireless critique to help me improve my writing.

Endorsers

Bob Moffitt, Marina Shakour Haber, Marsha H. Lupi, Camille Cira, Land Weyland, Josiah Dela Torre (Philippines), Veronica Hutapea, UKI Alumni, Jakarta, Indonesia, Edna Seckel, Richard DellOrfano, Wanda McLaughlin, Miriam Day, Dr. Hal Seed, Richard Campbell, Terri Williams Klapf, and Tony J. Selimi.

The Quantum Leap Team

A special thanks to the invaluable coaching, guidance and encouragement of **Steve** and **Bill Harrison**, **Martha Bullen** for tirelessly editing parts of my book and providing publishing guidance, **Geoffrey Berwind** for a great mission statement, **Brian T. Edmonson**, for his tips on creating a good website, and **Raia King** for advice on marketing and business. You all have made this book a reality.

Mastermind Team

A special mention to **Jack Canfield**, who took the time to read my manuscript and told our group, "It's a wonderful book." **Steve Harrison**, who encouraged me to tell my story and called me *The Miracle Worker*. Members of the Mastermind team, **Vincent James** and **Joann Pierdomenico**, **Nicolas Hauff**, **John Bellami**, **Christian Gregory**, **Amenoffi**, **Elizabeth Trinkaus**, **Blair French**, **Renae Baker**, **Janis Butler**, **Stephen Davis**, **Robyn DeLong**, and **Jonathan Yatsky** for your words of wisdom.

Thank you very much to all of you. Without your help this book would not have been published.

Table of Contents

Introduction

I still remember the tropical island that was my earliest home as a fairy tale place, fascinating and mysterious.

"Mammie, I can fly," I called out, rushing to my mother in the living room.

"What? Who told you that?" my mammie (pronounced mummy, meaning mother in Dutch) asked.

"In my dream. What does it mean?" I asked.

"If it's one time, it's nothing. Just a dream."

"No, mammie, I often dream of flying. All I need to do is jump, and off I fly."

My mother paused and sighed. "Then you have a desire to fly high like an eagle and soar to distant shores," she said.

"I can fly out of here?" I asked.

"Yes, you can. You need a lot of preparation. Most important, learn English."

"I can't speak Dutch? I know Dutch and Indonesian."

"Yes, but the international world speaks English," my mother replied.

And so my journey began, and with it the many miracles that guided my path.

I became my family's breadwinner at 21, and found myself in many unusual situations. Just one of them was to carry an airline bag filled with 82 million rupiah into a war zone to help a deteriorating church and its community near Medan, North Sumatra. I remember my grandaunt's outburst at the time, "Who do you think you are? The daughter of Jesus Christ?"

My goal in writing this book is to take readers on a journey that restores their faith in the power of belief and in God's miracles.

I had the desire to fly high, soar with the eagles, and so I did. You can too.

Chapter 1: My Early Years

I began my life in Jakarta, Indonesia, a Christian in a 90% Muslim country, its culture as diverse in every sense as the land I now call home.

Indonesia is an archipelago, comprised of five main islands, Java, Sumatra, Kalimantan, Sulawesi and West Irian, between Australia and South Asia, Singapore and Philippines to the North.

Jakarta is on the island of Java and serves as the Capital of Indonesia. One prominent national art form is woodcarvings, the best in the world. Jakarta, Indonesia, was my hometown until I lived in Los Angeles, and in Oceanside, California.

This tale follows my early life and young adulthood as the daughter of a traditional Indonesian-Chinese family of seven: father, mother, three younger brothers, myself and one older sister. It encompasses my deep faith in our Lord throughout those years, a faith I sustain to this day, and, as the title of my story suggests, the miracles He has showered upon me along the way.

So, I begin at the beginning!

"Hurry," said my sister Tina. "It will rain. Mom doesn't like you to get wet."

She waved and summoned me with her hand. We were on the way home from school. Dark and menacing clouds were forming in the sky. Tina's responsibility was to make sure we didn't get caught in the rain.

Tina was a sturdy girl with black hair, big bright eyes, taller than me. She also walked faster, and I had a tough time keeping pace with her. I was six years old, and my sister eight.

"Why?" I asked.

"Because you suffer from allergies and can seriously sicken from a simple cold. Come on, hurry. The rain is coming."

I looked at the sky; no doubt a storm was brewing. Tina didn't stop. She kept on walking, past Thalia, the movie theater.

"I need to stop by the theater first," I insisted. "Mammie (pronounced Mummy, the Dutch word for mother) wanted me to find out about the new movie. It'll only take a moment. Wait for me."

Tina didn't listen and strode on.

I rushed up the theater steps and went straight to the poster board. I looked at tonight's showing: *The Three Musketeers; actors were Gene Kelley, Lana Turner, and June Allyson.*

Oh yes, one more thing…was it in color?

I searched the poster board again. There it was…*color by Technicolor*. I stopped for a moment and tried to remember anything else my mother had asked me to look for. *Check*, I said to myself, and ran to catch up with my sister.

Just then, the skies dropped their load and I was caught in the downpour. No sign of my sister who was somewhere ahead of me so I ran home as fast as I could.

When I arrived, I heard Tina telling my mother she had warned me of the impending storm. "You told her to go to Thalia to find out about the new movie, Mam," I heard my sister report.

I was soaking wet. My mother told me to change my wet clothes and she made sure Tina and I drank some hot cocoa.

"Did you find out about the new movie?" she asked while drying my hair.

"Yes," I replied. I gave her all the information. I pronounced the words the way I read them—Yoon Alison, for one. With each mispronounced word, my mother corrected me.

"Good job," she finally said, "Next time, when you pass the theater, watch for the rain."

I nodded.

World War II was over for us in 1945. English books were hard to find. Reading the title of movies was one way to learn English. I became fascinated with the language.

My father introduced English to Tina and me through comic books which he enjoyed reading: Captain Marvel, the Lone Ranger, Superman, among others. As we grew older, Shakespeare comic books became available and were added to our library.

Every Sunday, our father took us to see re-run movies of Roy Rogers, Gene Autry, and Tom Mix. I developed an attraction to the lives of cowboys. They lived outdoors under the sky, watched the stars, and sang by the campfire. A fantastic life, I thought. So much so, that the adventures of these cowboys became a regular feature of my dreams.

As a child I never saw green pastures in my hometown, Jakarta. Sleeping outdoors meant sleeping on the street.

"Will we ever have a campfire, Mam?"

"No, and you know why," my mother said.

We lived in a small house, with a small porch connected to the living room through an entry way. Two bedrooms and a dining room, and a bathroom with an open-to-the-sky ceiling in the back part of the house,

Noor, our maid, cooked on a wood burning stove, using chopped wood which my father stacked on one side of the front porch. She occupied a small place in the corner and slept on a bamboo bed with a thin mattress. We didn't have running water and had to fill our three water barrels with rainwater.

Our house was the second one on the left of ten small houses facing each other, five on the left and five on the right, separated by a 10'wide street - a row of small houses for less than modest income families. It was a dead-end street, our playground, and bicycles were the only means of transportation.

My father's favorite pastime was reading comic books to my sister and me while we sat on either side of his armchair. I dared not interrupt him while he was reading.

Neighbors would come out or pop their heads through their doors. "There he goes again, with his foreign books and foreign language." They were used to my father's loud voice and understood it was reading time.

When my father was at work, I would sit in his chair and re-read the comic book of the previous day, pronouncing the words as I thought he had, imitating him.

One day my mother, hearing me, peered through the window. "What are you doing?" she asked.

"I'm reading this comic book," and lifted it to show her.

I sat next to her while she glanced through the pages "You need to improve the pronunciation," she insisted. "Are you interested in learning?"

I was excited and clapped my hands, "Can I, Mammie? Yes, please."

Comic books became my constant companions. I flew with Mary Marvel, and no distance was too far. The best comic character before Superman was Captain Marvel; Mary was his sister. Both could fly...and in my mind, so could I.

There were no schools open during the Japanese Occupation (1942 – 1945) and for a few more years. My parents home-schooled my sister Tina and me until they could register us at the new school in 1947. We had survived the war.

Indonesia was once the Dutch-East Indies; the Dutch ruled for 350 years. But on August 17, 1945, Indonesia became a Republic. Sukarno, the new President, and Mohammad Hatta, as Vice President, were recognized as the dynamic duo. Dutch remained the main language until 1950, when they handed over the government to the Indonesians.

Indonesian was the language used by domestic help. President Sukarno chose it as the national language. One nation, one language and one national anthem called "Indonesia Raya." Indonesia has over 13,000 islands and dialects; a national language would unite the country.

The Dutch language disappeared from the schools' curriculum but I continued to speak Dutch with my parents.

My earnest desire to learn English caused a stir in my parents' minds and my father questioned my seriousness. My mother said, "Let her try. She needs to satisfy her obsession with the language."

"Let's start here," my mother said. "First, you need to understand the alphabet."

"A, b, c." She pronounced each letter one by one. I followed her instructions. Afterwards came, "I, my, me, you."

Besides learning words, I also learned to count in English. My mother did not have to nag me to do my English homework because I always looked forward to the lessons.

Foreign words were like music to my ears. They were enchanting. I built my inventory of English words. Memorizing them was another challenge.

In 1947, a school opened in our location. It was a subsidized school sponsored by a group of wealthy Chinese. Most attendees were Chinese, with a few Indonesians.

Native Indonesian families could not afford the tuition fees, due to their poor incomes. They went to public schools, supported by the government. Tuition was free, and most students were Muslims.

My mother would take us to school. Sometimes we walked. Sometimes we rode in a pedicab, a three-wheeler pedaled by a man behind its passengers. Whenever we walked home, we passed the old movie theater, Thalia.

Often we stopped to read the glass-encased posters; lacking books in English, the posters were the substitutes my mother used to teach the language. And so it went:

"You see this poster board? How many are there?" she would ask.

"Five," I answered.

"Do all of them have the same movie on them?"

"They are all different, Mam. That one over there is for next week. The one by the main entrance is the only one with actors."

"All right. Now, how do you know whether the movie is in color?"

All I could do was shrug. "I don't know."

"Let's check this one," she said, pointing to the poster, "Go down to the bottom of the poster, and point at the words – *color by Technicolor*. That means the movie is in color, see that?"

"Oh." I nodded.

My weekly assignment when school started was to read the titles of the movies and ask for help with the words I did not understand. My parents didn't pressure me. I was only six years old.

Several years later, in 1950, my father came home carrying a package.

"What is that?" I asked.

"A radio."

"A radio?" I clapped my hands. As long as I could remember, we had no radio. My father then explained that radio networks were operational again after years of fixing and rebuilding the wires.

"Come to think of it," I continued, "why didn't we have a radio?"

My mother sighed. Recalling the past depressed her. My mother hated the Japanese occupation. During those three years the Japanese wrecked the network. They forbade us from listening to any news.

"The Japanese controlled the country by instilling fear in everyone," my mother said. "We remained indoors after sundown, and there was a curfew. The only way the Japanese could remain in control was to deprive us of all communications.

"Thieves were cautious. Should the Japanese catch them, they would chop off the thieves' hands. Murderers had to watch out—when the police caught them, the murderers had to dig their own graves. One shot to the head and they fell into their own burial ground. No chance of negotiation, no court appeals. Feeding bad people in jail was a luxury the Japanese couldn't afford."

My mother said the three years during the Japanese occupation were the quietest and most peaceful time.

"We felt safe for a while, until one evening...."

Chapter 2: The Raid

"What happened, Mam?" I asked.
The following is my mother's story.

"Your father and I were astonished when we heard loud banging on the door. We were relaxing in the living room reading comic books.

"'Open the door! We are Japanese officers here to inspect your house.'

"'Why?'" your father said. He jumped up from his seat. The frown on his face showed profound concern. 'Don't they have anything better to do?'

"I was wondering what they wanted when your father threw a glance at me and pointed at the radio.

"'Hide it?' I asked.

"'Pappie spoke quietly: 'No, leave it there. If you hide it, they will think we have something more to hide. It will be even more dangerous. I'm glad the children are asleep.'

"The banging on the door became louder and more impatient."

"'Open the door, or we break it down.'"

"The door opened before your father reached it. Four Japanese officers in uniform, each carrying a rifle, appeared in our small living room and began a search of the house. Noting the radio, they wanted to know whether we had been listening to the news.

"It was a simple radio, with two bandwidths. One for news, and one for music. But It was an old radio and in bad shape, with wires sticking out.

"However, Pappie had ripped the cables and dismantled the connection each time he finished listening. No one would know we could listen to the news.

"The Japanese talked in loud voices. They were shorter than the Chinese and Dutch men. Apparently they thought that by amplifying their voices, they would convey more power and authority.

"The Japanese officer asked, 'Why radio like this? You listen to radio?'

"Your father tried to explain. The Japanese officers motioned him to raise his arms and move away with his back against the wall. They threatened to shoot, another one raised his rifle to be ready to hit him on the head.

"My heart thumped faster, I was very frightened. I tried to calm your father. I gestured by moving my arms downward to show your father he should lower the volume of his voice and stay calm.

"Your father explained: 'Rats did that. They are hungry, want to eat, and chew the wires.' Rats were common sights in houses everywhere.

"'You want radio? Take it!' your father said, and continued to challenge them. He opened the palms of his hands and gestured toward the radio. 'Go on, take it.'

"The Japanese officer looked at the radio and left it alone. The rest of the officers, except for the one who was going through the house, opened cabinets, and did an intensive search.

"Afterward that officer returned to the living room, assembled his men, and conversed in Japanese.

"He talked loudly and rapidly; he scratched his head, shook it, and summoned his companions to follow him.

"One officer watched your father and me. I followed the others with my eyes. making sure they did not disturb you and your sister asleep in the bedroom.

"The officer pointed at the simple furnishings in the living and dining rooms; he opened the bedrooms and pointed at the bunk beds, and continued to the back of the house. They looked up and saw a natural opening-to-the-sky ceiling in the bathroom area. The military officer tried to turn on the water tap. It was dry.

"As you know, we collected barrels of rain water and cooked with chopped firewood.

"The officer pointed at the servant's bed made of bamboo. It had one pillow and a sheet of Indonesian batik serving as a blanket.

"He kept rambling, and all we heard was: 'Ah so! Ah so!' and all the officers nodded in agreement. They scratched and shook their heads, talked a little bit more.

"The leader lifted his right arm and motioned everyone to follow him. 'Sayonara!' Goodbye. He nodded to your father and me, and they left, leaving the radio behind.

"One thing your father and I knew for sure...once the Japanese officers were done: there would be no further inspections. They didn't have sufficient manpower to do the routine inspections and perhaps they realized this was a false alarm.

"We did not speak Japanese," my mother said. "From their gestures, body language, and pointing here and there, they must have concluded we were not rich, and there was no evidence that we were spies. They could have received the wrong information and discovered it was not worth inspecting further.

"After the Japanese left, your father hooked back the wires, and continued listening to the news.

"Our neighbors heard the commotion that night and didn't dare open their doors. They all talked together and asked several questions: 'How did the Japanese know? Who leaked the information?' We were a group of close-knit Chinese families, watching each others' backs. The mystery remained unsolved.

"Your father expressed the following words of wisdom:

"'No need to fight them, we will never win; Outsmart them, that's the answer.'"

Chapter 3: My Parents, Marriage and the Early Years

"Your father and I met at a Christian church, as choir members—I was a soprano, and your father, a bass.

"After a few years singing in the choir, our relationship bloomed into love, and we married in 1939. We received wedding presents from church members, friends and relatives.

"During those years, many businesses went bankrupt. Pappie continued to work part-time at the car repair shop. He could not pursue higher education due to his parents' meagre income.

"With seven brothers and older sister, things were not looking up for farmers, which is in the case of your grandparents. They're running short on funds.

"Playing soccer with his brothers and other children became a pastime, when the school expelled them from class every time they failed to pay tuition. He could speak fluent Dutch and basic English."

My mother excused herself to check on the baby in the bedroom. When she returned, she continued her story. "Compared to Pappie, my parents could support my education through High School. Women had limited opportunities to pursue higher education: Why bother to earn a degree when a woman's future would lead her to the kitchen anyway?

"During the turbulent times, we had no choice but to use our savings. Whenever necessary, I sold my sarongs and the wedding gifts.

"We felt protected in that tiny group of ten small houses. After the raid, we were very careful about any conversations with individuals outside of our community.

"To protect ourselves even more, we formed a neighborhood night watch by playing Mahjong, a card game comprised of tiles decorated with Chinese characters. Rich or poor, it was a popular game among both men and women in the Chinese community. This mahjong game served two purposes. First, to serve as a night watch in our neighborhood and, second, as a source of entertainment.

"We formed a mahjong club. It worked well and before long, the neighboring areas developed their own 'mahjong game neighborhood watch'.

"After three years of Japanese rule, World War II was over for us."

"Was everybody happy?" I asked, as my curiosity grew.

"People had mixed emotions," my mother answered. "It was a challenging time for everyone. We had no clue how and where to start. We all had the same need: find work.

"Indonesia gained its Independence Day on August 17, 1945. During the first years, the country had cleaning up to do. There was unrest everywhere, uncertainty about the future. War camps closed. Dutch and Jewish prisoners returned to the Netherlands or remained in Indonesia. They were searching for their relatives, hoping they had survived. The chaos and grief on people's faces were indescribable.

"Houses were burned, government buildings vandalized, archives destroyed and no schools were available.

"It was heartbreaking, and depressing for many people," my mother said.

"The Dutch occupied the Dutch- East Indies, a name for Indonesia, for over 350 years. They didn't expect Japan to attack.

Japan attacked Singapore, and subdued the British, Afterward they jumped to Indonesia, which is only an hour away by plane from Singapore. They spread themselves too thin.

"The Dutch wasn't prepared for a full force frontal attack by the Japanese, and surrendered as they didn't have sufficient time to call for reinforcement.

"In 1941, Japan bombed Pearl Harbor in America. Pappie said that was a gross mistake. They were cocky. Winning over the British and the Dutch in South Asia was not enough. At the time, America was not involved in the war. But due to this egregious act, America was compelled to join.

One of the Japanese generals stressed his concern that they may have awakened a sleeping giant. Moreover, they didn't expect America to retaliate with two nuclear bombs on Hiroshima and Nagasaki. The war ended because Japan was crippled. Therefore the short stay in South Asia.

"The Japanese stayed for three years, and left Indonesia in 1945.

"It was time to reconstruct and renovate. The Indonesian Government and the Dutch signed a Peace Settlement and the Dutch handed the country back to the Indonesians.

"Merdeka, Merdeka!,' (freedom) the people chanted. Pick up trucks cruised down the streets, honking, and waving the red and white Indonesian flag. Men with fists raised to the sky, chanted 'Merdeka, Merdeka,' after the Japanese surrendered in 1945.

"The excitement went on for days as the Indonesians needed to know they now have a country. Instead of the Dutch- East Indies, the country became the Republic of Indonesia. We resided in Batavia, and the name was changed to Jakarta. Sukarno as President, led the Indonesians to regain and strengthen the economy and communications network.

"Indonesia is comprised of five main islands, 13,000 smaller islands and dialects among the islands' inhabitants. Unity in Diversity became the trademark of Indonesia.

"Sukarno had a degree in Engineering, was an excellent linguist and a strong leader. He was intelligent and a good communicator. For the country to unite, he insisted on adopting and speaking just one Indonesian language.

"Be proud of your language," Sukarno said, and his voice echoed across the nation.

"It would make it easier for traders to communicate with people of the islands, thus boosting more trade and improving the economy.

"It did not mean everything would come to order quickly. The Dutch opined that being so long under Dutch rule and feeling oppressed, Indonesians would have a tough time adjusting to this newfound freedom. They would not even comprehend what to do and how to begin.

"There were still lootings and vandalism everywhere. Law and order was non-existent. The neighborhood mahjong game night-watch continued to serve and help protect the community."

Chapter 4: My Parents Became Christians

We felt secure living in our small block of ten households. There were moments we heard the sirens during the aftermath of the war. I recalled my mother telling my sister and me to crawl under the bed and bite on a rubber eraser, with cotton stuck in our ears. We were relieved as we were free of fear.

The neighbors started to come out of their residences and reach out to each other. They all learned about the Japanese raid and were glad we survived the ordeal.

Until a school could open in our area, my parents provided our education at home.

Deprived of schooling during World War II, many children were older in the first grade. I was six years old, and my sister eight. Some students were even three to four years older.

We could go to school riding a "*becak*" (pronounced bechak), a three-wheeler transportation pedaled by a man. When the weather was nice, my mother picked us up, and we all walked home from school.

I pursued learning English at home.

Private vendors became a common sight. They carried their fresh produce using a thick stick and two big trays balanced on their shoulders. I admired a blind man selling cooked food. He shuffled his way around, and letting his presence known by loudly reciting self-invented rhymes. Mammie always bought something. She said, "Be thankful you are healthy." Vendors always stopped at our house to let my mother choose. They parked under the tree in front of our house. My mother felt blessed, as she could cook according on what she could afford to buy.

After the war, a market opened near the movie theater. However, private vendors continued to serve the local community.

Retail-shops popped up on the main highway, for more exposure. New movies added to the scarce entertainment at the Thalia and Orion theaters. Orion was another movie theater a distance away. Tom and Jerry characters were our friends. We enjoyed Donald Duck, and Shirley Temple movies. The city came alive.

To my mother's relief, my father landed a permanent job at the Department of Economics as one of their department heads. His duties involved taking care of all applications for new retail businesses.

The government needed several creative, smart people. My father was one of them. He spoke Dutch, which was a plus when serving Dutch speaking business prospects.

We enjoyed the time when one of my father's business clients came to the house and brought delicious Chinese food. Sweet and sour fish, fried frog legs, egg fuyong, just to name a few. The whole family ate our first delicious meal since Indonesia's independence.

The owner of a shoe store invited us for a visit. He encouraged my father and mother to choose shoes for everyone in the family. So many choices, colors, and styles.

I asked my mother once: "How many business clients does Pappie have, Mam? They are all very nice, and give us many gifts."

My mother considered the question before responding: "They are all work-related."

I didn't comprehend the business relations part but delighted in their kind-heartedness.

My mother trusted Pak Amat, our 'becak' driver to take my sister and me to school whenever she was occupied with my two younger siblings at home. Pak Amat also picked us up from school. (The word "pak" pronounced 'puck' is a courteous address to male adults, used for Mr. as well).

My school education comprised of learning to read and write in Dutch and Indonesian, and Math. These were compulsory subjects. The State gave us a State exam at the end of every school year, which created a lot of pressure. Those who did not pass had to remain in the same class. Nobody liked the exam.

I continued to check the theater to sharpen my English. Except for comic books, other reading books in English were scarce.

The Dutch language tapered off. Bookstores sold less Dutch books until there were none. There was only one Dutch library called Erasmus Huis or House of Erasmus. My father collected the old reading books and hid them for future use. He realized that one day these books would be extinct.

On Sundays, our family returned to our Sunday activity, going to church in Chinatown. Arriving there, I told my mother that the church looked like a Chinese shrine.

"Well," my mother said, "It was an old Buddhist temple. The Church Board kept the building in its original architecture. They planned to renovate it. However, during the war, the building remained closed. People stayed home.

"An occupied building is always better than an unoccupied one," my mother said. "A church is no threat to anyone. When he was ready to sell, the owner preferred a church as the occupant."

Arriving in our pedicab, we entered the church by passing through an open wrought iron gate. A custodian would close and lock the gates at night to prevent vandalism.

The church contained a sanctuary with long rows of seats. Six doors served as exits, three on each side. Middle and high school age groups used the second floor, with kindergarten and elementary school age groups in rooms on each side of the sanctuary.

I loved stories. Period. I came to know how the world was created according to the Bible. I dreamed I saw God standing in the middle of nowhere, arms lifted and kaboom…land took shape, the sea and waves rolling in to the shores…poof…blue sky, trees. He pointed at the sky…whoosh…sun in the morning, the moon at night. A wonderful place to be. Then, the first man and woman…Adam and Eve. So romantic!

The bell rang. I breathed deep and looked around the room to say '*goodbye, till next Sunday*' to the pictures, and left the church.

At home, I yearned to know more from my parents: how did they know about this building? My mother called it our old church.

I asked my sister Tina, "Do you know how Mammie and Pappie came to this church? How they became Christians?" I followed her to the bedroom. She ignored me.

"Well, did Mammie tell you?" I raised my voice.

I irritated her with my questions, and she yelled at me.

"Why don't you ask them yourself? You, and your constant questions!"

I screamed back: "All right, I will ask. I thought you knew. You are older. And I was only asking a question. You don't have to be so mad." I left her and went to my mother. She was in the kitchen preparing lunch.

"Mam, how did you become a Christian?"

"What question is that?" was my mother's reply. She continued slicing carrots.

My sister caught up with me and interrupted: "That was what I asked her. Why the question?"

My mom examined the vegetables she was taking out of a basket, looked at us and continued with her cooking.

"All right, you two. Stop bickering. If you help me with preparing the vegetables for cooking, I can tell you the story. Agreed?"

"Yes! Agreed!" I said. I took the vegetables from her hand.

My sister did not look so enthusiastic. "Oh well," she said. Tina was assigned to cutting red onions, I cut the white onions (garlic).

"When I was younger," my mother paused, took the vegetables from my hand and put them into in a bowl with water to wash.

"Here, now break the veggies like this. Use your fingers." She showed me how to do it. It was my mother's habit to teach us cooking while telling a story.

I was growing impatient and kept on. "Well, what happened? Who started first? Oma? (grandmother in Dutch). Were Oma and Opa (grandfather in Dutch) already Christians?" I asked.

Mammie continued washing the chicken parts and cut the meat. I prepared the spinach and shredded the corn with a knife. I knew what she would cook.

"It is a bit complicated, and you may not understand. Anyway, I need to go way back when, as a young girl, I lived with my mother and father."

Mammie started the journey of her life. "Your Opa and Oma adopted me." Our eyes opened wide in disbelief, and my sister exclaimed:

"Adopted? All these years? How come you never told us?"

"I am telling you now," she replied.

"My adopted father's name was Piet (Peter in Dutch) Tan (his family name). He had Dutch citizenship. During the years before the war, your Oma could not conceive a baby. Don't ask me why, as I don't know."

My mother paused and looked at my work and my sister's. "Okay, give me the veggies now, and Tina, give me the rest of the spices you prepared for me. All right…red onions, garlic, dried shrimp.

"Where was I? Oh yes, during the adoption Oma and Opa were not Christians yet. As was the common Chinese tradition, they could go to this specific Buddhist shrine. There was a big Buddha statue, hands folded in front of his big tummy, in the middle of the shrine. Whenever a baby was cradled in his hands, it meant that the baby was available for adoption.

"The Chinese believed a child's genes could some times contradict that of his/her parents, especially if their baby was often sick, not strong enough to stay in the same house as the natural parents, and might die. Women who were barren and wanted to adopt a child, could claim the baby. The first woman to make that claim would become his/her new adoptive parent. The new parent could take the baby home." My mother paused. "Tina, give mam the bowl. I need to put this dish in there."

Tina got up and handed her the bowl.

"Wow!" my sister and I were dumbfounded.

"Will the baby see his or her parents again?" we both asked.

"No." My mother sighed. "That is the other condition. They could not see each other again."

"Ever?" we both inquired.

My mother shook her head. "Never."

She added: "That's how I became the adopted daughter of your Opa and Oma."

"Do you know where your real mother is?" I asked.

"No, I knew my two sisters, as they came for a visit after they found out who had adopted me. We kept in contact; however, I never visited my real mother."

"Wash your hands now," she said. "We'll have dinner and continue later if we have time."

Everyone was quiet during dinner. I was thinking of my situation, suffering from allergies and looking unhealthy. *Was I adopted?*

"Why are you so quiet?" my mother asked.

I replied: "Oh, nothing."

After dinner, we did our homework for the next day and went to bed. My mother had promised to continue the story the next day.

I couldn't concentrate at school. I kept asking myself, *am I adopted?*.

Sometimes children take stories too seriously. Anyway, I shared my feelings with friends at school I might be adopted. The news spread like wildfire, and my mother once again was called to the principal's office.

"I told you and Tina only; it was not for the school to know." She added: "You are our daughter, not adopted," while pointing her finger at me. "Do you understand me?"

I nodded.

"We became Christians and we didn't believe in the old traditions, (which she called mumbo jumbo)."

"Yes, but how did you become Christians?"

"My mother, your Oma, wanted to release me from the diseases that may have followed me. She didn't know what to do, until one afternoon a Dutch missionary came for a visit." My mother got up and went to the kitchen.

"What happened then? Are you coming back?" I said in my loudest voice. My mother answered, "I'll be back. Just want to get a cup of coffee."

While adjusting her seat and sipping her hot coffee, my mother added: "His name was Reverend De Groot. A nice, kind man in his forties. He always spoke gently to my mother. Because of his patience in explaining what it means to believe in the Lord God Almighty, your Oma understood the

Christian religion better. She needed to trust someone. She trusted Reverend De Groot.

"He explained to your grandmother that the old Chinese beliefs did not have to be followed and that she should not live in fear. Believing now in the Lord God Almighty, your Oma trusted God to give strength to her and her daughter. 'Pray, and ask for the mercy and grace of God. But you must believe in Him,' he said and left her with a Bible.

"To everyone's surprise, your grandparents and I converted from Buddhism to Christianity. Thus, we went to church, the old church in Chinatown. Your grandmother adopted a second child, Erna, from my uncle. We all knew each other. Erna, your aunt, didn't come from the shrine."

My mother concluded her story, "My father passed away a few years later. I was not sick anymore. And, don't make me visit the principal's office again."

I was relieved to know the heritage of my own Christian belief. No need to be fearful anymore as the Lord God Almighty would give me the strength to overcome all things. I was seven years old.

Chapter 5: Why Ducks Make Circles

There was one final episode with a classmate after my adoption rumors. I asked her whether she knew why ducks make circles in the water. She was annoyed and responded with a shrug.

I called her stupid. She cried and kept on crying. The class became chaotic and disrupted. My mother was once again summoned to the office of the Principal.

Miss Tuti (pronounced tootee), our class teacher, was there together with Mr. Ko, the Principal of the school. Ms. Tuti asked my mother where in the world did I come up with a question like that? She smiled, sat down, and Ms. Tuti offered tea as a courtesy.

Mammie sipped her tea and told the story.

"When Esther was younger, about four years old, my husband took her and Tina, her sister, on a bike ride. Esther sat in the back, and her sister, in front. When Esther stopped talking, my husband knew it was time to go home. Meaning, she had fallen asleep."

"Esther always liked pointing at everything she saw. What is the name of that fruit? Does that flower have a nice scent? Why are the flowers always red?" It was during one of these bike trips that my husband took them to a Chinese Club House, close to our neighborhood."

My mother paused a moment and sipped her tea again. "It was a big mansion, once occupied by a rich Chinese businessman. We lived close to Chinatown. The mansion was of Chinese architectural design and stood in the middle of the grounds, surrounded by lush landscaping with beautiful flowers.

"High wooden gates, and high walls surrounded this house. We couldn't see what was inside, unless we looked through the ceramic peepholes throughout the walls."

"After the war was over in 1945, local businessmen once again took over the building from the Japanese and converted it to a Chinese Club House called Sin Ming Hwee.

"The Board of the Club House opened the place as a Public Park. People could enjoy walking through the lush gardens and sitting by the man-made lake. The Club House could accommodate sports activities and weddings," my mother explained as she sipped her tea.

"Sports included ping pong, badminton, martial arts. Besides weddings, during holidays, families and their children could enjoy puppet shows, and during Chinese New Year, the dragon dance.

"An indoor cafeteria made it convenient for women to buy ready-made food to take home."

More teachers gathered in the Principal's office and grew more intrigued with the history of Chinatown. One of the Club Houses became the Chinese embassy," my mother said.

"There were several ducks swimming in the pond with their ducklings. Esther and her sister were watching them, when my husband asked, 'What are you looking at?' Esther was the first one to answer: 'Oh, those ducks; Pappie, why do ducks make circles in the water?' The question caught my husband by surprise."

The teachers in the room laughed, they were amused. "Well," one of them said, "does anyone here know the answer?"

The teachers looked at each other and shook their heads.

My mother sighed. "So…Esther kept asking anyone who would listen to her story. As of now, she has not received a satisfactory response. "My daughter was telling the truth. She is hungry for information.

"Does this explain the problem? Are we all right now?" my mother asked.

Everyone nodded. My mother got up, thanked them for the tea and left.

The bell rang; it was time to go home. Mammie told the story as we walked together, and I could not stop laughing. It was funny. I clapped my hands, walked backward, and danced around.

"Can you imagine?" I said. "Even the teachers don't know the answer to my question?"

A week later my mother reminded me of the new movie as Tina and I walked out of the house. "I thought I saw the workers at the theater changing the posters," she said.

"All right, Mammie, will do," I answered.

Tina said: "And I'll not wait for her, Mammie. She always takes her time and it's too long to wait for her."

"All right." My mother waved at us. "Watch for the rain."

At school, Ms. Tuty shared with us the delightful meeting she'd had with our mother. She learned a lot about the area of China Town. It was very informative.

I liked Ms. Tuty. A woman in her forties, she had salt pepper hair. She spoke fluent Dutch and had a delightful voice, but not as beautiful as my mother's.

After school, I trudged behind my sister, and kept reminding her I was to read the posters at the theater. Tina kept on walking. She ignored me. "Did you hear what I told Mammie this morning? I won't wait for you."

There was no use reasoning with Tina, so I decided on my own. I always did anyway.

When I saw the new posters, I began to lose track of time. I read: *Midnight in Paradise, Actress Merle Oberon.*

Wow! Her dress was gorgeous and covered with glitters. I would love to have a dress like that, I thought. Who doesn't want to look like a Princess? And who is that handsome guy beside her? Name, what's his name? I pointed with my finger and went all over the poster. I read a strange name "Turhan Bey." Oh well, I will ask my mother later.

Did I have everything? Check. Now I saw people running towards the theater.

I realized I'd taken too much time. I forgot about the rain. Why did it have to rain now? It was such a beautiful day this morning. No time to wait. I put my bag over my head and ran home.

I had just turned onto the street where we lived when I saw my mother coming out of the house holding an umbrella and peering through the rain.

"Mammie, I'm here."

She stopped and looked up, turned around and took my hand. I walked with her under the umbrella.

"All right, you're drenched again," she said. "Change your clothes, put something warm on, and don't forget your socks."

"Why my socks?"

"You may not notice it, but your feet are cold." My mother always noticed things. The hot cocoa would help warm me up.

Tina welcomed me, "I am glad I didn't wait for you."

"Oh, shut up," I hissed back.

The fun was over. I had time to tell my mother through a bout of sneezing about the new movie, and the handsome man with the strange name. My mother knew of him.

She said, "His name is Turhan Bey. He is from Turkey."

My sneezing didn't stop. It developed into a fever with labored breathing. My asthma kicked in. It was a mess.

"Go straight to bed," Mammie said. "I will ask Noor to bring dinner to you." She gave me some aspirin, rubbed my back with Vicks, and I remained in my room.

I didn't want to be sick, it was too close to Christmas. The church would decorate the Christmas tree with lights. The children would receive gifts. I didn't want to miss all those activities.

I miscalculated the seriousness of the cold, and the bout of sneezing. The diseases took a number. First, the cold, next influenza, then a virus set in. It developed into measles, followed by chicken pox.

I frequented Dr. Liem (pronounced Leem), our family doctor, who was always kind and patient. His big house accommodated a private practice and office on the first floor, with family quarters on the second.

My mother told me to listen to him when he discussed my health problems; he was a good doctor. She said to ignore him when he discussed Marxism; he was a Communist.

As the days became weeks, and the weeks became months, Dr. Liem became more quiet and serious. I tired easily and was skin and bones.

When I developed my fourth and final disease, mumps and whooping cough; Dr. Liem didn't lose his composure. He was always considerate and patient. Sometimes, when we ran out of funds, he would take the medicines from his own supplies.

My parents were frantic, not understanding why the illnesses were unstoppable. My sister was healthy, why not their second daughter?

I dreamed about going to the Buddhist shrine. In my dream, I heard my parents say, "So sorry it happened this way. Perhaps our genes are contradicting each other. You are much better off here."

I began to have nightmares.

Chapter 6: God Gave Me Life

"Mammie, what's going on?" I cried out, a faint moan. "I can't get up."

My mother rushed into my bedroom and found me lying on my bed in a splatter of dried blood. My hair clung to the cushion and my pajamas were spotted with blood stains. I had a nose-bleed.

"Oh, my Lord," my mother blurted out. "What happened to you?"

"I don't know, Mam. I can't move."

My sister came running but my mother stopped her, "Remain in the dining room until I find out what's wrong,"

She called out to Noor, our maid, to bring warm water in a bucket, and a clean dry towel. She dipped the towel in the bucket. "Boil more water, Noor, *cepat*…Hurry!"

My mother cleaned the blood from my face, then my hair, freeing it from the pillow. I looked at the bloody towel and cried.

My mother comforted me, "No need to cry, I am just cleaning your face; there's no more blood. You had a nose-bleed last night. Still, it's too much blood." She helped me dress.

"We're going to Dr. Liem again, Mammie?" I asked.

She nodded. I saw the worry on her face.

The Doctor concurred with my mom it was nothing serious. "Just a simple nose-bleed." He made me lie down with my head tilted back. "Put a cotton ball in her nose if it bleeds again," he said, summoning my mother to follow him behind the divider.

Dr. Liem told the nurse to watch me. "Make sure she doesn't fall asleep. I need to talk to her mother. Do the routine test on her. Check whether she is coherent."

"Open your eyes," said nurse Lan. "How many fingers do I have?"

I said "Four."

"All right, watch my fingers." Up and down, left to right. "She is all right, doctor."

When they returned, my mother had a frown on her face. Dr.Liem put his stethoscope to my chest, both sides, then my back. He listened attentively.

"All right." He patted me on my shoulder. "You can get dressed."

I heard my mother say: "Yes, doctor. You are right, doctor. She shouldn't be playing in the rain, naughty girl."

"Here is the prescription," Dr. Liem said, handing my mother a small package with medication for three days.

"Give her the cough syrup for her cough. She has whooping cough, and beginning pneumonia," Dr. Liem said.

I had to stay home. Both diseases were contagious. No school, and no heavy activities. Stay indoors and rest.

Before I left, the Doctor advised me, "Remember young lady, always stay away from the rain, and keep yourself warm, all right?"

I nodded.

It became customary for me…stay away from the rain…no evenings out… keep warm. My parents never confided in me about my health issues. They knew I would not understand anyway. Why make it worse? All they said was "Pneumonia."

My mother cooked more nutritious vegetables that cost more money. Chicken soup, comprising of chicken feet and chicken liver, was my main diet. Gone were my simple rice and fried eggs, or rice with corned beef. Dr. Liem insisted on foods with more nutrition.

My medication took a toll on my father's finances, to keep me alive. My mother had no choice but to sell her beautiful sarongs.

"The steam from the hot soup entices the fever to leave your body," my mother said. "These vegetables are nutritious." She pointed to the celery, tomatoes and carrots, among others. "You need these to fight the illness." Celery and carrots were all I remembered and learned to dislike. I learned to eat potatoes. My diet had changed dramatically; I never asked for food, everything was tasteless.

I thought I was dying. However, God had other plans for me.

I recall my mother taught me to recite the Lord's Prayer, once a day, every night before retiring.

"We need to ask God for help," my mom said.

"I will not go to the shrine, right Mammie?"

"No, you won't," she answered. "No shrine. Now go to sleep."

I dreamed of angels watching over me. Christmas was around the corner.

One morning I asked my mother if I could eat chicken porridge for a change. "Can I, Mammie?" My mother was brushing my hair. She stopped and looked at me with surprise since I had not had a good appetite for two months. After a moment she said, "You're sure?"

"Yes, I feel like eating chicken porridge, with the chicken liver. I love chicken liver."

My mother called Noor and asked her to cook chicken porridge, chicken soup and to feed me anything I'd like to eat.

"If we don't have it, buy it," Mammie said. "She needs to eat."

That was the day of my recovery. From that moment on, I became better. My appetite had returned. My strength and energy were restored. Now my mother could get me out of bed, to learn to walk again without help.

My sister and my brothers still communicated with me through my room's window, until the kind Dr. Liem gave my mother the green light that all was well.

Christmas went by and I missed the celebration and beautiful lights. My parents brought me my gifts. One was a mock-up of Jesus Christ, born in the stable. My mother told me I was blessed to have a house, no matter how small. Jesus didn't have one. I felt sorry for Jesus.

There was a gift came from the Sunday School teachers. It was a game of checkers that roused my competitiveness toward any games in the future.

I didn't know what medicinal shots Dr. Liem gave me, or what pills I had swallowed. All I knew was that a Communist Doctor saved my life. A man who didn't believe in God. He had a great heart. I never saw Dr. Liem again.

"I pray to God to give me all things I can enjoy...
God gave me life that I can enjoy all things."
Quotation unknown

Chapter 7: The National Geographic Magazine

My ordeal with my illness ended. I stayed at home for over three months.

Many Chinese people opened new shops and stores. My father's income had improved, and we moved to another location. The house was more spacious and had a front yard.

My parents thought it was time to leave the past behind—the Japanese raid, my illness—enough was enough. This would be a fresh beginning for all of us.

One thing I remember was a ritual that my mother performed before we took the beds out of our old house. She would go to the bedrooms, pat the mattresses, and say, "We are leaving now. Go with our body and spirit."

I asked my mother why she did that.

She said she wanted to make sure that our spirits followed us. "Otherwise, you will have dreams of past events." Her main worry was the Buddhist shrine incident. "You must move forward and consider the future."

"I saw the house, Mammie. It has an extra yard," I said. "We can play outside."

My father had other plans: perhaps buy a car; cover the yard with concrete, build an awning. "An awning is much better," Pappie said. "We can enjoy sitting on our porch on a rainy day."

Another happy event was when my father purchased a modern radio with more channels. We connected with the outside world through news and music. A lot of educational programs came on the air; one in English.

My mother shared the news that a radio station was introducing an English class, called "English for You."

"Wow!" I exclaimed. "How much does it cost?"

I was aware of my father's moderate income, and paying for my English lessons might cause financial hardship.

"Tuition is free," my mother answered. "We need to pay for the work books. It starts at 4 p.m., you will need to sacrifice your prime play time.

"You should consider moving your playtime to the next day. The English class is only once a week."

"Good idea, Mam, I can always play the next day," I said.

Breaking the news to my neighborhood friends was not as easy as I thought.

"Are you crazy? Why do you want to learn English anyway? Where are you going?" they asked as a chorus.

I shrugged.

"Good question. Where would I go after learning English? Which country? What would I do with the language?

The answer came soon afterward.

I overheard a conversation between two women after school, mothers of my classmates. They were discussing the possibility of going back to the Netherlands.

The Dutch government had given their citizens a second opportunity to embrace Dutch citizenship, those with a Dutch education. They would support them during the transition period. Some people had enjoyed the Dutch culture and education. They could serve in the Netherlands.

"Does that include us, Pappie?" I asked.

"Why do you want to go there?" he asked. "People think they can earn a better living in the Netherlands. Such a small country. If you want to move, choose a big country like America. That would make moving worthwhile. America is big, but not the Netherlands."

He waved his hand as if it was not worthwhile talking about.

I approached my father, and in my usual inquisitive manner, asked: "Why not in the Netherlands? What's the difference?"

"Nederland," my father explained, "was the Dutch name for the Netherlands.

"'Neder' means low. 'Land' means land. 'Nederland' means the low lands built below sea level.

"Using irrigation, the Dutch have expanded and enlarged their land toward the ocean. But, the country itself is small. I don't think the Dutch will welcome the immigrants, because the Dutch government will have a challenging time finding space to accommodate them."

My father's words lingered in my memory. At night I visualized how big America was. *America, that's where I would go with my English language. It already had the approval of my father.*

I started my English lessons by listening to the radio, which was a much more in-depth study of tenses and sentence structuring. I had already exhausted my mother's knowledge of the English language.

Every Thursday at 4 p.m., I stopped playing, washed my feet and legs to clean away the dust, and stationed myself in front of the radio. It was studytime.

In the meantime, my mother ordered and paid for the workbooks. No more stopping at the theaters, and no more getting caught in the rain.

I could still play with my neighborhood friends. I was ten years old. Life was wonderful.

Three months later a package came in the mail addressed to my father. Stamps read U.S. "What does U.S. stand for?" I asked my mother

"United States," my mother replied. My curiosity peaked. "You mean the United States of America?" I looked at the date.

"Wow! The United States must be far away."

"What makes you say that?"

"Look at the date. It took three months to arrive. America must be far away."

My mom laughed. "The package was sent by sea mail, silly. It would arrive much sooner if sent by airmail, but would cost more. The postal service sends magazines by sea mail. They are heavier than regular mail."

Well, I thought, my mother must be right. This package was heavier.

"Can I open it? Would Pappie be mad if I open it? My curiosity grew more intense.

"Go ahead, open it."

There it was… the most beautiful magazine I ever saw: the National Geographic Magazine.

I sat beside my mother and paged through the beautiful pictures: mountains with snow, green pine trees, strange animals too, streams and rivers. The magazine had many stranger English words. It took me longer to understand while pausing and asking questions to my mother.

I didn't even notice when my father arrived home. I was too busy reading the magazine.

The next day at school, I was full of stories, and of course caused a stir! Word got around. 'Esther wants to go to America.' My mother was summoned to the principal's office; a group of teachers awaited her. Where did Esther get the story?

"Are you going to America? When?" The teachers asked. "What made you and your husband decide on America?"

My mother smiled and told the teachers, "My husband subscribed to the National Geographic Magazine. Esther loved reading it; she fell in love with the pictures. She dreams of going to America someday.

"We have no plans of going anywhere. Esther was telling her friends about what she saw in the magazine. She is a dreamer and likes to share what she knows. She has a passion for the United States. I don't know why."

Chapter 8: California, My Future Home

I was paging through the National Geographic magazine when I saw a few friends run past my house. One of them was shouting, "They are doing it again," and pointed at the house two doors down.

"What are they doing?"

"Calling the spirit of a dead man," was the reply.

I had seen this performed many times at parties or local gatherings. My mother told me it originated in mainland China, centuries ago. Through the years, this pastime became extinct. However, a lot of Chinese traders had arrived in Indonesia, stayed, and married, bringing with them this entertainment which had become popular in our country.

I put my magazine down and joined the crowd. Some adults stationed themselves outside the fence to watch from the street. On the porch the owner of the house and their close friends were watching Yana, a young neighborhood girl, perform the ritual. We knew her mother but never knew Yana could summon supernatural spirits.

"What's the name of the man you want to summon? When did he die?" Yana ask.

"Lucas Hin," answered one of his close friends. "He was 25 years young, involved in a terrible motorcycle crash near the harbor two weeks ago. He was to get married in a month. Poor guy," said Daniel, another friend.

According to Yana, the spirit might still be present, and it would be easier to summon.

A simple woven basket with a handle, and covered with a blouse, was the medium used for communication. Yana attached a ring of keys to the handle to provide a jingling sound when the basket moved. Two persons held the basket on their open palms. They would lower their hands when the basket became heavier, as if holding a brick, signifying that the spirit had arrived and occupied the basket.

The question and answer session could then begin. One nod for 'yes,' or two nods for 'no.' A wooden pen with a long handle and brush was tied to the basket. The pen could write on a paper using the ink provided.

I was standing on the sidelines and watched the preparation. Goosebumps crept up my arms. I felt the tenseness of everyone present; it was like being hypnotized

Yana, at sixteen years old, was regarded as a 'wild girl.' She loved men and always tried to seduce them. She seemed to have an affinity for summoning the spirits of dead people. My mother told me to stay away from her.

"If you are here, nod once," Yana said. I saw the hands holding the basket move and drop. The spirit had arrived. The basket fell forward once.

"Is your name Lucas Hin?" The basket nodded once.

Everyone stepped back and expressed a surprised "Oh!" I moved farther away from the basket.

Yana asked the attendees, "Do you want to ask him something?"

"Do you remember me?" The basket nodded and then moved to dip the pen in the ink bowl. The hands moved with the basket and the pen wrote on the piece of paper that had been placed close by. "Daniel."

"Wow, he still remembers you," his friends said. "Incredible. It is him."

I ran home. It was too much for me. I told my mother about it. She shook her head in disbelief, looked at me, and in a stern voice said, "Don't play with the dead. Let them rest."

"I was only watching, Mam."

An hour later, I saw Yana come to my wired fence gate. "Can you come here for a second?"

I went to her.

"Hold this for me," and she handed me the basket.

"Where are you going?"

Yana ran away.

I stood there with the basket which still felt heavy. I looked at the basket and realized Yana could not get rid of the spirit. *Oh, dear me. What am I going to do with it?* There was no help in sight; everyone had run home. I was the unsuspecting victim.

My mother was preparing to go to the market when she saw me holding the basket and concluded what had happened.

"Where is Yana?"

"She ran home."

"She dumped the basket in your hands, didn't she? Now what?" My mother ordered me to put the basket down. She asked a question to the basket, "Are you still there?"

The basket nodded and moved on its own.

I was a scared ten-year-old, victimized by one of the neighborhood kids. *What if this spirit followed me around?*

My mother addressed the basket, "Look, my daughter didn't summon you here. She has work to do. Could you please leave?"

The basket nodded twice, meaning "No." It irked my mother.

"All right," she said. "Let's see whether I can *make* you leave. I made a polite request, and you refused." She sounded as if she were talking to herself.

She told me to open our fence gate, "Open it wider," and then, bam, she kicked the basket out of our yard. It rolled over several times and stopped in the middle of the street.

I froze and put my fingers in my mouth. "Mammie, the spirit might get mad."

My mother put her hands on her hips; I'd never seen her this upset. She waited a few minutes, went to the middle of the street and picked up the basket. I guessed the spirit might have left. What spirit could survive a kick like that? She turned around and went toward Yana's house.

"I will give Yana's mother a piece of my mind. You, young lady, get back in the house. Now!"

I ran into our house.

My mother was a strong believer in God. She was not afraid of any spirits.

"Respect the dead, and leave them be. That's why on the tombstone, you read R.I.P., Rest in Peace," she told me later.

I refrained from attending this kind of activity again. (Author's note: Due to many activities of today, this pastime had become extinct.).

As we started fifth grade, the school added new teachers.

Mr. Lim taught Chinese history and language. He was a great story teller, in his mid-thirties, medium build, and carried an old black leather briefcase. He used his arms and legs to demonstrate heroes fighting off the enemy, making the stories more fascinating to us.

"Be proud of your heritage," he said. "It embraces a great history and its interesting cultural values." He gave me a Chinese name, Mei Lan, meaning beautiful orchid.

Mr. Boon was a young teacher in his twenties, tall and slim. He shared with us his interest in the vocations of his students. "What would you like to be when you grow up?" He understood the diversity in ages and backgrounds due to the war. The class needed stimulation, new ideas, and one way to understand their minds was through essay writing.

I didn't know what I wanted to be. I enjoyed story telling; however, but in what school would l learn story telling?

Mr. Boon gave us a week to prepare. He asked me to read my essay in front of the class.

"I want to be a mother," I began.

The students laughed and chanted, "Esther wants to be a mother…"

"Why not, my mother is a good story teller." I said.

After class, Mr. Boon called me and wondered whether he could introduce my mother to the class. *Oh, no. Again?*

"What now?" asked my mother. "What have you done?"

"I don't know, Mam. Remember my essay? I wrote I wanted to be a mother, because I wanted to be a story teller like you. Maybe he wants to know what I am doing at home as I have no ambition. Other kids have big dreams, engineers, architects, doctors, and I want to be a mother." I sighed.

My mother visited our class the next morning and talked to Mr. Boon. Surprise, surprise. He was impressed with my essay. He thought it was a genuine story, from the heart. It was a compliment to my mother.

"There is nothing wrong with being a mother who becomes a role model to her daughter." Mr. Boon gave me a passing grade of eight (ten being the highest), for essay writing.

Sixth Grade started and we had an overloaded class, sixty students total. In Indonesia, due to lack of facilities, we had morning and afternoon school. I went to morning classes from 7.30 a.m. to 1 p.m. Better teachers, more hours and more studying, compared to the afternoon class hours from 1.00 to 5 p.m.

Since the afternoon class held less than the quota of forty students, they were merged with our class. The teacher's name was Mr. Ko. School went well, until a few months before graduation.

He decided to add English to the curriculum. It would be good to learn English before joining the Intermediate School. Mr. Ko became the English teacher.

I shared my concerns with my mother. "I have a bad feeling about this, Mam," I said. "He never spoke English, and we have to pay tuition too."

My parents advised me to go with the flow, as no other parents objected to the idea.

Mr. Ko meant well. The three month class was only an introduction.

My concern became a reality. He lacked the experience, compared to the instructor on the radio. I had studied English once a week for two years.

I didn't make a comment when he pronounced 'vegetable' as vege-table. It was not a table. It was a veggie. My classmates advised me to stay calm. After several repeats of faulty pronunciation, when he pronounced 'piano' as 'pie-ya-no', I lost the battle. I whispered, 'peeyano'. He didn't seem to hear; he continued with 'pie-ya-no.' This time I pronounced it a little louder...'pee-ano'. Mr. Ko stopped, turned around, looked at me, and walked my way. Fifty-nine pairs of eyes were watching.

"What did you say?" he asked.

The eyes of a 12-year-old girl looked back at him. I answered, "pee-ano (piano), sir, not 'pie-ya-no.' It is the name of an instrument. All countries call it pee-ano. The same goes for 'ray-dee-o' (radio), not ra-die-yo. Mrs. Stanya from the radio said so."

He drew a deep breath: "Can you ask your mother to come to my office tomorrow?"

Oh no, not again? "Yes, sir."

I didn't know what my mother told him, but I had no more problems. He listened, and we could discuss the words. My guess was that my mother shared with Mr. Ko that I had studied English from the time I could read and continued to take the class on the radio, longer than any students in his class.

By the end of the school year, I knew where I wanted to live when I grew older. I was holding the National Geographic magazine in my hands.

"Where?" Mam asked. I showed her the pictures.

"Look at this. See these rivers, fishermen, blue skies, and the sunshine. Look at the sea. Just like Indonesia," and I pointed, "Here is where I would like to live."

My mother looked at the pictures. The title of the page read... California. I was 12 years old.

Chapter 9: The Bicycle, Yohan and Coming of Age

"Today, I want to be Flash Gordon. I can shoot, and fly the space ship. I am bored playing Dale Arden."

No matter how hard I tried, the boys decided I could not play the character of Flash Gordon. I was Flash Gordon's girl friend.

"You are a girl," Mark said. "Your task is to follow me."

Girls in the neighborhood could not play on the streets. My friends were boys.

I was frustrated and we screamed at each other.

My mother heard the ruckus and appeared from inside. She held her hands up and demanded that we calm down.

"All right, kids, what's all this yelling about?" All at the same time, the boys tried to tell her. "All right, all right," my mother said, "Why, Esther, do you want to be Flash Gordon?"

"I got bored playing Dale Arden. The boys keep saying I can't because I am a girl. Being a girl sucks."

"Time for a break," my mother said. "Let it rest. You all go home now. Come on, everybody out." That was the end of the Flash Gordon and Dale Arden debate.

I had arrived at the turning point, from child to teenager, and had developed a mind of my own, in addition to demanding equal rights.

My next venture was learning to ride a bicycle. Our street was a dirt road and a dead end, an ideal place to learn. The challenge was to use my father's, as his was the only one around. But my father rode his bicycle to work. I had to be careful.

When he was resting in the afternoon, I took his bike from the stand and planned to return it before he woke up. My first try ended in a telephone pole crash; I shattered the bike light and bent the steering handle. I hurt myself and came face-to-face with the consequences of disobeying my father.

His words were, "If you refuse to listen, you must feel." My father was waiting with the rattan stick in his hands, and it landed it on my back and legs. I weathered the pain. I held my tears, afraid there would be more if I cried. The neighborhood kids scattered.

I went straight to my bedroom and waited for a lecture from my mother, but she let me be. She knew I was wrong.

My sister sat and watched me with her big eyes. She asked, "Why did you do it? You know Pappie doesn't like it when one of us disobeys him? Hurt much?"

I nodded.

My sister sighed. Tina never learned to ride a bicycle, for fear of my father. Well, no pain, no bike.

A little later Mammie came into the room and asked, "Why did you insist on learning to ride a bicycle? Who suggested it to you? The boys?"

"No Mam," I said, "it was my idea. The games bore me. With a bike, I could go to the club next door, and play there. I could also sit by the pond and watch the ducks. I could do it on my own."

My mother disagreed with my desire for more freedom. She only answered, "Well, we'll see about that." She tried to explain the anger of my father, why he had to give me a lesson for being disobedient. "That bicycle is your father's transportation to work. You broke it, and it will take days to repair. Now he has to take a different means to get to work. When Pappie is absent, he will not get paid, and it may result in no food on the table. Do you understand?"

Nodding and sobbing, I asked, "Why can't Pappie teach me to ride a bike? Terry's father did." Tears rolled down my cheeks.

My mother frowned, "Who is Terry?"

"Terry is the girl living on the other street, and she has a nice bicycle that fits her, a girl's bike."

"How do you know this?" Mammie asked.

I paused, wiped at my tears and answered, "Remember, when you asked me to buy stuff at the convenience store down the street? As I walked out of the store, I saw her learning to ride, with her father behind her. I watched her with Yohan."

"Who is Yohan?" My mother was increasingly intrigued.

I was irritated. "Oh Mam, you don't know anybody. Yohan is the boy who lives next to the convenience store. He lives there with his father and two sisters. The sisters played badminton every Wednesday and Saturday down by the truck garage." I pointed in the direction of the badminton court. The movement made me wince: "Ouch!"

My mother's eyes grew bigger, and she had a hard time responding. She took a deep breath, realizing that I was not a kid anymore. I had ventured into new activities, met new people. I had outgrown the children's games.

"If you don't believe me, wait until Sunday morning. Terry will ride by with her father at 10 in the morning."

"All right, I will," Mammie said.

Together that Sunday, we watched Terry riding by with her father. My eyes filled with tears, "All I wanted was to ride a bike."

After the incident, I became morose. The neighborhood boys thought I was sick. I read more magazines and became intrigued with the world of make believe, the movies. I read about the actors, the stories and gossip columns, in Dutch magazines, even though I was still underage.

Yohan was my new interest in the neighborhood. My mother wanted to know more and wondered why I was attracted to him.

"Yohan is different," I explained. "He doesn't play with the rest of the kids. I think because he is three years older. However, he always watches me from the steps of the convenience store and waves. I always know he is standing there."

I could tell that my new interest drew my mother's attention.

"If he doesn't play with the other kids, what game does he play?"

"Oh, I don't know, Mammie, it has a strange name…Chess? The game has weird looking figures, called the tower, the knight, king and queen."

"How did he come to know about you?"

"Oh, he has a friend called Billy Boy."

"Who is Billy Boy?"

"Mam, don't you know anybody at all? Billy Boy is the boy four doors down. He knew I was called Esther, but my teacher gave me a Chinese name. He has a Chinese name but not a western one. He asked if I were to give him a western name, which one would fit him? I thought he looked like a Billy and he is a boy. So, there you go. He is a good friend of Yohan's.

While I was watching Terry, Yohan greeted me using my name. He knew all the games I like to play, and he laughed when I wanted to be Flash Gordon. He thought it was funny. Yohan and I became friends." Yohan is a couple of years older than me.

"No wonder I had to wait half an hour before you came home." My mother then sent me to buy stuff from the convenience store. She came with me and talked with Yohan. She liked him. Now I could play chess.

Every Sunday I watched Terry ride by. Each time I looked at my father's bike, my sister waved her finger at me, and said, " Emh, ehm, don't even think of it."

I couldn't get the bike out of my mind, and grew silent. I didn't sing during the day anymore. 'Listeners Choice' on the radio had lost its fan. The house was quiet.

I had a thick book of 300 songs in it. Not once did I open it. My favorite song was by Bing Crosby, called "Far Away Places: Far away places, with their strange sounding names, are calling, calling me."

This concerned my parents. This was not the daughter they knew. I was not as gregarious as in the past, playing mahjong or card games. Games with the boys did not interest me as much. I played with them for only a short while. I always ended with "That's boys' games, you don't need me."

One Sunday afternoon, I heard my mother calling, "Hey, Mei Lan, come and look here."

Whenever she wanted me to see something different, she always called me by my Chinese name. I realized it could be something important.

There, in the doorway, I saw my father standing with…a ladies' bike.

"A ladies' bike!" Ha ha ha! I was laughing, clapping my hands, and jumping. "For me?

Let me try, let me try."

"Thank you, Pappie," and I took over the bike. "Can I walk with it for a while?" I forgot the days when I watched Terry. I seemed to lose the pain in my back and legs. They served as a warning not to disobey my father's wishes again. All I could see was my bike. *My bike.*

It didn't take long for me to get comfortable on it, even though it was twice my height. It had its challenges, but I conquered them. I was riding my own bike and my parents welcomed their lively daughter back.

My relationship with Yohan also had its challenges. He was a Chinese boy, but from a different background—more polished, and his father was strong financially. His oldest sister, Nancy, did not like me. Why, I did not know, except that I was playing on the street with the boys, and her brother liked me more than she would wish. Perhaps because I was the only girl Yohan liked.

She felt responsible for him, as they had no mother. I never saw his father either. Meeting and playing chess on his porch had become more difficult. He could not visit with me. I remember Nancy pointing at me with her badminton racket and instructing me to stay away from her brother. Whatever plans the family had for Yohan, as the only son, I was in the way and would not be compatible for him.

Yohan was smart enough to introduce letter writing. He called me Margaret, and he wrote in English. His sisters did not know he was corresponding with me.

My mother advised me not to be too close, afraid our relationship might cause disappointment and hurt. I was only 12 years old. Billy Boy volunteered to be the courier. I began to notice that boys in my life always caused problems.

I discovered the love of letter writing. Yohan began with "Dear Margaret." It had a nice ring to it. The word "dear" gave me a warm feeling. I could tell him what was in my heart, my aspirations, my dream to go to the promised land, America. Yohan understood and he shared with me that one day he would go to Singapore.

My mother was right. Yohan's relationship with me was short-lived. He was tutored in English to further his studies in Singapore, and one day he and his family departed. While I knew they would leave Jakarta, I didn't expect it to be so soon.

He wrote me one more time before leaving, explaining their sudden departure; he promised to write.

I was still holding his last letter when I heard my mother say, "I told you not to be too close, didn't I?"

I nodded. That night I said goodbye to my childhood sweetheart.

Chapter 10: A Miracle – The Lug Nut

I rode my bike and watched a group of young men, in their mid-20's, play badminton. Since Yohan's sisters and her friend had left the area, the group was looking for a new partner for Shelly, a 14-year old girl.

She caught sight of me sitting on my bike and taking notice of the game. She motioned an elderly man called Oom (uncle) Hwat and whispered to him. Oom Hwat was one of my father's mahjong friends.

He approached me and asked, "Would you like to play?"

"I don't know how," I said.

"If you care to learn, I can teach you. Then you can partner with Shelly."

I didn't need a second invitation. Shelly and I became the youngest members of the badminton club. My involvement in badminton had made me a special guest of the young men who were our neighbors. They invited me to watch the exhibitions of champions. My parents allowed me to go as they had known them for years and knew I was in good hands.

"Take care of her, guys. Don't stay too late," my mother said them as they pulled away on their bikes. I rode on the back of one of my neighbor's bike.

"Don't worry, will do."

It was entertaining for me to watch the prospective Indonesian champions play and practice. The men's doubles were great with swift arm reflexes and great footwork. What an evening!

These young men became Indonesian Champions for Men's Single, and Doubles. I followed their progress in the newspapers. Also the young men in our badminton club shared information with me as I was a member now. Badminton was and still is the main sport in Indonesia.

Sometimes I wondered what it might have been like if Yohan were still there. I missed him.

"Hey, Esther, focus. Hit the shuttlecock. You need to move and run to hit the shuttlecock." Oom Hwat was shouting at me. "You need to follow the birdie. Understand?"

I nodded. Once I figured out how the game was played, I progressed.. "Remember the footwork. Use your wrist, not your whole body."

I continued sharpening my badminton skills and partnered with Shelly.

"Let me know which school you have chosen as your Intermediate School. It has to be a Christian School," my parents told me.

"Yes, I have found it. It's a Catholic School. Still Christian, right?"

"Why a Catholic School?"

"No boys, just girls." *No headaches.*

"Just scout around. Don't register yet. Let me know what you have in mind."

"All right."

I went with several schoolmates. I liked the Catholic school. It was a white painted building with a large yard and trees, allowing shade for the students who already stood in line to register. I heard the teachers say, "When you return for the school year, remember to wear a blouse or dress that has sleeves. Wear pumps, no sandals. Understood?"

"Yes, teacher," my friends and I answered.

My mother said 'scout' and I determined to walk around and check the surroundings. I noticed a door and somebody going through it.

"Hey, Esther, where are you going?" Mandy asked when I moved away from the group.

"That way," and I pointed to the door. "I saw somebody going through there." "You're to remain here. Don't wander around."

"I'll be back," and off I went.

The door appeared to be unlocked, and I glanced inside.

Wow! This is a beautiful courtyard with an assortment of beautiful flowers. This is what a garden should be. The courtyard was rectangular with a fountain in the middle. Roses galore in various colors. A well-kept garden.

I carried on walking down the hallway straight into the garden, smelling the roses, and on to the statue of a lady with outstretched arms. A fountain and a bench completed the beautiful scenery.

I sat on the bench, delighting in the beauty and peacefulness of the place when I heard a voice, "Are you lost, my child?"

I jumped from my seat and looked straight into the eyes of a lady wearing a white head scarf, robe and a necklace with a cross. She had her arms folded inside her garment.

I was startled by her sudden appearance. She found me amusing, as I continued staring at her attire.

She smiled and questioned me again, "Are you lost, my child?"

"I don't know. What place is this?"

"This is a convent."

"What is a convent? Who are you?"

The lady in white was not angry. "I am a nun, I live here."

"Why do you live here? I thought this was a Catholic School."

"Well, next door, yes. How did you come to this area?"

"Well, through that door, over there."

"It should be locked."

"No, it wasn't." I got distracted, as I heard people singing. A group of ladies in black and white robes were walking down the other hallway and singing as a choir. Beautiful voices, and music.

"Are they choir singers? I sing in the choir too, but we don't have uniforms like them. Who are they?"

"Oh, they are nuns. They live here too. They are going to the sanctuary."

By this time, I was really confused. "Do I have to live here too, and sing with them?"

The lady in white smiled again, and said, "Well, when you have passed your High School exam, you can return, but not before. However, it's time for you to return back to your group." She then accompanied me to the door I came through earlier, and said politely, "Good day, my child."

She motioned for me to go through the doorway. This time I heard a click behind me, and I returned to my friends.

"Where were you? Are you still going to register?" Mandy asked.

"No, not now."

"Whom did you talk to?"

" I don't know who she was. She was dressed in white."

"Oh, it must be Mother Superior."

"Mother who?"

"Never mind. What else did you see?"

"A group of singing ladies wearing black and white robes."

"Those were the nuns."

Arriving home, I sat in the living room, overwhelmed with what I had experienced. I enjoyed the peacefulness. No boys. However, the place was isolated from the school. Obviously, they did not like kids. The lady in white wanted me to leave very quickly.

"Well?" was my mother's first question. "How was it?"

"I think I'd like to go to school there. And, after I graduate from High School, I could return to the Convent. The Lady in White said so."

My mother could not believe her ears. "And what do you intend to be?"

"I would like to be a nun."

My parents looked at each other. They were silent.

" A nun! It's all your fault; you gave the kids freedom of choice," I heard my mother say to my father.

The day after visiting the Catholic school, my sister and I registered at a Protestant School. This time Pappie came with us.

On Sunday, when I arrived home from the market with my mother, we found a car in our carport. My father's dream of owning a car had come true. It was a green colored jeep.

We could go to church in a car now, no pedicabs anymore. Also, we could explore the areas beyond our neighborhood. A little bit at a time, we traveled the localities where the rich lived, called Menteng, on tree-lined streets. We observed larger houses with beautiful gardens, wrought iron fences, and gates. Some of these houses accommodated dogs and cats. There were two cars in front of each house. Lots of shady trees. Streets were covered with asphalt.

We explored different areas every week. For the first time I became aware how spacious our city was.

"Tomorrow is Sunday, and we will go to the mountains after church," my father said. " We will walk around and try a new restaurant there."

"Yay," we all said, clapping our hands.

It was a wonderful trip. We drove on asphalt roads which made a huge difference. Where we lived, it was dirt road, not asphalt.

Everybody wanted to enjoy the day at Puncak, the name of the place. It was quite an experience for us. We returned late afternoon.

My father was cautious on the winding roads and, at one turn, we heard repeated honking. He glanced in the rear view mirror and realized two men were motioning him to stop. He slowed and let them pass by. One of the men was pointing at our car, and my father said to my mother, "Anything wrong?"

"Not that I can see."

 We continued our journey.

Arriving home, everyone got out of the car, and my father walked around to check it out. I was already inside the house when I heard my father call out my mother,

"Laine, come here."

My mother rushed out and asked, "What's going on?"

"Look!" My father pointed to the tire.

"Oh my God," my mother exclaimed.

I ran outside.

"What's going on, Pappie? What's wrong?"

By now, my sister and my brothers came running too.

My father picked up a stick from the ground and touched a lug nut on the wheel. It came off, and the tire rolled off.

"If that had happened on the mountain road, we all would have been dead," my father said. "Now I understand what those men were pointing at. They tried to warn us of the impending danger."

"God has other plans for us," my mother said, "If He didn't hold the lug nut in place all the way home, it would have been fatal. Pray before you go on a trip. Ask the Lord Almighty to help take care of us."

"My fault, Mam, I forgot to pray," I said.

"You may have forgotten, but I didn't," my Mammie said.

I accepted the power of prayer. Why shouldn't I? I couldn't help thinking about the time I was ill. My mother and I prayed too. The doctor had given up; however, I survived.

I was thirteen years old.

Chapter 11: Pak Tan

"Girls, this is Mr. Tan, your Principal of the intermediate school," Pappie said.

Tan Wai Tee was a tall gentleman in his forties with stern looking eyes. He wore a white shirt, khaki colored long pants, and stood with his hands folded in the back military-style.

"Well, Esther and Tina, you will both study in our school for three years. I hope to see you girls cheerful and enjoying your studies."

My first day in intermediate school was overwhelming. There were hundreds of boys and girls.

The teachers guided us to an auditorium and Mr. Tan stood in the middle of the room with his hands behind his back. He looked around the room. In his thunderous voice he said, "Welcome to our school. To those who haven't met me, I am the Principal. My name is Tan Wai Tee. You can call me Pak Tan. (pronounced "puck", a courteous address for all men in Indonesia). You all know this is a Christian school.

"I noticed that some of you are of different religions and cultural backgrounds. You need to choose for yourself whether this is where you want to be. We will start and end the classes with a prayer. We will have Christian studies, gospel songs, and celebrate Easter and Christmas.

"Should you have questions, please consult with the teachers you see in this room, or else you can come to my office. Whenever you have problems, let the teachers know at once, and we will work together to provide a solution." He motioned with his right hand to the teachers standing there. "Don't take matters into your own hands. Is that understood?"

"Yes, Pak Tan," answered the students.

"Let us pray."

We folded our hands, bowed our heads and together with Pak Tan we prayed. My intermediate school years began.

My sister and I arrived bright and early the next day and I claimed a spot in the front row. I chose the one in front of the teacher's desk, adhering to my parents' wish. "You need to focus," my father said. "Sitting up front would help you listen better and concentrate." My sister took the desk a few rows behind me.

We inherited our classroom from the Dutch. Everything was big. The classroom was well-lighted as there were big windows. They were high enough to prevent the students from daydreaming and looking outside the window. We needed to focus on the teacher, not on the street.

The writing board was large and wide, placed high on the wall at the front. A bench was provided for the teachers to climb and reach higher. *The Dutch teachers were probably taller than ours*; most of them were small in stature.

To the left, the room opened into the courtyard. All we saw were other classrooms, far enough away so as not to disturb.

A volley ball court decorated the middle of the courtyard. Male students played volleyball during recess time; the girls watched. We wore dresses and were not outfitted for sports that required jumping and falling or rolling on the dirt yard, which was unladylike.

We had a volleyball club, and students could return in the afternoon wearing the proper attire like shorts. Changing for sports was not possible for me since I didn't have personal transportation, and it was quite a distance from home to school.

I met Jenny, my bench mate, and we hit it off well. Gregarious and funny, she always wanted to try anything innovative. My type of friend.

As usual, due to the war, many students were two to three years older than me. They sat in the back of the class room, as they were taller than the girls; thus, they had an unobstructed view to the board and teacher.

Reverend Lie (pronounced Lee) taught religion. I knew the biblical stories as I read them in Sunday school.

I always pictured God as the ultimate magician. *Poof!* and your prayer would become reality. *Kaboom*, He divided land and sea. "Knock, and the door shall open." I wanted to be like Him.

Reverend Lie (pronounced Lee) loved telling us his stories beginning with "When I was in America…." His stories impressed us a lot, as nobody had gone to America. Hearing them, we could envision new horizons. It was also his favorite subject.

Every time he mentioned "America," Jenny leaned toward me and whispered, "What's so distinctive about America?"

I answered, "Oh, because no one else has visited America, I assume, and no one could contradict him. But, why not America? Better America than 'when I was in Russia'." I was imitating Reverend Lie.

We giggled.

Geography opened broader visions of the unknown. Countries that had shaved ice dropping from the sky, and temperatures that could begin with the sunshine and end in the evening with freezing cold nights. Wow! Now my National Geographic magazine made sense. I consulted the magazine every time I finished my geography class. My dream of foreign places came alive.

"In America, they have a fire in the house too," I commented to Reverend Lie. Everyone laughed. "Fire will burn the house down."

Reverend Lie quieted the students with his hands. "What fire?" he asked.

"Yeah, what fire?" shouted my classmates.

I stuck my tongue out. "I saw a picture of people eating around their dining table, and there was a fire burning. It's true, Reverend Lie."

"Oh, you mean fire in the fireplace," Reverend Lie said. "Yes, Esther is right. There is a fire in the house during their cold seasons called Autumn and Winter. which is October to March. The fire keeps the house warm. Indonesia, our country, lies in the Tropics. That's why we don't have fireplaces."

After the class, Reverend Lie asked me, "How do you know so much about America?"

"From a magazine called the National Geographic," I said.

"You read that magazine?" Reverend Lie asked again.

I nodded.

During recess, Jenny asked me "where did you get that publication?"

"My father subscribes to it."

"Any special interest?"

"Yes, I am interested in going to America."

Jenny just giggled and shook her head. "You are ridiculous. America is so far away. Have you ever thought about how to get there?"

My answer stopped her in her tracks. "Remember…Jesus said… knock, and the door shall open. Prayer, Jenny, through prayers."

Jenny sighed.

I told Jenny, "I love stories in the Bible. Jesus answers prayers."

One day, we had a new student, an Arab boy called Kamal.

He had dark skin and he seldom talked. When he did get the chance, he spoke in a loud voice as if he needed to exercise his vocal cords.

Sometimes the teachers told him, "Calm down, Kamal, we hear you. No need to yell."

I turned to look at him when he sat behind me.

"Oh dear, too close to the teacher. I don't like this." I heard him talking to himself.

"Why not," I asked, "are you scared?" It was the wrong question.

He got off his bench, flapped his arms and yelled, "I'm not scared."

I leaned toward Jenny and whispered, "If you want to see a crazy boy, you have one behind you." We giggled.

Kamal left and walked to the Principal's office. *Oh oh, bad news.*

When he returned, Kamal told me that Pak Tan wanted to see me. *I knew it.*

"So, Esther, how do you like your new classmate?" Pak Tan asked me as I entered. "Sit down and tell me."

"You mean Kamal? Not bad. He screams a lot. He didn't like sitting close to the teacher's desk."

"And what did you say to him?"

"I asked him whether he was scared, and he screamed and flapped his arms. That's all. I don't understand why he only mentioned my name. Everyone else was making fun of him. The more he screamed, the more they teased him."

"What did the other students say to him?"

"Hey, Arab boy, are you lost? You've traveled quite a long way from your village."

Pak Tan sighed and nodded. He tried to explain Kamal's situation in simple terms. "Kamal comes from a different family. He is an Arab boy and could attend a different school.

However, his parents wanted him to get a better education and must have thought a Christian school could provide that for him, more so than the government's public school. His first days have been devastating to him. He felt strange praying the Christian way, and he couldn't find another Arab boy to whom he could relate.

Is he scared? Yes. You would be too, if you had gone to a different school that taught a different religion. We need to make him feel comfortable. All right?"

I nodded and he let me return to class.

Pak Tan straight away addressed the situation. He came in and stood in front of the class in his usual military position, hands behind the back. "As Christians, I don't want to hear negative words addressed to newcomers. Remember what Jesus said, 'Don't judge, so you will not be judged.'" He went on, "Jesus said this on top of a mountain called the Mount of Beatitudes. He was teaching his disciples and I encourage you all to follow His principles. Kamal needs a friend, not enemies, and we need to make him feel welcome."

"Kamal," Pak Tan looked at him, "Next time, talk, don't scream. The students will understand you better, and you will not attract attention. All right?"

Kamal nodded.

Pak Tan looked around the class one more time, and said firmly, "Do I make myself clear?"

"Yes, Pak Tan," everybody answered.

I liked Pak Tan. He did not take sides.

Chapter 12: Ms. Leny – English Class

"She did it again, Mam," my sister said. Tina pointed her finger up and down at me.

"So, Tina, what did your sister do?" said my mother.

"She had a fight with an Arab boy, called Kamal. Pak Tan called her to his office. You might be too, Mam."

"Is that true?"

"I only asked him a question," I said. "He jumped up and down, shrieking at the top of his lungs, 'I am not scared.'"

My mother listened quietly while I shared the story. Then, "A time of adjustment," she said. "Let's wait to see what the teacher does."

"Pak Tan addressed the issue in class, Mam," I said. "He decided that we all have to work together. Kamal doesn't like sitting close to the teacher's desk. He sat behind me."

"You'll be called, Mam, I am sure of it. Just like in the other school," My sister loved picking on me.

I was uncomfortable, knowing my father would be displeased if my mother were summoned to school. It would be inconvenient for her as the intermediate school was farther away.

After dinner, I approached my mother, and said I would ask if Pak Tan planned to summon my mother to school..

"I need to know for sure. I don't want Pappie to be mad at me."

"I don't think Pak Tan will call me. Your father registered you, so he may call your father directly. Go to sleep, and don't worry. He handles situations like this all the time. Right? Go to bed now."

The next morning, I waited until I was sure Mr. Tan was alone in the teachers' lounge. He saw me, and motioned me to come closer.

"Well, Esther, you want to talk?"

"Yes, Pak Tan. I want to find out whether you want to call my Mammie now?"

Pak Tan stopped taking papers out of his bag, and looked at me with his stern eyes.

"Now, why do I need to call your Mammie?" he asked.

"In the other school the teachers always called her, causing my Pappie to be angry at me."

Pak Tan straightened up and seemed to think for a while, and then smiled. "Oh, I understand now. It was a different time, a different rule, and you were younger."

He sat down, drew a deep breath and continued: "In this school, we provide solutions. We take care of situations right away, often by meeting with the other teachers. Only when we have serious problems, do we call the parents. If I must call every Mammie and Pappie to the school, I would not have time for anything else. Are you worried about Kamal?"

"Yes."

"Well, don't be. We solved it yesterday." He sighed, stood up and said, "No, Esther, I won't call your Mammie." Time was up. He picked up his bag.

I still stood there. "Promise?"

Pak Tan smiled, "Promise."

The bell rang and I ran to into my class, wishing Pak Tan had been the principal of our elementary school.

During the second break, I did not see my sister. Her bench mate, Liane, also missed her.

"I don't know where she is, Esther. I wish I could tell you. She will be back in class soon, I'm sure."

A few minutes later I saw her come out of Pak Tan's office.

I stopped Tina and asked, "What happened? Why does he want to talk to you?"

"He wanted to know everything about our elementary school, and why Mammie was called in."

"And?"

"I had to tell him. I had no other choice. He thought it was funny you were helping Mr. Kho with his English class."

"That's it?"

"Oh, one more thing. He asked why you wanted to be a nun." Off she went to Liane, who was waiting for her.

I felt more comfortable now. I focused on an array of sports activities. Soccer was the number one activity for the boys. Girls were the cheerleaders. We didn't understand the rules and regulations and we cheered for almost everything. Perhaps we just wanted to exercise our lungs. The cheering was fun. Soccer was our pride and joy; our school had the best soccer team.

As the government already leaned toward socialism, the national soccer team called "Persija", invited international teams from socialist countries to play, Russia, Hungary, and Yugoslavia. My father took my sister and me to these games to give my mother a break. There were five of us then. Two girls and three boys.

A year passed by, and new teachers were added. Ms. Leny became our English instructor. A new algebra teacher, Mr. Boon, joined the staff. He was also my former fifth grade teacher.

Jenny still sat with me. She giggled, and said "I hope they like soccer."

I stopped studying English through the radio. Kamal continued to the eighth grade and liked sitting behind me. He became more expressive and we had become friends. Life was peaceful, as it should be. Until one day....

Miss Leny surprised us with an English test. "Close your books, we'll have a test."

"Oh no, no Miss Leny, that is not fair," we all responded.

Miss Leny distributed the test and said, "The subject is the possessive pronoun. We had it last week. Those who studied will not have any problem. I want you to be serious about this."

"Oh, my goodness," I heard Kamal grumbling.

Once we started the test, everyone was quiet. An hour later, Miss Leny clapped her hands and said, "Time is up. Now, give the test paper to the person behind you and we will check the answers together. Is that understood?"

"Yes, Miss Leny," we replied. Papers rustled. Everyone was serious about checking the test paper passed back to them, as Miss Leny called the answers one by one.

Kamal gave me the lowest score. Ten was the highest.

I rolled the paper like an ice cream cone and hit his desk. "You dare give me a one? Are you insane?"

Kamal snapped. He jumped up from his bench and yelled at the top of his lungs. "You made a mistake. They were all mistakes."

The students were laughing, they found it amusing.

Kamal didn't like it and pointed his finger at me, "It's true. She did them all wrong."

I felt like hitting him. However, before I could do that, Miss Leny approached us, and asked Kamal to forward my test paper to her. Kamal was still defending himself: "Esther did it all wrong."

"Sit down, all of you and calm down. Let me check this paper. Open chapter 8 of your book, and study on your own. Quiet, please."

I returned to my seat, and watched Miss Leny check my paper. She was gently shaking her head, a faint smile appeared on her face; she sighed and stared out the window for a while. Then she stood up, and motioned me to come to her.

"Have you had English classes before?"

"Not really."

"How did you come to all these answers, then?"

"Oh, I learned English from the radio," and I told her what I had done.

She smiled. "That figures. These were not wrong. It's only that I haven't taught it before. See me after class."

"Yes, Miss Leny."

"All right, class." She put her finger in front of her lips. "Sshhhh, I checked Esther's paper, she didn't make a mistake. It's only that I haven't taught it before."

Kamal defended himself. "How could she know something you haven't taught?"

"Never mind, Kamal. It's a long story. For now, Esther's score is a 10."

I turned around to look at Kamal; however, Miss Leny put her hand on my head and stopped me.

Jenny giggled. She giggled at everything..

After class, I went to see my English teacher. "Remember, out there, not many people know as much English as you do. When you have your final exam, try to go by the books. Otherwise, the examiners will not know whether your English is correct. Their knowledge may not be as extensive as yours; they only follow the books."

Chapter 13: Kublitsky vs. John Wayne

"God doesn't answer all prayers," Mr. Boon commented. He wasn't a believer, and it was beyond my comprehension why he chose to teach at a Christian school.

"Yes, He does," I contradicted him.

"How do you know?"

I shared with him and the class our excursion to the mountain and the loose lug nut.

"It was a coincidence," he said.

Jenny was tugging at my hand, trying to silence me. "Don't argue with him."

The class knew there was bad blood between us, and sometimes I felt a 14-year old girl shouldn't challenge her teacher. Mr. Boon disliked challenges from a girl.

Jenny approached me during the break and shared with me she had a new hobby. Ever heard of autograph hunting?" Jenny asked.

"What is that?"

"A group of kids in my neighborhood went to the hotel where the best Russian soccer team is staying. They brought with them their best goalkeeper in the world."

"And?" *I was not interested.*

"They asked for the soccer players' signatures, and talked to them."

"Talked to them?" *Now it caught my attention.*

"Yes, you know English. I think it will be fun. You get their signatures and meet with the best goalkeeper in the world. Interested?"

"The best in the world, huh? Let me think about it. My mother doesn't like me to go to hotels." *I needed to verify with my father. He knew most of the soccer teams in the world.*

At home, I talked about Jenny's new hobby. Since my parents knew her parents, the conversation was positive. I told my father that the Russian team brought with them their best goalkeeper in the world.

"Kublitsky." My father jumped at the name

"You know this guy?"

"Who doesn't? If you can get his signature, it is well worth it. Wow, Kublitsky, huh?"

I clapped my hands. "All right then, I'll get his signature."

It was a challenge. Indonesia loved soccer. A goalkeeper as famous as Kublitsky only came once in a blue moon. Many teenagers and adults were waiting in front of his bungalow to get a glimpse of the best goalkeeper in the world.

"We need to do something, Jenny. We'll never get our turn this way."

To get their attention I waved and talked in English, perhaps the only teenager who dared to speak a foreign language. A man saw me and motioned me to come closer. I dragged Jenny with me.

"You speak English?" he asked.

"Yes, sir."

"You are the only girls here; why the interest in football?" he asked.

"I've watched a lot of soccer games, sir, and my father is a fan."

"Ah! You want to meet Kublitsky then, ya?"

"Yes," Jenny and I answered. The crowd did the same and pushed forward. Some of them shouted, "We were here first."

The gentleman appeared to be the Russian team's coach. The team members, swarmed by a group of young men and two girls, found it amusing.

Speaking English helped. We both laughed and danced around at our achievement. We were perhaps the only two girls in our school who had met the world famous goalkeeper and got his signature too. We were proud of ourselves until the news arrived at school.

The word was out: Esther and Jenny shook hands with the world's best goalkeeper and got his signature too. We were the talk of the town. I was quiet in class when Mr. Boon entered. He started with "I have your scores from the last test. I can guarantee you that Esther will like the signature of Kublitsky more than the score from me. Right, Esther?" Rustling of test papers, and I kept quiet.

"What's your answer, I'm asking you a question?" he asked.

Silence. *It was a stupid question, and I didn't like being put on the spot.*

Jenny nudged me and whispered, "Just say anything, otherwise he will get mad."

"He will get mad anyway, no matter what I reply," I told her. It won't be favorable to him," I said. "He pokes at me every chance he gets. If I answer 'No, I like your score better,' he'd think I lied. If I tell the truth, 'I like Kublitsky's signature better,' he'll think I am mocking him."

I drew a deep breath. At this moment a frontal confrontation was imminent. There was total silence in the class.

Suddenly, I heard his thundering voice. "Out of the class." Mr. Boon's face was red and he pointed to the door.

It was only a signature. What's the big deal?

Without a word I left my seat and headed straight for the door with my head held high. The whole class reacted with "Ooh."

I was fed up with his attitude.

What now? The activity lounge would be an excellent choice. Nobody there. Whenever students wanted to play ping pong, that's the place they would go. I needed my peace and bought shaved ice with syrup from a vendor stationed close by.

A group of young men came in and found me sitting alone enjoying my ice.

The leader of the group was Teong Lee, a ping pong champion of our school, and a regional champion.

"Hey Esther, what are you doing outside of class? Doesn't the teacher like you? Who is he?"

"Algebra teacher."

"He's jealous of Kublitsky."

"How do you know this?" I asked.

"The algebra teacher likes you, but you like Kublitsky more. He gets mad. Understand?"

"Ewww, he's old."

"Everyone is talking about Kublitsky, and how you got his signature. Makes other people jealous too. Want to play ping pong?"

"I don't know how."

"Come on, it's easy, I'll teach you."

A champion wanted to teach me? What have I got to lose? I discarded my shaved ice, and said, "You're on."

He took out several ping pong bats and balls from his duffel bag.

"Wow, you carry lots of them in your bag," I commented.

"I have to," Teong Lee answered, "for the just-in-case situations…broken bats, lost balls. Take off your shoes. You cannot play in those shoes."

When the bell rang, my class ran out and saw me rigorously playing ping pong, doubling up with Tiong Lee and friends. That was the ultimate fun I remembered while attending intermediate school.

Jenny came looking for me: "I thought I would find you crying after that confrontation with him."

Tiong Lee passed by and commented, "Hey, Esther, try the next tournament for girls. Stay after school and practice."

"Are you kidding me?"

"No, I am serious," he said. "You have potential. Good footwork and arm reflexes." He left.

I looked at Jenny and said, "Hmmm". I was already considering Teong Lee's suggestion. Maybe I could be a champion.

"Apologize to your algebra teacher." Jenny woke me up from my dream.

"Why? I did nothing wrong. He was picking on me. He could have asked you the same question. Why only me? I stayed quiet and refrained from all conversation with him.

"He could flunk you," Jenny said.

"No, he can't. If I do my homework and get good grades on the final exam, he can't flunk me."

I finished the school year becoming the runner up for the girl's ping pong championship. Not bad for a first try. That became my trophy during my intermediate school years.

I kept my promise and stopped communication with my algebra teacher. The only way to confront him was to do my homework and do well on my algebra tests. Nothing else mattered.

My parents came to know about my disagreement with Mr. Boon. "How did he find out that you got Kublitsky's signature? Somebody must have leaked it to him.

"Next time, keep some things to yourself. Tell Jenny if you need to, but tell her to keep it private. Some people could be envious and make ugly remarks. You are too honest with your feelings. Some students are older than you and more mature. They use your words and twist them. Be careful," my father said.

"You have what they don't have, the confidence to speak English. Deep in their hearts, they want to be like you. Next time, remember, don't be too honest."

"Yes, Pappie." I remembered my father's wise words and advice.

When the new school year started, Mr. Boon came to see me in my ninth grade classroom; we shook hands and made peace.

Pak Tan must have been behind his friendly gesture. He said to all of us, "You may not see each other again. Make peace and separate as friends." I liked Pak Tan.

Despite my father's suggestion to study economics rather than languages, I continued with languages, art, and history.

My attempts to become a ping pong champion faded with the departure of Teong Lee who moved to a different school.

"Did you hear the news? John Wayne is coming to Jakarta. Let's get his signature," Jenny said.

Soccer teams from Socialist countries had lost their spark. I grew tired of listening to their countries being the best, without God.

Pak Tan commented, "Without God? No can do. Always walk with Him."

I agreed.

John Wayne's signature remains the best autograph hunt I ever had, besides Kublitsky. Seeing him was an enjoyment and a challenge. Jenny and I had to compete with people from all walks of life.

As a celebrity, he was afraid of being mobbed and remained in his room on the second floor of his hotel. He would step out on the balcony, wave, and say, "Thank you for coming…" The thought of him coming down to meet with us was an impossibility.

"How are we going to get his signature now? It is unlikely he will come down to meet us," I said to Jenny after an hour's wait to no avail.

I had to find a better way and walked around the compound of the hotel, where I came across the husband of my dancing teacher, Ronny. He worked at the hotel.

"John Wayne's signature, huh? A challenge, for sure," Ronny said. "He is well guarded. I have an idea."

Ronny motioned to a waiter who was carrying a tray. They talked for a moment, and I saw Ronny switch with the waiter. He said to us, "Put your autograph books here on the tray." He left.

When he returned, he told me to hush. He didn't want to get mobbed by the people standing there. John Wayne had signed my album: "Good Luck, John Wayne."

Jenny and I kept it a secret; we didn't share it with anyone. I wanted to keep my peace for a change. I followed my father's advice.

"How did you know Ronny? If it hadn't been for him, we could have returned empty-handed," Jenny said.

"His wife, Aty, is my modern dance teacher," I told Jenny.

"Is that all the activity you have now?"

"No, I have girl-scout, gymnastics and piano. My father is inviting a Dutch piano teacher for Tina and me. We will have lessons at home."

"Wow, with the homework we get, you will have no time to play." Jenny was right. We were growing up.

My parents wanted me to have activities closer to home. I returned to playing badminton as the club was close by. Twice a week would not disturb my studies, and give me enough exercise.

During my final badminton game, it drizzled. I persisted, and finished my game in the rain. I arrived home drenched, and Pappie was furious.

He looked at me and said, "You couldn't come home before the rain started, could you? You want to die?"

I was shocked. *Die? Because of the rain?* I stared at him with wide eyes.

"You didn't know, did you? When you were seven years old, you were sick with Tuberculosis, not Pneumonia," he said. "How you survived, we don't know. That's why we forbade you to play in the rain."

My mother rescued me and took me to the bathroom where I got out of my wet clothes.

I asked my mother, "Is it true I almost died?"

My mother nodded. "Yes, we didn't want you to know, as you were too young to understand."

I remembered the Lord's Prayer my mother and I did together. *Could it be our prayer?*

It was the day before Christmas when this happened...

Chapter 14: The Marriage Proposal

"Here we are, Christmas holiday. Do you have any plans for what you would like to do?" Jenny asked.

"My family will go to church, and watch a play," I said. "There will be refreshments and an exchange of gifts. You should see our church's tree, decorated to the top, where an angel gazes down on all of us. I believe Christmas will substitute our traditional Sinterklaas and Black Peter."

"What a pity," Jenny said. "I like Sinterklaas."

"I do too. Sinterklaas was the traditional celebration during the Dutch occupation, originating from Spain, called St. Nicholas."

My mind flew back to that time when my teacher told us the story of a rich and good-hearted nobleman living in Spain. Once a year, on December 5th, he rode his white horse dressed in a red robe, and disguised his face with white whiskers and a long beard. He distributed presents to the poor peasants around his estate. His tall red hat had a cross on it. On his right hand, he held a shepherd's rod. He was accompanied by his helper Black Peter who carried presents in a big bag."

People said he had a list of all the good and bad children. Black Peter would swing his broom and pretend to spank the naughty kids. It was a fun day. Our elementary school held this entertainment every year. This tradition faded after we gained our independence from the Dutch. I missed it.

"Pappie invited Sinterklaas to our house for several years," I told Jenny. "We were delighted to see him at our house, and the kids in the neighborhood also enjoyed seeing him. Oh well! Merry Christmas, Jenny. See you next year."

I was 15 years old and attending the final intermediate school year. Tina and I had a new dress for Christmas Eve, and we were about to leave for church when our maid told my parents we had visitors.

"Visitors? Are you expecting anyone?" my father asked my mother.

"No. Wonder who they could be."

Our visitors were an entourage comprising of three adults: father, mother, and daughter in her thirties, called Linda. They came on behalf of the only son and heir to their Shoes and Bags industry.

Linda informed my parents that they were visiting to extend a marriage proposal to my parents' daughter. They didn't realize there were two daughters.

My mother and father were caught by surprise. "A marriage proposal?" My father said. He thought they meant my sister, as she was already 17 and had a boyfriend, called Chris. This entourage could be his parents, but they were in the face powder business.

Still bewildered with the situation, Mammie rushed inside.

"Come on, dress up, we have guests, and they want to see you."

"Both of us? That's strange. Why?" I asked.

"Never mind. Just hurry," Mammie said.

We both entered the living room and were introduced to the guests.

I felt like a cow being dragged to market.

"This is Tina, my oldest daughter, and this is Esther, our second daughter. Which is the one your brother mentioned?" she asked Linda.

"Which one of you play badminton?"

"That would be me," I said. "Why?"

"That means you were the one my brother saw playing badminton and wondered whether there could be a bonding."

"You mean, me marrying him? Just like that? Out of the blue? I don't even know who he is and what he looks like." I started fidgeting with anger, made a fist with my hand, ground my teeth, and frowned.

I could see a storm brewing in my father's eyes. He was assuming that I was sneaking behind his back while pretending to play badminton.

"How could your brother have an interest in my daughter?" Pappie asked. "Has he talked with her?"

"No, I don't think Esther knew he was watching her from behind a tree. Our house is next to the club house."

"You mean he has never talked to her but wants to marry her? She is only 15 years old." Pappie shook his head in disbelief.

"Fifteen? She looks more mature than fifteen," Linda said

Hey, I know my age, OK? I am here, talk to me.

"You think I don't know my own daughter? Yes, she looks more mature, because she likes games of sport. She is bigger in size than most girls. Taller too," my father commented.

The meeting went on: Where did I attend school, what was my major subject, and other activities besides badminton.

These visitors were talking about me, but ignoring me as if I weren't there. *Hey, you, ask me. I'm here, I'll tell you.* I disliked them already.

Linda said we could come to a satisfactory arrangement on both sides. Could my father come to a decision, in perhaps two weeks?

Hey, you, whatever your name is, I am here. I can hear you. Ask me. I don't want to marry your brother, why didn't he come himself?

Another thing bothering me was that Linda's parents were silent during the entire meeting. Perhaps they were too busy speculating whether I was worthy enough for their son.

By now, I was raging mad. I stood up and looked at my parents. "Just like that, huh? I have nothing to say," I said, hands on my hips. "I don't even know this guy, and I hate being a girl. Nothing to say, huh? If I am forced into this... marriage, I will leave this house. Just you wait and see. What if I don't want to marry a Chinese man? All these traditions make me sick. I will leave this place. I am going to America."

My mother took me by the arm and hustled me out of the living room to avoid further embarrassment.

"How old is he anyway?" I asked my mother

"Twenty-six," my mother replied.

"Ewww! Can't he find a girl his age? He is too old for me."

My sister had to rub it in. "Well, you love handbags and shoes. If you marry him, you can have them galore. Think of your sister."

"Oh, shut up. Why don't you marry him? Your boyfriend has not asked you yet. So, how's that, Mam? Why not Tina? She is of marrying age."

"You really didn't see him standing there behind the tree?" Mammie asked.

"I was concentrating on the game, Mammie." I said. "I wasn't watching him. I saw somebody in a white shirt and long pants standing there. But I thought he was interested in the game."

We continued our arguments on the way to church. How my father could drive with the ruckus in the back seat was beyond me. Tina and I stopped arguing when we reached the church. Respect the church, make peace, no arguments.

Two weeks passed by, and no news. Nobody talked about the marriage proposal. My parents were quiet and calm. It was about me, and it drove me crazy, not knowing what decision my parents would make.

I went to my mother and asked brusquely, "So, am I to be married off now?"

"No, you are still too young," my mother replied. "Pappie asked them to wait two years, at least until you complete high school."

"And what happens then?"

"Nothing. They've already declined. So, calm down, and continue your daily duties. No more threats of leaving the house. You're going to be married some day. Are you going to make a big fuss like this all over again?"

"It has to be a man of *my* choice, not arranged by a stranger," I said.

Chapter 15: Good Deeds

"I cannot imagine you as a married woman," Jenny said, shaking her head. I told her about the marriage proposal when we returned to school in January. She giggled.

"I'm glad your parents rejected him. I can't imagine you marrying him. What will happen if he doesn't like sports? And you do." Jenny said

I told her that this man stood behind a tree and watched me play badminton. He was too shy to come forward and introduce himself. As a traditional Chinese man, he had to ask his sister and parents to propose.

"Rather than introducing himself?" Jenny asked.

"That is not the Chinese way, Jenny. Girls have nothing to say. Our duty is to follow and obey our parents. My mother said one day I would marry. Why the big fuss?"

"What else do we girls have to do to be ideal contenders for marriage?" Jenny said in a mocking way.

"The three attributes: cook, bake, and sew. A woman needs to care for her household."

"Does Tina have to do all these?" Jenny asked.

"Yes, she does, because she will be engaged after finishing high school. Remember, she's 17 years old, marrying age."

Jenny murmured, "Better to stay single. No headaches."

I made Jenny promise not to tell anyone about my marriage proposal. She agreed.

Pak Tan entered the class and spoke to us about doing good deeds.

"Like what, Pak Tan. What is a deed?" Effendi asked.

"Doing something good to make someone happy," was his reply.

"How many must we do?" Effendi asked again.

"One a day."

"That's it?" Everyone asked.

"Does anybody know how many days there are in a year?" Pak Tan asked.

"365 days. Wow, that means 365 deeds a year. What if we miss one? I asked"

"All right...let's assume you miss the target. How many will you miss?" He put his right hand by his ear while pointing his finger at the students. "Anyone?"

"100." Effendi answered.

Pak Tan went to the green board and wrote 365 minus 100 equals 265 deeds. "Okay, that leaves 265 good deeds. Right? It is still a lot of good deeds. Now write your list."

"It is difficult to do," said Pauline.

"Pauline?" Pak Tan turned to her. "Why is that? Can you tell me?"

Pauline thought for a moment: "I don't know, it's just difficult."

Pak Tan helped our task with these wise words, "When you walk through life, don't always look up. Look down occasionally. If you keep looking up, you will envy people who have more than you. You'll be unhappy. Look for people who have less. They'd love to be in your shoes, to have what you have. Do good to people in need."

"Like the Good Samaritan from the Bible," Liane said.

We were all quiet.

As a Christian, I found a lot of good deeds in the Bible. Jesus restored the eyesight of a blind man, He revived Lazarus from the dead, He cleansed the lepers—to name a few.

A young woman called Esther became Queen of the Jews. She saved the Jews because she dared to intervene. She had done her good deed.

"Well, you've done a lot," my mother said while I was doing my homework. "Everyone in this household has done a lot of good deeds. Except you did them spontaneously, and didn't recognize them."

"What have I accomplished?"

"You helped around the house, went to the market and carried my bags. Negotiating with the Chinese vendors helped a lot to get the discounted price.

"Both you and Tina helped me cook in the kitchen, clean the house. You do your homework. You make us happy. See? You never considered those as good deeds, but they are.

"You babysat our neighbor's baby when her mother had to run errands. Remember what she named her baby?" my mother said.

"Oh yes, she called her Esther. Now I understand. We reached out to the neighborhood kids and took them for a drive. Their parents didn't have a car. We took them to the roadside restaurant and ate chicken porridge together," I added. "Their parents never did. Right, Mammie? Some of them had never seen the ocean before we took them there."

"You remember Yohan?" My mother asked.

"What about Yohan?"

"You played chess with Yohan. He was a smart but lonesome young man, who did not have many friends to play with. He only watched from afar. You said yourself, he had a peculiar game. How many girls in our old neighborhood understood how to play chess? You gave him joy that no girl could."

I compiled my list. I became attentive of events taking place around me. Perhaps that's what Pak Tan wanted us to be aware of. I learned to feel content with God's blessings. The neighborhood kids didn't have what we had. Yet, we were not rich.

Pak Tan's words rang in my ear, "Many individuals would yearn to be in your shoes."

My mother put it in different words: "Feel blessed you have a roof over your head. Feel blessed you have food on the table. Be thankful you have clothes to wear. Thank the Good Lord you have a family. You have a lot for which to be thankful.

"Don't grumble, be contented, others don't have what you have."

I realized the significance of the words when our Handicraft teacher explained further with a quotation:

"I have no shoes, and I murmured, until I saw a man with no feet."
Quotation unknown

Our intermediate school years ended. The school organized a picnic in the mountains. The students were looking forward to it, when I got word from my sister that our father forbade us to go. I was depressed.

Pak Tan called me into the office during intermission.

"Your father forbids you and your sister to join the picnic. He came yesterday when you were in class, and asked me whether I could guarantee your life. The answer was 'No', only God can. We have several teachers joining, thus assuring your safety."

I left the office. Before I closed the door, I said, "I'll bring the money tomorrow, Pak Tan. I want to go."

Mr. Tan shook his head and took a deep breath. It was our last picnic together.

At home, I asked my mother. She shook her head. I went to my father. He was annoyed that I pressed the issue.

"What in the word NO don't you understand? You want to defy me?" asked my father in his thunderous voice.

"I don't understand why you asked my teacher whether he could guarantee our lives. Only God can. Remember the time we went to the mountain and we had a loose lug nut? You said yourself if God hadn't held on to the lug nut, we would have fallen into the ravine and died.

"Remember Mammie? You said yourself, we need to pray. Why can't we pray now? If I were meant to die, it would have been a long time ago. Remember when I was seven years old and I was gravely ill?"

Tears of frustration sprung in my eyes and I struggled hard not to cry. "I don't understand anymore. I prayed for a safe picnic and you still forbid me to go. What good is praying?"

An absolute silence fell in the house. My sister refused to cooperate with me. She was afraid to face my father's fury. The next morning, when I passed the living room, my father called me and handed me the fee for the picnic.

"Here is the money. Just be careful and come back safe," he said.

"Yes, thank you, Pappie." I laughed. "How about Tina?"

"There's sufficient payment for both of you," my father said.

"Come on, Tina, we'll join the school picnic."

Tina couldn't fight for herself. I helped her get the approval from my father. I'd done my good deed for the day.

It was a wonderful picnic.

Chapter 16: Trending to Communism

"Where are you going for tenth grade, Jenny?" I asked.

"I guess the same school as you, another Christian School. However, I will follow trade and economics." Jenny answered.

"I will pursue languages, art, and history," I said.

"Tina and I will attend the same class," Jenny said.

"Are you sure your father let you choose languages?"

"No, he wants me to go into trade and economics, so I can work after graduating," I replied. "There are no companies using the English language, except the American and British Embassies." I sighed.

The new school was going great; however, the country's politics were on a downhill trajectory. Possibilities for jobs and specific studies became limited with communism creeping into the country and more government intervention. Indonesia was and remains a Muslim country. No one understood how Muslims and Communists could become united.

Tina followed my father's advice and decided on the C department following economics and trade, so did Liane, Tina's close friend and Jenny. I took the A Department following languages, art and history. Different Departments, but the same school.

I was sitting in my backyard letting my thoughts fly free like a bird when my mother found me.

"What are you thinking about?" she asked.

"What it will be like to be in tenth, eleventh and twelfth grades. I could stop pursuing my studies after high school and try to find a job, or go to college. Some of my classmates have already made their choices and have gone abroad. Their parents are well off."

"With the uncertainty in our politics and the country trending toward Communism, there may not be too many choices, unless you want to go to Russia," my mother said.

"Russia? Are you serious? I don't like Russia," I said. "My choice is still California, no matter what. I already know English. Russia is too cold."

My future remained a mystery.

My father's moonlighting business selling cars had picked up pretty well, and we had two cars. Mammie used the car with a driver to pick up my brothers from school.

My high school was within walking distance, and Tina walked straight home after school, while I went window shopping. I would venture alone to explore new areas around the school and the shopping strip. Soon enough I became an expert in shortcuts, and became familiar with new routes to get home.

Tina and I pursued new activities: ballet, gymnastics, and girl scouts. They kept us busy. I loved Morse code and tying knots.

I seldom talked to Jenny as she was in a different class; however, her classroom was opposite mine on the other side of the school's courtyard. I could see her and wave. I shared my bench with Hanna.

Reverend Lee became our new religion teacher. He graduated from a theological school in America. A tall man in his fifties, he was open-minded and charismatic. He shared real life stories. One of them was regarding blame.

"How do you provide a solution when being blamed for something you didn't do?" I asked during his weekly session.

Reverend Lee thought for a moment and replied, "Interesting question. Well, when that person blames you, he points his finger at you. Correct?"

"Yes, sir," the students answered and gathered around. Curiosity set in.

"It is only one finger. Now, point your forefinger at me." So we did.

"What are the other three fingers pointed at?" We looked at our fingers, "At us, Reverend Lee."

"Right. Therefore, when anyone blames you for anything, remember, that three fingers point back at him/her."

"Meaning?" I didn't understand.

"Nobody is perfect. It is easy to blame others; however, the person blaming you may not be without blame."

Reverend Lee had won my respect.

Before he left the class, he told us of the new church he would lead. "I suggest you attend. I will explain more about the blame game."

As I matured in age and experience, the image of Pak Tan (the Principal of my intermediate school) faded into the background. He was right. I would find a substitute.

The church led by Rev. Lee catered to younger audiences and opened new Sunday activities for me. I attended his service on Sunday, and he explained why people should refrain from pointing fingers at other people.

"He explained the subject at school, Tina. I want to know the stories he'll come up with," I whispered to my sister.

Tina said, "Shhh, be quiet. I want to listen to him, not you." I stuck out my tongue..

Reverend Lee read the story of Mary Magdalene. She was a whore, a slut, the lowest of the low. She had sinned, and people wanted to stone her to death. No one would help her. The Israelites asked Jesus, "Master, Master, can you help?"

Jesus answered, "Let the one who has never sinned throw the first stone."

Everybody had sinned, and nobody dared cast the first stone. When Mary Magdalene approached Jesus to thank Him, Jesus said, "Go, and sin no more."

I remembered the story so vividly and refrained from judging people and pointing fingers.

"Learn to forgive," Reverend Lee said from the altar. "Jesus did."

My father followed the news closely, as he didn't like where the government was going. Communism couldn't be trusted. Too much propaganda and empty promises. The Government didn't follow their own rules and regulations. Corruption and bribery were a way of life.

My father told us we needed to be careful with our spending. Through the grapevine, he heard that too much Indonesian currency was floating around, and it was possible the government might consider a devaluation.

I also heard the rumors at school. However, the teachers mentioned nothing, afraid of creating unnecessary panic. After a while, we forgot and concluded that perhaps the government had changed their mind

One morning after church, Tina and I found our house empty. After a few hours my father, mother and brothers returned and told us they went to Chinatown.

"What were you doing in China town?" I asked Mammie.

"Oh, we were checking the Banyan tree movie theatre. Remember the one that showed cowboy movies?"

"Yes. What about it.?" I asked.

"Well, the place has been closed. The theater got hit with the new regulation which requires the showing of more movies from socialist countries. The community preferred cowboys, and lost interest. What a shame. We miss Roy Rogers and Gene Autry." My mother sighed.

I was thinking more about the local people who didn't have money to pay for tickets to the big theaters. Even with old reruns, the movies served as their only entertainment. I felt sad. We had fond memories of the place.

My mother and I saw as many western movies as possible at the other three theaters near our house before they disappeared.

It was difficult to procure tickets. The queues were long. Everyone had wanted to see the movies before they disappear.

"This is impossible, Mam," I said. "Who can stand in line for a whole day? Some people with three maids could do it by replacing one another. There must be another way."

"Black market tickets," my mother suggested.

Tina said, "Not me." She shuddered.

"Let's try. The next movie is *Ben Hur*," my mother said.

"I read the comic book. Judah Ben Hur had a girlfriend. Her name was Esther. I will become an instant celebrity," I told my mother. Hmm, Ben Hur's girlfriend. The thought amused me. I laughed.

I ventured out to buy movie tickets 1through the black market and became good at it. Ben Hur was worth fighting for!

"Be careful not to get caught," my mother said.

I avoided the crowd.

Classmates asked, "Where can you buy tickets without standing in line?"

I pointed at my head. Meaning, "think."

My mother, Tina and I watched *The Ten Commandments;* the last one we saw was an Elvis Presley film, his one and only film before the government shut down Western movies. Still, from that one showing, we understood why Elvis Presley became the King of Rock and Roll. My classmates and I were heart-broken when there were no further Elvis movies.

Toward the end of the year, Indonesia imported more movies from socialist countries, Hungary, Soviet Union, and China among others. Western International Sports organizations had been substituted a few years earlier with Eastern Europe Sports Organizations starting with Kublitsky, the Russian best goalkeeper in the world.

The next step by the government was to shut down western music. Dutch books and magazines were non-existent. Fewer and fewer stores carried English reading materials. Gone were the comic books, which included one of my favorite series—Mandrake, the Magician.

Western dances disappeared. Private house parties could provide dancing. However, Boogie Woogie, Rock and Roll, and the Twist were capitalist dances and were forbidden.

I remember attending a birthday party. As the late afternoon turned to evening, the music heated up and guests were dancing the Twist. Doors and windows were closed to keep the sound inside the house.

With no warning, the police raided the place and the dancers were instructed to leave the premises. The party came to an abrupt end. My friends and I guessed that uninvited and envious neighbors might have tipped off the law enforcement. The raid brought back bad memories.

We listened to the radio programs and news from radio Australia, and made sure we lowered the volume. Gradually, entertainment became extinct; we were denied the pleasure of Western entertainment for many years.

Chapter 17: The Inner Voice

"Who has gone on a field trip?" our teacher, Pak Sugita, asked.

"What is a field trip?" I inquired.

"It is an educational tour away from home, to provide students with experiences outside their everyday activities. It is to explore the history of an area or place. We will have lectures built-in as we go along. Books are scarce, we need to see the subjects of our studies."

"This trip will take more time to prepare and I need to meet with the teachers and Principal for their approval. We will print and distribute flyers, including the itinerary. You all need to show and discuss the contents with your parents.

"Get their approval, and bring back the signed form as soon as you can. I can then make a head count," Pak Sugita concluded.

I loved to visualize the places we would visit, historic temples, tourist spots among others, visit local manufacturers that specialized in hand-painted *batik* materials. Badminton rackets were another specialty, as badminton was and remains one of Indonesia's favorite sports.

"You look so deep in thought," Hanna said. "We will see the beauty of nature and learn Indonesia's history in a visual way. I am looking forward to this event. Are you coming?"

I shrugged, and mumbled, "That would be nice."

Everyone was excited. The trip was something new. The teachers believed it was a brilliant idea, and all were for it.

It would be almost an impossibility to get my father's approval. A day trip would be all right, but a week-long?

I came to learn the complexities of this journey. Pak Sugita told us we would go to Central Java, three to four hours by train, and a bus would take us to our destination. We would spend the nights in schools. As there was no running water and pumping water was a necessity for our showers.

I looked forward to the lectures in open spaces close to the historical sites, with no comforts of home. "Don't forget to wear hats," Pak Sugita said.

My father listened to my presentation. He sighed but didn't answer. A one-week trip was too far-fetched. His daughters should remain close to home. He was over-protective. Pappie still remembered how sick I was as a little girl, that I almost died.

If I were healthy like Tina, I thought, I wouldn't have this problem. Pappie would let me go. He's worried I might get sick on the trip, and he wouldn't be there to help me."

My mother recognized my determination to join the school's field trip, but this was an almost impossible challenge to win. She knew I wouldn't succumb without a fight, like a thunderstorm threatening massive downpours, or a volcano on the brink of bursting.

My sister joined the conversation and suggested that I give up the plan. "You are aware how infuriated Pappie will be."

"So, you suggest I should go to the teacher and say, 'with all due respect teacher, I cannot go and I will pass the final exam. Thank you very much. Troolaloo! Have a nice day.'" I used various intonations to show my frustration, and walked around wiggling my butt.

"Why don't you tell the teacher that Pappie forbids you to go?" Tina asked.

"I am 16, Tina. There will be 39 students in the class besides me, and seven teachers are chaperoning. No problem there. I am trying to figure out what other reasons Pappie could have for not letting me go? I won't accept a plain, 'No' as his answer."

"Don't be too hard on your father," Mammie said. "He knows your weaknesses. Besides your health and allergies, you carry your heart in your mouth.

You are too honest with your feelings. He's told you that many times. He feels uneasy you will lose control and cause problems. The speed of words, spitted out, is like lightning. Twenty of the fastest horses in the universe can't catch the words and bring them back. What I mean is… be careful with what you are saying.

"Okay, fair enough. What else? Come on, Tina, help me out. What else?"

Tina shrugged. "Isn't that enough?"

"It would be a shame not to try. Should I drop the idea just like that?" I snapped my fingers, and I felt hopeless.

"Perhaps you should leave it be for the time being. Approach your father again later in the week," my mother suggested.

This time, I needed a miracle to make it happen.

"Master, Master, wake up, calm the storm." I stood up and lifted my arms to the heavens. It has become a habit of mine when I'm at the end of my rope.

"What are you doing?" Tina asked.

"Just like in the Bible. The disciples were in a boat on the sea while Jesus was sleeping. A storm was brewing, and the boat rocked up and down. The disciples felt hopeless, like I feel hopeless now—in a rowboat without oars. Without my compass, I lose my direction…where is East, where is West? The sky is dark, no moon in sight. Just dark clouds."

My mother and sister realized I wasn't making any sense. They left me alone.

To make matters worse, three months before the departure date, the biggest train crash in the history of Java happened. Many people were killed and injured. My hope for an approval had crashed like a glass shattering on the floor.

"So, Esther, are you joining us? What's holding you up? Where are your signed papers?" Pak Sugita woke me up from my daydream.

"I'll bring them, it's still two months away."

I tried alerting my father about the trip again during dinner time. He was sitting in the living room and I had to compete with the voice of the newscaster. I talked in a loud voice as if I were going somewhere.

"The educational trip is essential for my final exam, and we will not have another opportunity like this. Other schools don't even have this special program."

My sister frowned and asked, "Did Pappie let you go?"

"No."

"So, why are you talking as if you were going?"

"I'm hoping he will change his mind. Why don't you help me talk to him?"

Tina stared at me for a long time, then shuddered. "You are looking for trouble again," she said.

My father remained the ultimate authority in the house.

Another month flew by. At school, Luanna said, "You have to join us, Esther. Otherwise you will be the only one left behind. No fun."

"After tomorrow, it will be too late for you to join us," Pak Sugita said. "I need to deposit the funds." He added: "Is there anything I should know you haven't told me?"

"Her father forbids her to go," Luanna said.

"So, you are not going then?" Mr. Sugita looked at me.

"I *will* go, I'll bring the money tomorrow."

Pak Tan, our intermediary school principal, flashed across my mind; he was shaking his head. "War brewing with your father, again?"

At home, I went to my room and checked everything, books, clothes, question and answer sheet, vitamins, inhaler, cold medicines. I studied all the educational requirement.

I launched a short prayer. "Please, Father, show me the way."

My mother breezed into my room. "Do you know the story of the man who rode a tiger?"

"No, what happened?"

"Well, life won't always be smooth and without problems. It has its trials and tribulations. When life gets rough, it could be like riding a tiger. If you get off, the tiger will kill you. However, if you remain seated on his back and wait until he gets tired and falls asleep, you can get down and walk away unharmed. But you won't know when the tiger gets tired. You need patience."

"You aren't helping me, Mam. I'm running out of time, and need the money now."

"I suggest you take a deep breath," Mammie said, "Face your father, and stay calm. All right?"

I stood up and took a step toward the door. A strange inner voice said, *"Ask your father to join you on the trip."*

"What?" I replied.

"Go, ask him." The voice answered.

In the living room, I confronted my father and said, "I would be the only one left behind, and I wasn't planning on failing my exam."

My mother positioned herself between my father and me. She didn't look at either of us. In case the situation took an unexpected turn, she would be ready to intercept.

The same inner voice returned, this time with more pressure, *"Ask him to go with you."*

I clasped my hands together as if in prayer, and put both hands against my chest, and asked, "If you forbid me to go with the school group, can you promise me you will take me to these places yourself?"

My father looked at me in disbelief, and left the room.

"Why on earth did you ask your father to go?" My mother asked.

"I didn't, Mam, my inner voice did."

"What inner voice?"

"There isn't any explanation, Mammie." I said. "It came before I confronted Pappie, and again when I was in front of him. This time I followed it."

My mother paused, and looked at me.

Mammie said that during her wedding ceremony, the pastor of her church left her with golden words to hang on to during her married life. My mother's life wouldn't be easy, but God would send a helper to her. She thought the helper would be a man or woman, an adult. Perhaps a friend or a family member.

After the incident with the inner voice, she realized the helper was me.

Chapter 18: Devaluation

My mother had shared with my father that the inner voice guided me to the final question. She shared the biblical quotation, *"If God is for us, who can be against us?"*

The trip was a huge success. Nobody complained about the poor accommodations, the heat, long walks, and lectures. It was a once-in-a-lifetime experience.

Pak Sugita was great at sharing the background of the historical sites. He knew the stories by heart, and never carried a notebook. The history came alive and was a huge asset to our educational needs.

For the first time, I observed the scenery around me. This is my country. The greeneries on the mountains, the blue skies, streams, colorful flowers and fruits in abundance served a richness of its own. President Sukarno once said: "I have been to other countries in the world, but nothing compares to Indonesia. Be proud of your country." He was right.

My Sunday school teacher, Mrs. Lian, once stated, "You want to see the greatness of God? Look at the beauty of nature."

My family was waiting when I arrived home.

"You look darker than when you left, too much sun? Were you sick during the trip?" Tina asked.

"How was the accommodation? Did you have to pump water?" my brothers inquired.

I smiled. "I had a wonderful time. Beautiful weather, and a wonderful experience. It was a one-of-a-kind experience, and I *will* pass my exam."

I wiggled my butt and went to unpack and crash. Home sweet home.

Why was happiness short-lived? I was on cloud nine when I went on the field trip…why must this happen?

My family faced some serious financial difficulties. My father worked for a government office, and word got around that they would release the older generation of Chinese employees without their pension. He took an early retirement which also meant a reduced paycheck. He didn't trust the government anymore and didn't want to wait until they ended his position.

Devaluation of the currency was another scary thought. My father counseled my sister and me that we might have to work, instead of continuing our education. I wanted to pursue college. Tina and her boyfriend planned on getting engaged right after graduating from high school.

A few weeks later we received devastating news.

Our Principal, Mr. Lim, instructed everyone to go home. "When I say 'home', I mean stay home."

Unpleasant news had a habit of being released over week-ends. When the school instructed the students to leave the premises, we could expect the worst of circumstances.

"What happened, Mr. Lim?" I asked on the way out.

"Go home, and you will find out," he said.

I looked for Tina, and asked her whether she had received more information.

"No, the teacher told us to go home too."

We both walked as we knew my mother would take the car to pick up our three brothers. We passed the shopping strip which was quiet and deserted. The owners of the shops closed early, afraid of vandalism. There was no one on the streets; it was like a dead city. Tina and I walked quickly. My heart thumped even faster.

Arriving home, I saw my mother sitting at the dining table, head bent. My father sat opposite her. Everyone was quiet. Our driver had gone home too.

"What's going on?" I asked.

My father tried to make sure the children understood the situation. "The Government has devaluated the currency with no warning. All the bills are now worth 10% only. I had already changed the money to small bills a week ago. However, I forgot to tell your mother. She changed the bills back to large ones. Now we only have sufficient savings for three months. I had to let the driver go, and we must sell the car.

"You girls could help to make ends meet, and look for a job. Esther, you have been taking classes in typing and shorthand. They may come in handy."

I watched my mother. She hadn't moved or even looked up at us. I guessed she felt guilty and was at a loss.

"So, what else can we do in the meantime?" I asked my father.

"Rumors have it you can still change the old currency to the new currency, for ten percent more in value; however, it is dangerous to try."

"What must we do?"

"People who know how can try and go to the shopping strip and wait there. I received information that a man would tap you on your shoulder and ask if you need to change money. Just say yes, and he will take you to a place where you can change to the new bills."

"What other choices do we have? Can we trust the man?"

"We need to pray that all will go well," Mammie said. "Let me go. It is my fault we lost our savings. The military suspects all men folk," she added. "I can at least try."

"Laine, you cannot do this alone. You could get caught. You need someone to go with you," my father said.

I looked around. Tina looked as if she would cry, and my three brothers were too young to understand. I saw the frown on my parents' faces.

This was not the time to feel sorry. There must be something I could do.

I stood up and said, "I'll go with you, Mammie. Let's do it while we still have light. The place is close by, and we can pretend that we are waiting for Pappie to pick us up."

"You?" my father said.

"Yes, why not me?" I looked around with my hands on my hips. "I know the place and I know the area. Ten percent more is better than nothing. Let's go, Mammie. We should not waste time." I motioned my mother to get up.

My father handed the bag to her. I was sure they both had counted the total amount. I was sure they had been debating the best way to change the money. "Laine, be careful," he said.

Mr. Lie, our Indonesian language teacher, once nicknamed me "Mrs. Major", as I took charge most of the time. Now, I felt like one.

Off we went straight to the shopping area in a pedicab. The driver had known us for years. "Please be careful, ma'am. People are desperate," he said.

My mother nodded. We went to stand at the corner of the shopping strip, and waited.

It was an eerie feeling to see a vacant shopping strip, so quiet, not a soul around. We were the only ones on the strip. A once bustling shopping strip had become a dead zone. The breeze blew papers along the street, the last purchase receipts before closing. The sun had gone down, darkness was enfolding us.

We heard a voice behind us: "You want to change money?"

Before we could answer, a military jeep came around the next corner toward us.

The man disappeared.

"Ma'am, what are you doing here?" the officer asked.

"Oh, we are waiting for my husband, sir. He is a little late. As soon as he arrives, we will go home," Mammie said.

"Stay home, do you understand? It is not safe on the street."

"Yes, officer."

The strange man reappeared. "You still want to change money?"

"Yes," my mother said.

"Follow me," and we followed.

"Did you pray?" I asked my mother

"Yes, I did."

"Good."

The stranger went into the alleys, turned left, and then right. After several turns, my mother stopped and looked around.

"What's the matter, Mammie? Why are you stopping?"

"I am not sure what area this is."

"We are still in the same area, he only went by way of the alleys. Don't worry, I know the area well. We are still in the same shopping strip," I said.

"You know this area?"

"Yes."

The man returned: "What's the matter? Hurry, we need to continue before the military finds us."

A few minutes later, we heard, "In here." A door panel slid open, and we entered a small, empty store. My mother felt relieved, as it was a Chinese store. Three men were sitting at a table. A big bag on the side.

"You have the money?" One man asked.

"Yes," my mother said.

Another man took the bag from my mother and poured the money on the table. All three men helped, and they put the counted money in a different bag. I could tell they had done this many times. *Where did they get the automatic counting machine?*

My mother watched them sorting without missing a beat. One man put the new money in our bag and handed it to my mother. We didn't need to recount as they did that with the machine. We went out the door. However, before I left, I turned around and asked the men a question, "Where are you going to dump the old money? What good will it be to you?"

"We will use the old money in the villages. Buy commercial properties and land. The news will reach them next week."

I felt like someone had stabbed me in the stomach.

"Did you hear what he said, Mam?"

"It's not our problem."

"To some people, it will mean certain death."

It was the most devastating era I could remember. The media reported the many tragic incidents as a few accidentals.

It was a day to remember. College seemed far away.

I heard my mother's voice singing softly: Rock of Ages, cleft for me...

Let me hide myself in Thee...

Don't worry Mammie, 'If God is for us, He will give us strength to overcome all things'.

Chapter 19: College Years and the Interview

The devaluation era was the worst in history. People felt robbed of their life savings. Death and unrest were everywhere. Those in the villages suffered the most. They felt blessed when city people offered them more for their properties. A week later their world fell apart; their hopes and the future of their children crashed to smithereens.

As young as I was, we couldn't ignore the unfortunate events. I felt the anger in my father as he sat at the dining table, covering his forehead with his right hand. Perhaps he had a throbbing headache…there was no way out. Fifty-year olds had no place in the workforce, neither did teenagers.

Mammie liked watching movies. Tina and I accompanied her. Now we could only sit at the back of our house and talk about movies we read about in the newspaper. Gone were our cars and driver. I curtailed my badminton activities. We were home before dark. Whatever we had to do, we did in the morning and afternoon hours. It was unsafe to be out at night.

Aargggh!

"Why must this happen?" This was a cry heard throughout the nation. Parents who couldn't provide for their children anymore killed them while they were sleeping, and then kill themselves. They didn't want their children to suffer in someone else's hands. Family suicides had become a tragic ending for many. There was no future, and no trust in the Government. All I could do was pray.

My life had changed, and college seemed only a dream. Responsibility laid heavy on my young shoulders.

I talked to my father about continuing my studies; he could offer no solution.

"You need to find a job. It's of the utmost importance right now."

There were no job openings for adults, let alone high school graduates. Period. There were too many people looking for work and I couldn't compete with them. We were fortunate to have a roof above us, and felt blessed to have food on the table, and a family to come home to. I learned to count my blessings even more.

My part-time jobs included teaching English to two children, and teaching Indonesian to a returning Dutch-Chinese family. That, and my father's pension kept our heads above water. I also became a guide for the Thai World Champion badminton team. It was fun breezing through the gates with the world champions of men's singles and doubles, and sitting in their VIP lounge with my college friends.

The most interesting job I wanted was to become an English interpreter for an international conference in Jakarta. CONEFO (Conference of the New Emerging Forces, Communism) would provide me with free tuition, and I thought it was worth the experience. It could help to pay for my college tuition too.

After passing all the tests and various levels of interviews, the Committee disqualified me. They needed graduates with Master Degrees, not a second-year college student. I felt like somebody had popped my balloon. *Poof!* Back to basics. I was nineteen years old.

The diversity of part-time jobs turned out to be lucrative enough for me to continue my studies in College, and I attended the Christian University of Indonesia, English Department, in Jakarta. We had teachers from foreign countries, including British, American, and Australian.

The University was in its beginning stages, but its English Department was accepted as the best. It was subsidized by the Government. The location was farther than desired, too far to walk, and I had to take public transportation.

Wow! College…a dream come true. I stood and looked with pride at the old building with its big rooms and large auditorium. My college. Now I could see my Bachelor's Degree, still a long way to go.

The Christian University's prominent neighbors were the University of Indonesia, opposite us on the other side of the Boulevard, the Council of Churches, and the Bible Institute on our right. I kept my peace with the Christian community.

Stage acting was on my menu for several years with training by a well-known Director/Actor, called Steve. Perhaps I may become an actress some-day? With the uncertainty of the workforce, I had to diversify myself for the future. Acting boosted my self-confidence in public speaking and on stage. I was able to face the public without fear. I called it survival.

Buying study books was a challenge as there was only one bookstore that carried the English books. The store owner had to wait three months for the shipments to arrive from America or England. It was 'survival of the fittest' to get the first supplies.

I had to watch my expenses. The books were expensive. But, without the books I would have to withdraw from school. After some thought, I figured out that instead of buying ten books for the school year myself, why not divide the costs among seven college girls? It would be do-able. I networked and gathered seven girls to form a study group. We shared the books, and we were thankful to continue our studies. Nothing was to deter me from getting my degree.

The difference in age and backgrounds turned out to be a serious situation for the professors. The temptation to be absent from class among senior students, to watch a movie and shop, was hard to avoid.

My drive to finish my studies in the quickest time possible, and the lack of funds, meant perfect attendance. The Dean elected me to be Head of the

Class. The teenage students loved me, more hated me because they were adults. *So what?*

To keep order in the classroom, I had to keep the attendance record, and make sure all students understood the seriousness of poor attendance.

I stood in front of the class (this was one of the moments when my acting experience helped me). I raised my arm, attendance book in my hand, and said, "Here's an attendance book, given by the Dean to keep track of *your* attendance. Let me make it simple. Whether you are present or absent, it's up to you. "I will jot it down in here," I said, touching the book…"No excuses.

"Should you wish to see a movie, lunch with friends or go shopping… it's your choice. My duty is to mark you as absent in this book.

"I haven't much money and time. I want to pass my final test as soon as I can, and I won't let you"…pointing at the senior girls…"stand in the way. Capiz?"

There was lots of jealousy and anger but I hoped one day they would thank me. Some of them did.

One girl, Susan, tried so hard to be in favor with the teachers. She would spread gossip and lies about me. I didn't let it deter me from my studies and focus. After a while, however, her gossip appalled me. I told my mother that one of these days I would smack her in the face.

"Whoa, no smacking," said my mother. "Keep your hands clean. If you are faultless, someday someone will smack her for you."

"Are you serious, Mammie? Who will smack her for me?" I said.

"Just wait and see."

A week later as I was doing my homework, I heard voices in the living room, "Auntie, is Esther home?"

"Yes, she's in the back." Susan entered and she raised her arms when she saw me, and asked for forgiveness. Then blurted out what had happened to her, being smacked by a military man.

"What did you do?" I asked.

"I didn't like him to cross my path" Susan said.

"Don't you know that the military own the streets? Stupid girl."

She wanted to confront the man to apologize. Instead he smacked her cheek. She was breathing heavily and rambling. I asked Suzan to calm down.

"Want a drink of water?" I asked.

She waved her hands in front of her face, and said, "No, no, I wanted to tell you the story. I thought of you right away. How I had wronged you. Please forgive me."

My mother was right. Susan and I became friends.

On one interesting occasion, Susan approached me before the final exam. "Esther, can you help pray for me?"

"Why?" I asked. "You can pray to God too."

Susan said, "God listens to you."

"Oh, come on. Where did you get that idea?" I said. "If you study well, you will pass. I can't pray and expect God to make it happen right away." I lifted my hand and said "*poof!*" Do you understand me?"

"God is not a servant. Prayer is like planting a seed. You break the ground, then nurture, water and fertilize it. After some time, the seed will blossom. Like a prayer, it takes time. My former teacher, Pak Tan, said, 'God is not your butler.'" Susan looked dismayed and didn't bother me further. I heard she passed after the second try.

I came close to going to the United States when Ms. Liz approached me and offered me a scholarship. "Would you go?" she asked.

"I'd love to. Let me get together and discuss this with my parents."

"Go, and never come back," Pappie said. "Whatever you need to do in the States, do it, but never come back. Your future is there. Don't worry about us. We'll manage."

Mammie disagreed. Her teenage daughter going to the States? So far from her family? How would she live out there on her own? How about monetary needs? I needed a prayer. *Can I go, Lord?*

News got around about a returning graduate. A hush hush sad story. He had received a scholarship, and returned home a doctor. His mother worked as a vendor of baked cookies to make ends meet and help support her son. She went door to door selling her goods, and was proud of her son fulfilling his responsibilities in an impeccable manner.

The Government wasn't prepared to successfully administer returning graduates. His appointment was to one of the big islands. Instead of a blooming career, the doctor was murdered. His mother had a mental breakdown.

Scholarships may have come as a blessing. But the graduates were at the mercy of irresponsible government rules and regulations.

It was devastating for me to decline the scholarship.

Soon college years passed by. There was no fanfare, or the song *'Gaudeamus Igitur* (played at every college graduation) echoing in our ears when we graduated. I was hoping at least the Faculty would celebrate our graduation with a ball.

After graduating and getting my Bachelor's Degree, I visited the Faculty once more to pick up my Diploma. I met Ms. Liz, one of my professors.

"What now, Esther? Are you going to continue to the fourth year?"

"I wish I could, but I need to find a real job, Ms. Liz. I'm picking up my Bachelor's Diploma," and I showed it to her.

"Remember Mr. Charles Grant, your former conversation teacher?" she said. "He works for the Council of Churches. His office is next door. If you are interested, you can meet with him to apply for the secretarial job. I can arrange it for you. Interested?"

"Yes, thank you. That would be nice."

Ms. Liz left, and I heard her talk with Mr. Grant. When she returned, she said, "Ten o'clock confirmed, the day after tomorrow. Tell him that I recommended you. Good luck." She smiled, shook my hand, waved and returned to her office. That was the last time I saw Ms. Liz.

I told my parents about my forthcoming interview. It was like a silver lining within dark clouds. It was also intimidating. This would be my first American boss and I could speak English every day. Just like in America.

My father coached me on the art of negotiation.

"Ask for 10,000 rupiahs (roo-pee-yah). Exchange currency of Rp.100 per US$1. No less. If he counters less, it would still be manageable for us."

"I have no experience, Pappie."

"Well, do the best you can."

I had had interviews before, only for short-term assignments. This time it was different. Our livelihood depended on it. I perspired and dabbed my forehead as I entered the Council of Churches.

"Mr. Grant is on the second floor," the receptionist told me. "Commission on Inter-Church Aid."

I walked upstairs to the second floor and looked for his office. *Here it is… Commission on Inter-church Aid.*

I took three deep breaths before I knocked on the door.

"Come in," I heard a man's voice say.

I entered and Mr. Grant looked up.

"Oh yes, Ms. Liz recommended you. Take a seat." I sat down.

His office was large enough to accommodate his desk and the desk of his secretary, if he had had one. Nothing fancy. A wooden cabinet against the wall on the right with documents stacked on the shelves. Next to the cabinet were two dark grey filing cabinets. In another room, two sofas, two end tables with lamps and a coffee table formed a complete ensemble of furniture. I was the only other person in the office. A second desk and typewriter were in another room.

Through a connecting door I could see a third room with a long oval table and chairs around it, a conference room. A map of churches in Indonesia hung on the wall. Mr. Grant was the Representative of the Church World Service in New York, and the Director of the Commission on Inter-Church Aid. His friendly manner and supportive attitude made me feel right at home in the office.

It was a comfortable interview. He made me feel relaxed and asked general questions . "Do you live far from here? Activities? Church? How did you get here? " I told Mr. Grant I took a bus.

"Are you Chinese?"

"Yes, I am."

"What's your Chinese name?"

"Mei Lan."

"All right, I will call you Mei Lan." Mr. Grant shared with me he had a Japanese wife. When they first met, they communicated using Chinese characters called *Kan-Ji*. His wife spoke no English and he spoke fluent Chinese, but no Japanese. I thought it was interesting to meet an American who spoke fluent Chinese and Japanese

Mr. Grant was unusual.

As we were continuing the interview, a Japanese lady entered and said "*Ohayo gozaimasu.*" (Good morning in Japanese)

Mr. Grant introduced her as "Iko, my wife."

Both spoke for a few moments in Japanese, glancing at me, and then Iko excused herself.

"*Sayonara.*" She looked at me, nodded and left.

Mr. Grant shared with me the job description of his secretary and for a while I was quiet, as I had heard no offer to the post yet. He had not yet asked me for my experience in the workforce.

"Oh," he said, "Can you pick up the phone?"

"Sure." I picked up his phone and asked, "Where do you want me to put this?"

He realized he wasn't specific enough in his request. If he noticed that I'd misunderstood him, he kept it to himself.

He smiled and took the phone from my hand. He put it where it belonged and picked up the receiver.

"This is what I meant with 'picking up the phone'."

"Oh. Sorry." *I could lose the job, Stupid, stupid.*

"Next step, experience," he said. Tell me where you've worked before." *What should I tell him? Tell the truth? 'Honesty is the best policy,' I remembered my English teacher, Ms. Leny, saying.*

"Not much," I said, "Teaching English and Indonesian, stage acting and talking on the radio during student years. I am learning to type, shorthand and a little filing. However, I can perform any work provided you teach me."

I nodded with satisfaction after giving my answer. *Check.*

"All right, fair enough," he said. "How much do you think you are worth?"

Without hesitancy, I said, "10,000 rupiahs." *The least I could do was try. I imagined a frown on Pappie's face, if I didn't do as told. I needed to report to my father.*

"What makes you think you're worth 10,000?" (Equivalent to US$ 100)

"Because I can learn."

Mr. Grant grinned. His face turned red and he tried hard not to laugh. He found my answers amusing.

"So, Mei Lan, you have no experience, you cannot type, no shorthand, but you can learn, huh?"

"Yes sir, I can."

"Let me tell you what I can do for you," he said. "You will get 15,000 rupiahs a month. Plus medical coverage. When you are sick, and you have doctor's bills, let me know, and I will reimburse your medical expenses. One more thing. You are taking the bus to work. Give me the receipts for your travel expenses every week and I will reimburse that too, until we have a company car. Afterward, you will have no more bus rides."

I've never heard of a company or man who would give me or anybody more. I looked at Mr. Grant in disbelief, and asked him, "You are pulling my leg. Why do you want to do that?"

"Say yes, Mei Lan."

"Why?"

"This is why," Mr. Grant replied. "I've interviewed ladies for the job, and they all gave me raving resumes. The results were disappointing. You, to the contrary, told me what you couldn't do, and you will learn. We can throw away all these old files, and start fresh. We will establish a new filing system and I will teach you the American way of working in an office."

"Great. When do you want me to start work?"

"Yesterday."

"If you wanted me to start yesterday, why interview me today?"

I saw Mr. Grant's first great smile, and he said, "You and I will have a great working relationship." He clapped his hands and stood up.

"See you Monday, Mei Lan. Welcome aboard," and we shook hands. "My wife was right."

"How so, Mr. Grant?"

"My wife is a good people reader," Mr. Grant stood up and put his hands on his hips. "She saw my disappointments with the former candidates and she volunteered to attend this interview with you."

"And...?" I asked.

"She said, 'This time you have won the jackpot.'" And he laughed.

"What is a jackpot?" I inquired.

"Never mind," he chuckled and mumbled, "Blessed innocence."

Arriving home, my parents watched me flop into a chair. No words, just a big sigh.

"You didn't get the salary?" my father asked.

"No, I didn't," and I told him what happened.

My father said, "Why did he do that?"

"I asked him the same question, Pappie, and he said 'because I am honest.'"

Like in the theater, the curtain went up, and a new era began.

At 21 years old, I became the breadwinner of my family.

Chapter 20: Mr. Charles Sharp Grant

"*Cao an*, Mei Lan," Mr. Grant greeted me.

"Good morning to you too, what's going on?"

He put his arms on the table.

"Let's talk about you. I'd like to know how you are doing."

"What do you want to know?"

"Everything."

I talked about how after the liberation in 1945, food was scarce, and school had limited tools. We depended a lot on our teachers. I went through my life again, from when I was a child and almost died of pneumonia, and my passion for learning English

"How did you survive, food-wise?"

"I hate to talk about it, sir. However, you may understand more about your projects and how the people live. Their story may be like mine."

"Right you are."

"Rice is our main meal, the same way you eat potatoes. We had a continuous supply of rice. Food was served cold, as we used wood burning stoves and sometimes the wood supply was low. My mother only cooked once in the morning for lunch and dinner. Our family of seven shared the food. We could not afford to buy meat or chicken. It was too expensive. We ate chicken feet soup, shredded beef soup with red beans. We ate a meat dish when funds permitted. Vegetables were cheap, and we consumed more vegetable dishes or salads. We had no refrigerator, and couldn't have leftover food.

"How about fish or another kind of sea food?"

"No, sir. My mother chose dishes we all could eat together. Fish were small. The big ones were expensive. I remember we ate fried frog legs or snails, cooked in turmeric. During tough times, my mother only cooked rice, sprinkled with a little bit of salt, and rolled in banana leaves. We ate them as delicacies. Rice made us feel full, so did eating soup and salad. We were lucky that my mother was a creative cook."

"We eat to survive," my father used to say.

"Yes, you eat to live and do not live to eat," Mr. Grant replied.

I nodded.

"Feel blessed we have a roof over our head, and food on the table," my mother always reminded us. We ate whatever my mother put on the table

"Ever had sandwiches before?"

"When finances were better, we would go to a restaurant on Sundays that served western food, for us to try sandwiches. We liked ham and cheese, or just plain egg sandwiches, nothing fancy. My father liked to introduce us to a variety of dishes, perhaps to prepare us for the future, in case we could not have Indonesian or Chinese food. Now, with my job, I can contribute to enhance our food quality."

"How about hamburgers? Have you tried them?"

"I don't know. What is a hamburger?"

Mr. Grant looked up and waved his hand. "Never mind."

"I heard from Ms. Liz that the University offered you a scholarship to the United States and that you rejected the offer. Why?"

"More politics. The Government is not ready to administer to returning scholarship graduates. They are at the mercy of the Government in the choice of placements. I heard horror stories.

"What horror stories are you talking about?"

I shared with Mr. Grant the story of the bakery vendor and her doctor son. He ended up being murdered in Kalimantan. His mother went crazy. All the years of going door-to-door, selling food to help ends meet and the dream crashed, in one day. That boy was her only son. Nobody can deny that fact. But we heard nothing more, as the media covered it well."

Mr. Grant shook his head, and murmured, "What a shame."

"When you can spare a moment, look around the area, Mr. Grant, see how many people are beggars. These are the homeless. They came in vast numbers from outside Jakarta, and hoped to find better jobs and more income for their families.

Evening vendors showed up when businesses closed around six p.m. Their porches became portable restaurants to sell their products. It was a second income for them.

Mr. Grant listened, sighed and said, "The people wanted freedom so badly, but the dignitaries couldn't manage it."

"The first ten years were building the economy and communication when two brilliant men led the country. President Sukarno spoke at least four languages, Indonesian, Dutch, English and his own language, Javanese. He was charismatic, and he created unity in diversity.

"My geology teacher once said Indonesia is as large as the United States, except we have sea surrounding the islands. President Sukarno united the country and its people by introducing one language, one flag, and one national anthem.

"Through the years, the government became used to their power. The people lost trust in their leaders to govern and lead. The soft seat of government and abuse of power turned them to corruption and bribery. It became a way of life. The country and people's needs remained in the background and faded, overwhelmingly taken over by selfishness and greed. Poverty set in."

"How did you commute?"

"I took public transportation to college. Not the best way, but the only way.

"There was an occasion when I became scared while at college. Shots were fired, and nobody knew where they came from. Classes were ended and the faculty instructed us to go home, which was nothing new to us. The streets were empty, no vehicle in sight. I walked from the University to the bus stop, however, it did not stop. I felt uncomfortable when it got dark as the University was quite a distance from my house. It was impossible to walk.

"How did you get home?"

"I felt blessed when I saw six students from the Legal Department who finished their class late, walking toward me. They needed transportation themselves. I told them how frantic I was when no vehicle would stop."

"How did your friends stop the next vehicle?" Mr. Grant asked.

"Eddie and his five friends forced a bus to stop by blocking the street. Since they were all husky men, the vehicle had to stop and they instructed the driver to take us where we needed to go. They made sure I arrived home in one piece. That was quite a scary experience for me. My parents suggested an alternative."

"I'll bet. What did your father suggest?"

"My father bought a second-hand Vespa motor scooter for me. I had to get my license. That worked well, and I wasn't scared anymore."

Mr. Grant nodded and sighed again.

"Now I understand why you were excited to have transportation included in our arrangement."

"I was, sir."

Working with Mr. Grant taught me a lot about responsibilities, good administration, problem-solving, communication and a good filing system. Whenever the office was quiet, he would talk about America.

Soon our office staff grew with Tae Yo, a Field Representative to lead North Sumatra's Dairy project. And an Accountant, Mr. Ko, an elderly man in his fifties. He was excited to be accepted, and felt he was one of the lucky people to acquire a post. *Yes, you can say that again.* Another Field Representative from Akron, Ohio completed the first group. Matthew Lester led the Pig project in Bali.

Mr. Grant introduced the immigration lady, Mamiek, and me to a taste of upscale living at the International Club, where more foreigners entertained themselves with tennis, swimming, or conducting business meetings.

Upscale living intimidated me, as I had never visited these places before. Mr Grant understood: "Once you are used to it, you will no longer feel intimidated or uncomfortable."

I recognized that the opportunity to work with someone like Mr. Grant was a great privilege. He was 42 years old, slim and about six feet tall. A good-looking man and always dressed in white, even his white canvas shoes. He had had his share of stress in the United States for marrying a Japanese woman after World War II. In Virginia, people still remembered Pearl Harbor.

"Too soon to forget and forgive," he said. His missionary work took him to third-world countries, where his marriage was better accepted. His duties included assisting churches and improving their farm needs.

Together with the two field technicians, Mr. Grant would take us to conventions. He suggested we get to know the pastors and their staffs better.

"People will be more receptive when you care about them," Mr. Grant said.

One of the unusual tasks he gave me was narrating a documentary movie.

"Do you know what a narrator is, Mei Lan?" Mr. Grant asked.

"Yes, sir. The background reading for a documentary movie, or plain reading of a story. Once, I took training at the American Embassy to work with the Indonesian Students Group, to be a radio announcer. Similar, isn't it? Why do you ask?"

"The Church World Service (CWS) in New York was impressed with the outcome of their Outreach Program in Indonesia," Mr. Grant said. "They took advantage of it by implementing projects that engaged youthful delinquents from farm areas in the United States. Opportunities arose for them to assist under-developed countries to improve their farming systems. Every session took three to six months.

"Well, the CWS archived those activities in a documentary. We need to translate the documents from Indonesian to English.

"Ms. Liz confided in me you wanted to become an interpreter during your freshman year. The committee disqualified you due to your early age. You didn't lack skill. The Indonesian Film Network proposes to use a male narrator, which is standard practice. I'll take my chances on you. Can you translate and narrate the movie for us?"

"Delighted, Mr. Grant."

He handed me the documents. "Let me know when you are ready."

The Council of Churches became an approved member of the CWS with the documentary film archived in New York. It was the first documentary film with a female narrator archived at the Indonesian Film Network.

I attempted any task entrusted and gained much experience while working with Mr. Grant. The training I received from him catapulted me into a better career.

I was 23 years old.

Chapter 21: Coup d'Etat – The Mission

Communism was at the door. All English-speaking magazines and letters were often undelivered or censored. Packages never arrived, perhaps lost or stolen.

People talked about President Sukarno in a negative way. He had three wives, the third one was a former geisha from Japan. His first wife, Fatmawati, felt betrayed. She left the palace and lived in her personal house with their five children, vowing never to return to the presidential palace. His second wife, Hartini, lived in his second presidential palace in the city of Bogor.

It was not a good example for women. The men followed suit for their own entertainment and *this* caused distressed marriages and families.

The President's "skirt chasing" became well-known in the international world. Sukarno admired beauty. He made promises, but he didn't keep them. "Eat more corn, people," but the President ate rice.

He watched movies from western countries, but the people couldn't. His earlier governing promises to the Indonesian people, that is…for the people and by the people, were long forgotten. Sukarno had accumulated power for self-gain.

My father alerted us that the past month's unrest was brewing in other parts of the islands. The reports were only by word of mouth. There was also an exodus of ethnic Chinese to other countries. "That's your sign, watch your back," my father said. "It will get worst. Make sure you're home before dark."

Our office, the Interchurch Aid Commission, continued assisting the churches as best we could, considering the circumstances. The government could shut us down..

My income had boosted my parents' household finances and my brothers continued their education. My sister got married.

A year later, on September 30, 1965, on the way to work, I passed the Presidential palace and saw the military wearing a yellow sash. I asked my driver whether we were expecting a VIP. He shook his head. I wondered what could be happening.

Frans, our Office Manager, relayed to us that Mr. Grant and his family had gone to Singapore for a few days until things in Jakarta settled down.

"Why, Frans? Is there a problem?" I asked.

He said, "Last night there was an overthrow of power, a coup d'etat. The new government stripped Sukarno off his duties and he is no longer active President. Six generals were killed. Suharto is now Acting President."

"Are you serious? How do you know, Frans?" I asked.

"The news on the radio announced it last night. Rumors went around that should the Communists win, we (employees of the Council of Churches) could be their first target. I am glad the Communists lost. "

"Why us, Frans? Because we are Christians?" I asked.

"Maybe. Mr. Grant wanted to close shop until next Monday. That's why he's not around."

Everyone in my family was home when I arrived. We lived in the capital city, Jakarta, which was well-protected and heavily guarded by the military. No riots, shootings or killings took place. From my perspective, it was a quiet and peaceful takeover.

In the office, the only topic for the next week were the rumors floating around and how dangerous the situation had become. Frans said the media had covered it up. The government didn't want the world to stamp Indonesia as a lawless breed.

"There was a mass killing, and many have died, perhaps hundreds of thousands," Frans said.

"Where?" The employees arrived and listened to Frans relaying the message.

Frans shrugged. "Americans helped overthrow the government, so the rumors go, because they didn't want the communists to block the international passage in South Asia, but is it true?"

Everyone lived in uncertainty. My mother purchased a lot of canned food and rice.

Our office building was close to the University of Indonesia, and we could see trucks with men shouting into their microphones roaming the streets: "Stay close to home. For your own safety, stay home." This had become a common sight.

That devastating day was the 30th September 1965. It became a movement, nicknamed Gestapu. The killing reminded people of the Nazi's Gestapo.

"Gestapo killed millions of Jews, Is the same happening here? Millions of people killed, not hundreds of thousands?" I asked Frans.

Again, he shrugged. "Everything is possible."

Sukarno was under house arrest. He wasn't put on trial, as the government still recognized him as the first person to unite the country and lead Indonesia to their independence. There was unrest everywhere. Villages burned.

The killings were long suppressed in history and textbooks. The new Suharto government took over power in stages through the next months.

Suharto said it was a failed coup d'etat, as Sukarno still led the country with limited power. In March, 1966, Suharto, from Acting President, became President of Indonesia. (Author's note: Sukarno died a few years later due to natural causes.)

Mr. Grant returned to the office on Monday. It was during this period in March 1966 that Mr. Grant asked me to undertake an important and dangerous mission.

"Esther, I need to talk to you." *Whenever Mr. Grant called me by my Christian name, he had something serious to share.*

"Yes, sir?" *No more bad news please? Will he be leaving? I hate moments like this.*

In retrospect, he said, "You believe God is with you and for you.?"

"Yes, sir, "I said. "Why do you ask?"

"It is important for what I need to do," he said. "When you were a child, you became a Christian due to your parents' belief, and baptized as a baby."

"Yes, sir," I said. "At 17, I was to confirm and accept my belief. But, I needed to make sure that this was what I wanted. I postponed the confirmation until seven years later. I attended worship places of various denominations, and returned to my old church. The confirmation took place on Christmas Day. I was an adult."

"Do you think non-believers could follow your steps to find God?" Mr. Grant asked.

"I don't see why not," I said. "I have wise parents and had great teachers, who cared about us as children and students. We followed the same path to learn more about Christianity. I followed the teachings with conviction, as it was for our own good, and I believed God would be there for us.

"I could be angry with the Government, but we weren't the only ones suffering. Millions of people were worse than us. We still have our family and food on the table. That's why my mother said. 'Be thankful and stop complaining.'"

"Wow!" Mr. Grant shook his head. "You are leading an interesting life, and you are in the right place.

"You aren't mad at God? He could have prevented this devastating time," Mr. Grant asked.

"Yes, God could be blamed every time riots took place, killing and suffering, Mr. Grant. My teacher, Pak Tan, said God is not our butler. He will protect us against evil. Like the Bible said, 'If God is for us, who can be against us?' Bad times are a risk in life. So far He has been there for our family. I didn't know I would meet you, and things would get better. You lifted us. I think God sent you to help us. That counts for something, doesn't it?

"Are you worried, Mr. Grant?" I asked. "Why all the questions?"

"I am mulling over a situation that is happening and how to solve it. It won't be an easy task. Have you ever traveled by plane?" He then asked.

"No, sir."

"Ever taken a vacation somewhere outside the city?"

"No, where would I go? I can't afford it. I went on a school field trip once to Central Java. That's about it."

"Well, I'd like to discuss a serious matter. You have three weeks to decide. No rush. Consider it, and talk it over with your parents. Understand?"

I nodded.

He sighed and said, "Remember the Dairy Project in North Sumatra? They need help. Buildings are in need of repair, they need to buy more seed and more cows—farming needs. Should the Project fail, a whole community will die with it. We need to deliver funds to help them. They have waited for over a year. Banks refuse to do a transfer due to the amount. The same applies to any man handling this task. Church World Service needs pictures. We have received no reports since we started the project two years ago.

"As an alternative, I wonder whether you could help to hand-carry the funds. You know the situation; I wish it could be different, but I have no other choice. That's why I asked questions about your faith. You will need it."

"How much money are we talking about, Mr. Grant?"

"82 million rupiah (pronounced Ru-pee-yeah), equal to US$ 450,000."

"82 million Rupiah? Wow! A lot of …" I clasped my hands together and released them with the palms facing outwards."

"I will put the cash in an airline bag," Mr. Grant continued. "You need to hand it over to the pastor of the Batak Church, and no one else. I want you to be certain you are up to the task. Should you wish to decline, I will understand. Do you have any relatives in Medan, North Sumatra?"

"Yes, I have a grandaunt, aunt, and uncle."

"Good. Can you stay with them?"

"Yes, I'm sure they wouldn't mind."

"I have the tickets. Let me know as soon as you can. Send your uncle a telegram and advise him of your impending visit, just in case. And don't forget to pray, Mei Lan."

"That's number one on my list, sir."

It was easy to guess what my father's reaction would be, and I wasn't wrong.

"Are you out of your mind?" he said. "Going to a dangerous area so soon after the unrest? Doesn't your boss have anybody else to do the job? Why you? You don't even know what is happening out there. Don't you understand why the bank refused to send cash to North Sumatra?"

"It is the stronghold of the communists. A lot of killings have occurred across Indonesia, the worst in Central and East Java, Northern Sumatra. There had been an outflux of Chinese to other countries. Many didn't return. What does it tell you?

"Law enforcement scrutinized the Chinese and linked them to the communist party. Medan swarmed with Chinese. The Government will check you upon arrival. What will happen if they find your 82 million in the bag? Have you considered that? How about the risk of being shot as a spy?" My father shook his head, and couldn't believe I was even considering the task.

The room seemed to swirl around me. It felt hot in the living room and I felt the sweat trickling down my face. I sighed and stayed in my room. As usual, my mother confronted me and asked what I would do.

"I will ask my other Father," I said, pointing at the ceiling. "He will let me know whether I should go. Many lives depend on the funds."

"It's not your problem. I don't think it's wise of Mr. Grant to ask you to do this job. Too heavy for a girl your age."

"I have three weeks to decide, Mam," I said.

"If I'm meant to do this task, Father, please give me a sign." A simple prayer for a not so simple task.

I couldn't explain it, but the next day an ambience of peace and calm embraced me. I felt more confident and free of fear. God had given me the strength and faith to fulfill my duty, and I knew He would be there all the way.

I shared my feelings with my mother and sent a telegram to my uncle.

In the office the next day, when I told my boss I would take the assignment, he said: "Are you sure, Mei Lan?"

"Yes, sir, I am. God wants me to go, and He'll be there with me."

Mr. Grant drew a deep breath. He was worried, but knew my faith would carry me through. It was not an easy decision to make, but he had no other choice. This was the life and death of a community.

He met me at the airport on the day of departure and handed me the Cathay Pacific airline bag.

"I trust the money's all there," I said.

Mr. Grant nodded. "You can still cancel this trip. You don't have to go." A frown appeared on his face."

"I will see you in a week." I said.

"Enjoy your reunion with your grand-aunt and family," my boss said, and whispered, "Please be careful."

He added, "Oh, here are two rolls of films."

I nodded and he handed me the introduction letter from the Chairman of the Council of Churches.

I put the letter in my bag and waved goodbye.

Three hours later I landed in the middle of a war zone.

Chapter 22: Medan, North Sumatra, the War Zone

"Hurry, down the steps, ladies and gentlemen. Tourists on the left side, locals and returning citizens on the right."

Medan was new terrain for me. I glanced over the area from right to the left of the tarmac while descending the steps of the plane, and followed other passengers to the terminal. Law enforcements personnel; police, military, and security guards were everywhere.

The tourists' line comprised of people entering the city. These were the group they focused on, checking bags and persons for concealed weapons. Law enforcement wanted to make sure that there was no possibility of spies and rebels sneaking in from the outside. Mr. Grant was right, there were no foreigners arriving in Medan.

I approached one man coming out of the interview room and asked, "Who are those people inside?"

"They are uniformed personnel. They will be asking questions to men and women in the interview rooms," he answered.

"What questions did they ask you?" I asked.

"The usual. My name, where I came from, where I'm going, and how much money I carry."

"Money? Why do they ask about money?"

"Ma'am, this is a war zone," he replied. "Anybody bringing in money could be construed as a spy aiding the rebels, and could be executed." Before he could say anything more, an officer approached us, and he left the scene.

"Move it, move it, you are holding up the line."

I was a naïve, inexperienced young woman, and didn't recognize the danger involved. God would be there with me. He would never leave me to face my perils alone. *If I had wanted to escape, how would I do it without being shot?*

Cold sweat trickled down my face, and I my breathing was labored. I said a short prayer, "Please Lord, help me through this ordeal."

My father's voice rang in my ears, "What if they find the money? How will you explain the 82 million rupiahs?"

There was no escape, only one way to go, forward. I had to face the consequences of my actions, and be cautious in managing the interview.

I held my composure, breathed deeply and entered the interrogation room, a small room with a table and three chairs. A woman in green uniform—plumpish, hair held in a bun above her head, a person in authority—was sitting in one chair. She looked up as I entered.

"Good morning, ma'am," I said. She didn't answer. She motioned me to sit down. Her questions were short. She asked my name, who I was visiting, purpose of visit, how long, and then the dreaded question: "What's in the bag?"

"Money," I replied.

"How much?"

"82 million rupiahs."

"Who for?"

"The Batak Church, ma'am."

"Papers?" she asked.

I showed her the letter from the Chairman of the Council of Churches. She read it, and returned it. She drew a deep breath, and said," You need to report to the Colonel next door on this money. Leave the bag here!" It was an order, not a request.

It was a hard choice for me. *Keep calm, look her straight in the eyes.*

The same feeling of peace embraced me, and I said, "I'll be glad to report to the Colonel, ma'am, but the bag goes with me. He needs the evidence." I reached out to pick up the bag.

She stood up from her seat, took a quick step forward, and put her hand on the handle of the bag. I did the same thing, refusing to let go. I couldn't. It was my responsibility to guard it with my life if necessary. She gave me a defiant look, and raised her voice, her chest heaving up and down.

"Leave the bag, and report to the Colonel. Do you understand me?"

"I understand, ma'am, but I can't leave the bag. I'm sorry."

"Do you dare to challenge me?" I felt her breath close to my face. Before she could spit out another word, a man in uniform, complete with medals, breezed into the room, and interrupted the investigation. His face was round and his shirt bulged slightly at the waist, and he was holding a wand under his armpit. The Colonel, I thought, I wasn't afraid of him, and wondered what would happen next.

He took a quick look at me, and then at the military lady, who saluted him. "What's holding up the line?" he asked.

"This woman, Colonel; she has money in her bag."

"How much money?"

"82 million rupiahs, sir," I answered.

"You have papers?"

"Yes, sir." He watched me closely while I took out the letter from my bag and handed it to him.

I feared he would agree with his uniformed counterpart, that he'd grab the bag, push me out the back door and make me disappear. Nobody would ever know I existed. The outside world wouldn't know what had happened in Medan and vicinities. Communication was cut off.

I was a foreigner, a naïve messenger going into a dangerous zone, oblivious to what could happen to me, the money or anything else.

I understood I had a challenging task. My feelings of peace stayed with me. I believed God would never leave my side during this trial because He had promised to stand by me.

Like Mr. Tan, my intermediate school principal, once said, "If God is for you, who can be against you?"

The Colonel folded the letter slowly. He looked down at me, a frown on his forehead, as if he were debating how to handle a situation such as mine. He walked around in a small circle, scratched his head, fanned himself with the letter, and looked down at me again.

After a long pause, he handed back the letter, and addressed his counterpart, "She has papers, why are you holding her up?"

He then turned, looked at me, nodded, and said, "You're free to go, ma'am." The Colonel didn't see his counterpart's wide open eyes, her look of surprise, and the drop of her jaw.

I picked up my bag, said thank you to the Colonel, nodded, and left.

Outside the interrogation room, I stopped and put my hand on my chest, trying to catch my breath.

I looked up to the ceiling and whispered, "Thank you, Father."

Now I had to look for my uncle. I'd already sent him a telegram three weeks earlier informing him of my visit.

What if he didn't receive my telegram? Oh, not to worry now. It's too late anyhow. The question was, what now?

I looked around after picking up my baggage, but no uncle in sight. I needed a telephone, and rushed to the information booth.

"Can I use your phone, sir?" I asked. The officer nodded. While waiting for the phone to ring, I looked around again. This was what a war zone looked like. Military people all over, combat ready with heavy rifles, tanks outside the terminal and people standing by on the look-out. All I heard were the shouts from the military, "move it, move it. Get the line moving", and the footsteps of people leaving the terminal in a hurry.

"Come on, uncle, pick up the phone. Pick up, pick up," I whispered. I was anxious and hoped it would be better once I arrived at my uncle and aunt's house.

"Hello?" I heard my uncle's voice on the other line. I straightened up.

"Hello, uncle, this is Esther from Jakarta."

"I don't know any Esther."

I remembered he never knew my Christian name. "Uncle, this is Mei Lan, Sis Laine's daughter from Jakarta."

There was a pause, and he recognized me. "Ya ya! Now I remember. How is everyone in Jakarta?"

"Uncle, I am at the airport. Can you pick me up?"

Another pause. "At the airport? Why?"

"Can you pick me up first, and we'll talk later?"

"Ya,! I will pick you up. "

I heard Chinese spoken in the background, and then 'click," ending the conversation.

My uncle wasn't expecting me; it was obvious he didn't receive my telegram. I thanked the security guard and headed toward the exit.

It seemed like a lifetime standing alone and waiting for my uncle. Every time anyone looked in my direction, I imagined they knew I had 82 million cash with me. *Come on uncle, hurry up.*

As I had guessed, my uncle was surprised by my visit and he didn't recall receiving the telegram. "The rebels cut all communication lines," he said.

When I was settled in his car, he asked, "Now, Mei Lan, what's so secretive about your visit?"

"I have to deliver cash to the Batak church."

"Cash? How much?"

"82 million."

The car screech to a stop in the middle of an intersection.

"82 million? Did I hear it right? 82 million?"

"Yes, uncle. Can we move away from the intersection, please? Also, something smells of burning in your car."

"No, my car is all right. The burning smell is from all those," and he pointed at everything around us. Houses, trees, shops, cars, everything burned to ashes.

For the first time I had a chance to look around. "What on earth has happened here?" I inquired.

"The city was on fire, and the rebels burned the bodies too."

In my mind, I seemed to hear my pastor saying "…and Rome was on fire." It wasn't only in the Bible. Here was proof.

"Oh my God." That's all I could say.

"There was a massive massacre, Mei Lan. Thousands of people slaughtered. Dismembered body parts were everywhere. A sign of power by the rebels. Thousands of Chinese and Christians killed. Those who had financial means took the first flight out. Everyone else stayed indoors. Bodies thrown in the river, and the water ran red with blood. We refused to eat fish. Vandalisms and lootings by the insurgents. Chaos and death everywhere."

I had never heard such a horrific story. I experienced the visual destruction. The rebels had destroyed everything they came across. All that was left was rubble and more rubble.

"Do you think this happened everywhere too, I mean the other islands?" I asked.

"I wouldn't be surprised," my uncle replied. "The media covered it well."

"Jakarta is well protected by the military, uncle. We heard nothing of this massacre."

My uncle gave me a short tour through the burned areas; smoke still filled the air. Some houses were boarded with wood to cover their damaged doors and windows. People were still throwing water on top of their roofs to protect them from more fires.

I found it sad to see the hopeless look of people going through the debris for things they could salvage. When we came to my uncle's street, I saw two houses side by side still intact.

"These two houses are nice, they look all right, untouched."

"Those are our houses," my uncle replied. "One is mine, the other your grand-aunt. That baffled us too, why the insurgents spared our houses."

I wasn't surprised at all.

Chapter 23: Miracle Mission Accomplished

"Hello, Grand Aunt and Aunty Lee-Ann. How are you?" I tried to be as jovial as possible. A cold stare and silence welcomed me. Misery and fear and disbelief looked me straight in the eyes. *It was the wrong greeting.*

Both shook their heads and asked questions. My Grand Aunt prevailed, being the eldest, "Did your father tell you the danger of traveling?

"Never mind," she waved her hand, and answered herself, "I'm sure he did, and you," pointing her finger at me, "you wouldn't listen. Wasn't that the case? You always disobeyed your father.

"Did your father tell you that you are crazy? This is not a good time for anything. Last Sunday the city was burning, like in Hell."

Breathing deeply, I said, "Yes, uncle told me. Jakarta had lost communication with the outer islands, we were oblivious to what had happened here or anywhere. Otherwise, The Council of Churches would have sent the money a year ago."

"Money? What money?" My grand-aunt asked.

Oops...too late...like my mother once said... ten fastest horses in the universe couldn't catch the words coming out of my mouth. I waited for the upcoming storm. It wasn't looking pretty.

My uncle intervened and addressed his mother-in-law and wife in Chinese. I'm sure he was filling her in on what I told him during the car ride here.

My grand-aunt put her hand on her chest and frowned as she asked me, "Who assigned you to this job?"

"My American boss," I answered.

"American. Bad news! Oh, my goodness! " She gently pounded her forehead several times with her fist.

I looked around and saw my uncle engrossed in a discussion with my aunt. I guessed he must have told her the amount. My aunt gave a shriek and covered her mouth with both hands and looked at me. She froze. My grand-aunt saw the horrified expression on her daughter's face and approached her.

"Lee-Ann, do you know something I don't know? Come on, out with it."

My uncle intervened again and talked in Chinese to my grand-aunt. Since I didn't speak a word of Chinese, I could only assume my uncle did his best to explain the importance of my assignment, and how much money I was carrying.

"82 million rupiahs," she blurted out.

My uncle jumped forward and shifted a chair in time for her to flop into it. She breathed deep and wiped her forehead with a handkerchief.

Shaking her head, she muttered, "I knew you were crazy fighting your ancestral traditions, but I didn't know you were this crazy."

I felt bad. I tried to calm everyone down. "You don't have to worry because I prayed to God already. He promised to stand by me," I said.

"How do you know your God heard your prayer?" my grand-aunt, always the skeptic, asked.

"It's a long story, Grand-Aunt." I shared with her what happened at the airport. "God sent a Colonel to help me through the investigation. He could have killed me, thrown me in the river, and confiscated the money. Instead, he let me go without even touching and opening the bag. That was the strangest thing. The Colonel knew I had a lot of cash; but he wasn't curious at all.

"His counterpart was different. She tried to get hold of the bag, but God sent a higher official to intercept her actions, and I left the room with no trouble. God spared your two houses because He knew I would come here. That's why I wasn't surprised to see your houses still intact. God is looking after my safety."

Silence in the room. I looked around. My uncle paced up and down as if he were deep in thought. He held one arm across his chest, the other rubbing his chin. My aunt stood still, overwhelmed by all the excitement. My grand-aunt looked at me in disbelief.

"So, young lady, what are you telling me?" She stood holding on to her chair. She raised her voice: "Who do you think you are now? The daughter of Jesus Christ?"

I felt hopeless. "Look Grand-Aunt, I guess this is the wrong time for a visit. Since I am already halfway through my assignment, allow me to finish it. I'll return to Jakarta the day after tomorrow. It hadn't been my intention to make you worry about me. I am sorry."

"Everyone calm down." My uncle raised his hands and continued, "Let Mei Lan rest and unpack. Everyone take your afternoon nap. We'll talk about this later." Turning toward me, he said, "And you, stay put. Not one step out of the house, understand? Tomorrow I will take you to the church in my car and, together, we'll deliver the money. I have to work now. And remember, stay put."

He nodded to his mother-in-law, took one look at my aunt and said, "Hide the bag and lock the door behind me." He left.

I drew a deep breath and followed my aunt to my room. She said, "I have to lock the door and windows, make sure all is secure. You can unpack and hide the bag."

I nodded.

The room was neat and clean: a bed with fresh bedsheet and cover, carved armoire, large enough for a week's clothing with a drawer underneath for shoes and slippers. Two ornate carved end tables with lamps, and one lounge chair near the window with standing lamp completed the furnishings.

Where could I hide the bag? There was no place. *Under the bed, maybe? The first place the rebels would look.* This was hopeless.

My aunt came in and watched as I paced the floor and talked to myself. "What are you thinking?" she said.

"I was thinking about where to hide the bag. The only safe place I can think of is the church."

"The church? You aren't thinking what I'm thinking you're thinking?" My aunt looked at me with wide eyes, both her hands on her cheeks.

"It may not be a bad idea. Who would know? Grand Aunt is resting. Uncle is at work."

"Your uncle said to stay put. He'll kill me if I let you go."

"You're not letting me go, we'll go together," I said. "How far is the church from your house?" I showed her the address.

"Not that far, but your uncle said he would take you tomorrow in his car, it's safer."

"You mean, you prefer to sleep with your eyes wide-open, like a person suffering from insomnia, knowing the bag of money is under my bed, ticking like a time-bomb? What's the distance in minutes if we go in a pedicab?"

I mentally measured the distance. If a man pedaled in a normal manner, meaning without rushing for fifteen minutes, the church was reasonably close.

"Fifteen to twenty minutes, maybe?" I asked.

She nodded.

"Get dressed, Aunty. We are taking a pedicab ride to the church. Come on, hurry, while it is still light."

My aunt hurriedly looked through her closet and changed her lounge dress to a one with flower designs. She was nervous. She brushed her hair, put some powder on her face, lipstick, all the while imitating her mother... "Oh my goodness, now I believe you *are* crazy."

"C'mon, hurry," I said.

"Don't rush me. Now where are my shoes?" she asked, as she looked around.

"In your drawer," and I helped take her shoes out.

My aunt was only a few years older than me. She was rebellious to her mother too. She loved venturing into unknown circumstances. As I had guessed, she concurred with the idea.

"Ready?" I asked.

She nodded, and whoosh we went to the church. The streets were quiet. Only burned areas and nothing around. It was a dead city.

"Visiting a family, Miss?" the pedicab driver asked.

"No, we're going to church to speak with the pastor, you know…all this…" I pointed at the devastated areas. My aunt rolled her eyes.

After a while the driver stopped in front of a church with tall gates.

"Here we are, Miss." He shouted to the guard, "These ladies want to talk to the pastor."

I waved at the guard, and he opened the gate, then guided us to the sanctuary. I put the bag on the table at the front of the pews and waited. The church was still intact.

Five men approached us. One of them appeared to be the pastor. After introducing myself as the Representative of the Commission on Inter-Church Aid, all of them said…"Aaaah."

The pastor smiled and shook my hand, "I am Pastor Hutabarat. Nice meeting you. Is this lady from the Commission too?" he asked pointing at my aunt.

"No, she's my aunt, she lives here about 20 minutes away. I asked her for help."

The pastor thanked my aunt for her assistance.

My aunt nodded and smiled.

"So Nona (means Miss) Esther, you are the one chosen to deliver the funds to us."

"Yes, sir, I was." I said.

"I knew the money would arrive since a year ago. However, it was beyond our wildest expectations a young woman would deliver it. May I?" The pastor gestured to the bag. The staff members waited in anticipation. Some of them rubbed the back of their necks, scratched their heads, waiting impatiently.

"Sure."

The staff members took the bundles out, perhaps to feel and believe the long-awaited funds had arrived. I had never seen so much cash laid out in front of me. They all looked thankful and happy. Smiling, and laughing at the same time, they lifted the cash above their heads and looking up said "Hallelujah!" I joined them feeling relieved. I had performed my good deed for the day.

I remembered the signature required, and I pointed to the line for the pastor to sign. He took a deep breath, signed the document, complete with date and time. He handed the document back with a thankful smile.

"While you are here, is there anything we can do for you or Mr. Grant?" he asked.

"Yes, I need to take pictures of the Dairy Project, as the Church World Service has received no news or reports. Pictures will be of great help."

The pastor thought it was essential to have a ten minutes break to meet with his staff. The Dairy Project was a half hour away from the city through danger zones.

"What time shall we pick you up tomorrow?" he asked

"Nine o'clock will be fine," and I handed him my aunt's address.

It was my turn to smile and take a deep breath. I had successfully fulfilled my important and dangerous mission.

My aunt was smiling too, happy she could preserve the safety of her family. Pastor Hutabarat asked his driver to take us home and promised to pick me up tomorrow.

We shook hands and left.

"I am sure you have a feasible plan on how to break the news to your uncle tomorrow, right?" my aunt whispered.

"It crossed my mind," I replied, as I imagined a new storm rising.

Chapter 24: The Dairy Project, North Sumatra

The next morning, my uncle said, "I can take you to the church to deliver the money now."

My aunt stopped eating, turned her head and glared.

Lee-Ann had trouble swallowing her breakfast. "What are you going to say to your uncle?"

I shrugged and continued finishing my breakfast. Then I stood up to take my plate to the kitchen.

"Ready?" my uncle asked.

"Yes, and no. Yes, I'm ready, and no we need not go." I looked at my uncle. "Uncle, I delivered the money yesterday afternoon."

I heard a crash. My grand-aunt dropped her ceramic cup, smashing it to smithereens. My aunt Lee-Ann cupped her face in her hands, and peered through her fingers. Everyone was quiet, and I loved the silence. Nobody spoke. It was blissful.

A few moments after the shock subsided, the three of them talked simultaneously in Chinese. My grand-aunt and uncle realized that I had slipped out of the house with the help of Lee-Ann. They didn't approve.

The doorbell rang. I raised my hands and tried to make myself heard. "Calm down, everybody. The doorbell, shall I open the door?" My uncle jumped up, walked to the right to the front door, and asked, "Are you expecting anybody?" He looked at me.

"Yes, I am."

"Who?"

"Pastor Hutabarat of the Batak church."

"Why?"

"He will accompany me to the Dairy Project. I can open the door."

"No, you don't. We might not know who is behind that door. I'll open it." He made a gesture, "Step back behind the wall." He composed himself and opened the door.

"Good morning, can I help you?" my uncle asked.

"Good morning, I am Pastor Hutabarat, and I am picking up Miss Esther to visit the Dairy project." Four church staff members were standing at the door.

"Just a minute. I'll call her."

My uncle whispered to all of us. "Where is this Dairy project?"

"It is a tiny village called Pematang," I said.

"You know how far that place is?" my uncle asked again.

"No, maybe you can tell me."

"Half an hour at most, quiet highway on partial asphalt, primitive. The rebels launched a fierce attack to the neighboring villages last week, and people regard the place as unsafe. And you want to go there with these strange men? Are you out of your mind?"

"I should have sent you home yesterday," my grand-aunt said. "I am worried now. Can you cancel this trip?"

"No grand-aunt, it's my job. God...." I stopped in desperation. No need to go that route before creating another panic. "It will be all right," I said, trying to convince everybody. I still felt peaceful and calm.

Lee-Ann said, "Let her go, Ma, she believes in her God. Otherwise she wouldn't be here. We haven't seen her for several years. It is only for one more day, a few hours, and four men will accompany her. What could go wrong?"

"Five men," I corrected.

"Five?" my grand-aunt asked.

"Yes, you didn't count the driver." More discussions in Chinese, more whispers.

My grand-aunt agreed to let me go. "You believe this God of yours will take care of you?"

Yes, grand-aunt, my God will take care of me. I nodded.

My grand-aunt knew about Jesus Christ. She knew our family were believers. She believed in the Buddha.

"All right, then go, there's nothing more we can do. Just be careful and come straight back, you hear?"

I gave my grand-aunt the "Gosh, I am 24 years old" look.

I went to the door after grabbing my bag, hat and camera. "Good morning, Pastor," and shook hands. "Good morning everyone. Ready for the adventure?"

The men laughed. Good humor. *It will be a wonderful day.*

As we departed, three concerned faces peered through the window. I waved.

"We need to strategize the seating in the Jeep, Miss Esther, for protection. That's why we took one of our staff in uniform. We won't know who we will meet on the way." My uncle was right. This was perhaps a wrong and dangerous time to travel.

Next to me, in front, a man sat at my feet facing the right side of the vehicle. He was holding on to the canopy of the car.

The Pastor said from behind the driver, "Keep your eyes on the road, Sonny. We can't be too careful." Sonny nodded.

"Can you sit facing the back, Eddie?" he asked the man in uniform. Eddie jumped out of the car, looked around and said, "So far so good, Pastor. I can move to the back if I need to."

The Pastor sighed. I realized they had seated themselves strategically to protect me from harm. I said a short prayer, "Father, please keep us safe."

"Everyone ready?" The pastor asked his group.

"Ready, Pastor."

"All right, let's go. Drive normally so as not to attract attention. Not too fast, and not too slow. Keep your eyes open, everyone. We will be there in half an hour." The streets were quiet.

"People still fear the return of the rebels, Miss," Eddie said, addressing me. "They run when they see a vehicle approaching. See that man over there? He was lurking behind the tree, hiding."

"Gosh, you're very observant, Eddie. I didn't see him," I said

"A pity for these burnt fields. Takes time before they can plant again," Eddie added.

I kept quiet and listened to the conversation. "No shops are open. How can these people live with no income?" Luki, another staff member, said.

My grand-aunt had given me a sandwich for the road and a bottle of water. There were neither street vendors nor street cafes along the way.

"Fifteen minutes to go, drive slow around that bend, Sonny. The road will become bumpy," Pastor Hutabarat said. He had been over this road many times.

"Bumpier when we turn to the Project, sir." Everybody laughed.

Good, they could still keep their humor. Then I heard it, a baby crying.

"Stop, stop the car. Did anyone hear the cry? It sounds like a baby crying, or a young child. Look around and tell me what you find," Luki said.

Eddie jumped out of the car, with his rifle ready to shoot, and walked around. He walked toward the gutter on the other side of the road. He followed the sound, then motioned us to come and look.

"Abandoned kids. I wonder how long they have been here, and where the parents are. Typical results of …damn!" Eddie cursed.

"Watch your mouth, young man, we cannot get emotional. We need to help. Anybody have suggestions?"

"Yes, Pastor, we take them to the Project. They will be much better off there. The women could take care of them. We cannot leave them here, and it's the humane thing to do," Sonny said.

Two children came on board the jeep. The men fed them snacks and water. They gobbled them.

"How old are you and your brother?" the pastor asked.

"I am six years old and my brother is four."

"Where are your parents, and how long have you been there?"

"We don't know, sir. Two, maybe three, passersby gave us food. Our parents never returned." The children cried again. The pastor shook his head. He covered the kids with his jacket when he saw them shivering.

Soon enough we turned into a side road that became bumpier. "Sorry, people, hold on for another five minutes, we're almost there," Sonny said. A few minutes later we saw a gate made of thick lumber.

"The villagers needed to protect everything when the riot started a few months ago," Eddie said. "Gone are the flowers and the fruit trees. It used to be so beautiful."

"Open the gate, man, the Pastor is here." Sonny pointed at the Pastor who stood beside the vehicle waving. The guard waved back and gave an order to open the gate.

"Tae-Yo, Tae-Yo," I called out and waved to a man coming out of the barn. I stepped out of the jeep and continued waving to attract his attention. Tae-Yo turned around and just glared.

"*You!* What are *you* doing here?" he asked. The basket he was holding crashed to the ground. I was the least expected to visit the project.

"Good morning to you too, Tae-Yo," I said, ignoring his question. "Mr. Grant is worried about you. No news, no pictures, plain silence. What's up?"

We tried to talk on various subjects at the same time. Tae-Yo tried to find out what I was doing there. From his perspective, he had heard nothing from us in the main city.

I followed his arm gesturing to the dilapidated walls, plastic covered roof, and to lean cows. "Only four cows left, out of ten. We ate them through the years. The city was too dangerous to visit or for us to buy supplies. The insurgents could catch up with us, kill us, and take the supplies away. Last week it was hell. Didn't you hear?"

Tae-Yo stopped to acknowledge the pastor, shook hands and greeted him, "Good morning, Pastor."

"Nona Esther (Nona is an Indonesian word to address a young unmarried woman) heard the news after she arrived, Tae-Yo," Pastor Hutabarat said. "It was her request to visit the Dairy Project, to check on you, and take pictures as per Mr. Grant's request."

"Take pictures? We require money to fix…" he said, pointing at the crumbling walls, fences that needed repair, buildings in need of rehab.

The Pastor and his staff smiled and nodded, "Mr. Grant knew."

"All right then, did he transfer the funds? We have been waiting for over a year. Wait…" He stopped and looked at me, then at the Pastor. "Wait, don't tell me *you* delivered the money…you didn't…did you?"

Pastor Hutabarat laughed and said, "She did, Tae-Yo."

"How? Don't tell me you hand-carried it? Is Mr. Grant crazy to send you here? No other person to do the job?" he asked.

I smiled. "No, nobody else. That's why it took over a year before he asked me. I was his last hope," I replied.

The pastor intercepted, "I guess Nona Esther had the faith to carry out this task. Her obedience in allowing the Lord to lead resulted in her smooth passing through the entry investigation. It must have been a difficult decision for Mr. Grant to even ask her to do it.

"All right, Tae-Yo, take Nona Esther around to finish her task and afterward join us for refreshments here," he said, pointing at the primitive but adequate coffee table and chairs under the banyan tree. Pastor Hutabarat motioned his staff to follow him.

I enjoyed walking around the Project to take pictures and felt honored that Mr. Grant had chosen me to capture this historic moment. Blue sky with no clouds, cool breeze, and tranquility. Green rice paddy fields showed the self-sufficiency of the villagers. Overgrown weeds filled the empty patches of land which once were rice paddy fields. I raised my camera: *click*.

"I don't see many people living here. Too far from town?" I asked.

"No, we had to fire them due to lack of funds. Accommodations have been empty for the past 10 months and in dire need of repair."

I went inside the house. Tae Yo was right; I saw buildings with dilapidated walls in need of repair and paint, stained ceilings from water damage.

"We slowed production, causing loss of income, " Tae Yo continued. "The villagers moved away of their own accord. There was nothing we could have done and no way to provide for them. The financial aid from Church World

Service will help in rebuilding the Project. Darn the disturbances." Tae Yo said. I took another picture. "This place was once full of life, happy families and children playing around. Lush landscaping, great production for the community.

"We were considering construction of a church and a school, to better help the community. The dream and all hope crashed," Tae-Yo said.

The situation affected him. Another click of the camera showed the dryness of the soil in need of a good irrigation system.

"You can help them better now that the Pastor has received the funds. We will see you back in a few weeks," I said.

"No, that's not possible. I can't," Tae-Yo answered. "I have more things to do now. Say hello to Mr. Grant for me. His collaboration couldn't come at a better time."

The foreman and his family came out to greet us, and the children we picked up on the road waved at me. It left me with a warm feeling. They wore hand-me-down clothing on skin-and-bones bodies, but otherwise were healthy. The Pastor took the time to talk to these children and promised to help find their parents.

"Hey, Tae Yo, take my picture here with the cows and the staff. Mr. Grant would love to see what the Project had become. I'm sure he won't mind seeing smiling cows."

Tae Yo raised the camera one more time…*click.*

We sat down under the banyan tree that provided lots of shade. These trees grew wild in the villages and their dense leaves were used as natural roofs. Warm tea and the cookies that Luki brought with him were on the table.

We sipped our tea and enjoyed the cool breeze and tranquil surroundings when the conversation trailed to the investigation at the airport. Everyone wanted to know the real story. The Pastor's concern was getting the money through.

"We knew the military was short on cash. Who didn't need money? How did you take it out, Nona Esther?"

"As you said, Pastor, it was difficult. My concern was that the Investigators would open the bag. If they had seen all that cash, my life would have been in immediate danger. No doubt about it. I was praying throughout the ordeal. The Colonel didn't open the bag."

"The Colonel," Luki said. "That's strange."

"Why?" everybody asked.

"Yes, why would a Colonel be strange, Luki?" Tae-Yo asked.

"Well, I tried to help when I heard rumors that the money had arrived in Jakarta. I inquired whether there was anyone at the airport to help ease the messenger through. I was unsuccessful. Without knowing the exact date and time of arrival, it would be hard for my informant to stand by at the airport. Would the messenger be a man? Or woman? He mentioned he knew of someone in uniform."

"So, it could be the Colonel then," I said. "He was the only one helping me. When he read the letter, he walked around for a short time, looked at me several times, and then returned the letter without even touching the bag."

Everyone was shaking their heads and mumbling, "What a strange coincidence."

I heard Pak Tan's words again in my ear, "If God is for you, who can be against you?" God had helped clear my path and guided me through the airport with ease. My father and Mr. Grant worried, and the Pastor was at a loss and thought the solution was hopeless, but God made it happen. "You can help make this Project a hope-filled place again, Tae-Yo. See you in Jakarta."

He nodded

My grand-aunt drew a deep sigh of relief to see me return unharmed, and I said goodbye to the Pastor and his staff. "Thank you, Pastor Hutabarat, I couldn't have fulfilled my mission without your help. Thank you again, everyone. I am returning home soon."

"Say hello to Mr. Grant," the Pastor said, "and extend our deepest gratitude for being persistent in getting the funds to us. Thank you to you too, Nona Esther. Visit us again in a year's time to see the improvements yourselves."

We waved goodbye.

My grand-aunt changed her mind; she wanted me to stay and enjoy the last days of my vacation.

"You might as well visit the relatives you've never met. They live in Siantar, an hour away. We can stay a few nights with them and have a picnic by the lake."

I raised my eyebrows and looked at Aunt Lee-Ann with my 'what now' look. Lee-Ann shrugged. I understood Siantar was a quieter place, and less affected by the riots.

"All right, if you say so," I replied.

The next four days were great. My relatives had a camera shop. I asked them to develop my films. We spent time at the famous Lake Toba, listening to the echo of people singing in a medley. The Batak people were famous for their colorful attires and beautiful voices. After a wonderful time at Siantar, it was time to go home.

My grand-aunt stopped me at her front door when I was about to depart, and she apologized.

"What for?" I asked.

"Well, when you arrived I mocked you for saying you are the daughter of Jesus Christ. Remember?"

I nodded.

"I feel right now you are the daughter of Jesus. A week before you arrived, this place was hell, with fire and chaos everywhere. After you arrived, for the whole week, there was not one shot fired. It has been such a peaceful place, and I hope your God helps in keeping it this way."

I gave her a hug, and said goodbye.

The daughter of Jesus Christ still echoed in the back of my mind as I looked out the plane's window and dozed off.

Chapter 26: Mr. Grant's Departure and the Divine Guidance

"Good morning, is everybody happy?" I entered the office smiling. I took a few skips and hops, and concluded with "Ta-ta!" my arms stretched upwards.

Mr. Grant looked up, "Mei Lan, you are back! No news from anyone and thinking about the dangers. You look all right. My wife never ceased to remind me should anything happen to you, I would carry your soul on my head." He sighed, showing relief, and leaned back in his chair.

"Serves you right, Mr. Grant," I said, pointing at him. "The Pastor sends his regards and deepest gratitude for the funds. Tae-Yo is all right and looking forward to helping rebuild the Dairy Project. Things around the city and its surroundings were still uncertain, and the Project desperately needed supplies.

"Oh, here are the pictures I took," I said. I emptied my purse and put the pictures on his desk. "These will give you a better idea how they will administer the funds."

"Any picture will do," Mr. Grant said. "At least Church World Service will know their funds will work wonders at a time like this." Mr. Grant looked through the photos, and ended saying: "You are a good photographer, Mei Lan. Thank you."

"My pleasure, sir," I replied. "Anything interesting happen while I was away?"

Mr. Grant and the rest of the office staff grew silent.

"Oh, oh, it can't be that depressing?" I said.

"Well, let me be blunt," Mr. Grant said. "I got the news that Church World Service has in mind to transfer me to another under-developed country. I've worked here for over four years.

The world stopped turning for me as he spoke.

"The projects in North Sumatra and Bali are operating to satisfaction.

"I won't be going right away, but soon," Mr. Grant explained. "I neither know my destination nor how long I will be away. CWS didn't discuss who will replace me and whether this political turmoil will get worse." He looked dismayed.

"I will try my best to keep my post. However, It's beyond my authority."

He stopped talking and clapped his hands to awaken us from our bad slumber. "Come on, back to work. Chop chop. Don't look so glum, I will keep you informed," and he ended the discussion.

Everyone avoided eye contact, there were no comments, only deep sighs from me and my colleagues.

I tried to divert their attention. "Hey, want to hear what happened at the airport in Medan? It's a creepy story." Nobody reacted and all I got were blank stares. Everyone returned to their offices. They walked like zombies. I walked behind and imitated them. *Nobody cares. What now?*

The future looked bleak. I tried to hold my head high, pretending things would get better. What if I couldn't find a similar job? Who would train me the way Mr. Grant had with his all American system? What if his substitute were less dedicated and compassionate? Where could I find an American company to speak English?

I felt as if I were sitting on an airplane and heard the pilot say, "We're about to crash, ladies and gentlemen, brace for impact." I had an anxiety attack, cold sweat trickling down my neck, clammy hands, and a run-away heart-beat.

"Mei Lan, wake up." Mr. Grant saw the frown on my forehead and said, "It isn't the end of the world. It may not even happen. Right now I am going home to sleep. I haven't slept in a week worrying about you. Will that be all right, hmmm?" he said, crossing his eyes, and sticking out his tongue.

I couldn't help but smile, "Sure, I'll hold the fort."

He gave me a long look. Did I see a glitter of sadness in those eyes? Mr. Grant straightened up, nodded, patted me on my shoulder as he walked away. He seemed to know more than he would share with us.

He stopped at the door, turned around and mumbled, "We'll talk more tomorrow."

I looked out the window and saw clouds gathering. Even the weather expressed the gloominess of my feelings. How was I supposed to break the news to my parents? What if my salary decreased? My family! What will happen to my family if I couldn't continue in this position?

"Aaarrgggghhh!!"

I said a short prayer, "Father, please help Mr. Grant keep his post." Could I make a request like that? It sounded so selfish.

The next months were uncertain. Mr. Grant received news that Tae-Yo was missing. He went to get supplies in the city and vanished. Mr. Grant was on the phone, even from home, talking to the Pastor and authorities in Medan. However, so far no news. He was a typical shepherd, looking for his lost sheep.

Making a telephone call was very difficult in those days as Jakarta didn't have enough telephone lines to support the big city. The telephone company put a limit on the length of conversations, and callers took turns.

The silence about Tae-Yo was killing us. First the departure of Mr. Grant. Second, Tae-Yo. What would be next?

One morning I asked Mr. Grant, "You can't, or won't return to Indonesia, Mr. Grant?" I asked.

He didn't reply. Instead, he shared with me the demise of his sister Nancy. "Remember her, Mei Lan?"

I nodded.

Mr. Grant continued, "I tried to get you out of Indonesia to the United States. The only person I trusted was my sister to help you. She passed away of a heart attack, and I failed." His gesture caught me by surprise.

"I am so sorry for your loss. Why did you want to help me?"

"You should have better opportunities and you deserve better. I'll be on vacation for a few months and return to New York. Promise me you'll stay here until you hear from me. I'll know more by then about my next destination, and will let you know. I want to see you here. If I fail to return, promise me you'll leave. The bonuses from CWS will continue for the next three months until they decide where to place me. Afterward, your salary will decrease by half. Do you understand what I am saying?"

"Yes, sir, but I've prayed for your return."

The Grant family left Indonesia with no fanfare. A handshake and well wishes to all of us, and then "Sayonara."

Words from Shakespeare came to mind, 'Parting is such sweet sorrow.'

His towering figure and white uniform were two distinctive features I would always remember. His empty desk reminded me that once a great man sat there, compassionate, dedicated, a teacher and leader. Sudden emptiness gripped my heart.

The staff meeting was sluggish. Since the political situation didn't improve, there was a possibility the Inter-Church Aid Commission would be dissolved.

Two months passed by. I became restless.

One morning I arrived at the office and remembered the Bible in my desk drawer. My prayer concerned one subject only … for Mr. Grant to return. After my prayer, I opened the Bible. The pages parted and stopped at the Book of Jonah. It read…"Go, to the land of Nineveh!" I closed the Bible, and couldn't believe what I read.

God wasn't listening. It wasn't for me, Father. It was for the return of Mr. Grant. I hate leaving my comfortable workplace. It would be easier for my boss to return than for me to search for a new job.

I went home and shared with my mother what I read.

"So you must leave your workplace. Find out where Nineveh is," she commented. "If you disobey the Lord, the whale will swallow and spit you out in the Land of Nineveh, just like the Bible says."

"Thanks for the warning, Mam. I have to wait for Mr. Grant's letter. He might still return, you know."

"I doubt it. God has already said, 'Go.' That means, 'You go.'

The long-awaited letter arrived. I was bracing for bad news.

"There's good news and bad news.," Mr. Grant started. "The good news is that a Batak Church staff member found Tae-Yo through a friend in the higher ranks of Law Enforcement.

The military became suspicious of Tae-Yo purchasing supplies large enough to feed a battallion. Pastor Hutabarat assured the Commander-in-charge that Tae-Yo was a member of their Project. His supplies were for the Batak Church to rebuild their Dairy Project. The Commander-in-charge released him. He supported the Church's cause. Something came alive after the horrible destruction caused by insurgents.

"Now the bad news... I regret to announce that a transfer to India is imminent; CWS rejected my appeal."

My heart broke into pieces. *It couldn't be. I had already prayed. Why didn't God listen? What had I done wrong?*

Mr. Grant further stated, "The Council of Churches will take over the Inter Church Aid Commission. Due to political disturbances, they thought it would the best for everyone to select a local Pastor to replace me. Your salary status will change to follow the Council's payment plan. Good Luck in your future endeavors, Mei Lan. Keep your good spirit and enthusiasm. I feel confident your strong faith and experience will lead you to a much better future." Signed Charles S. Grant.

In my mind I heard the hollow sound of heavy doors closing, and marked the no turning back of my life. A new era was about to begin.

"God, please help me, I need divine guidance," I whispered. My first prayer was last week at my desk in the morning hours. I read my Bible. Perhaps I should choose a different Bible, room, and time of day. These gestures could show the Lord how serious I was on my second request. I felt sure God would understand.

The Bible Institute was down the hallway and could provide me with a new Bible.

The Secretary at the desk greeted me, "Yes? What can I do for you?"

"Can I borrow a Bible? I will return it as soon as I am finished. I work next door."

The Secretary replied, " I know who you are. We are giving free Bibles to whoever needs one. Here you are, still fresh from the printing office. Keep it, and may God bless you."

I returned to my office, and in the afternoon chose the Conference Room to read. After a short prayer I opened the Bible, and the pages parted again, on the Book of Jonah. "Go to the Land of Nineveh."

Chapter 27: The Interview, Arrival at Nineveh

Where is Nineveh? The city of temptation? Where is Nineveh? I wallowed in my defeat. I felt helpless, and needed direction.

Like my high school years before leaving on our field trip, I once again felt tossed around in a boat with no direction and surrounded only by darkness. *"Where is Nineveh, Lord? How can I get there?"*

My mother was cutting vegetables at the kitchen table. It was Sunday morning and we had returned from Church.

"Thinking back, the preacher said, 'Go, and spread the gospel all over the world.'" He pointed his finger at me."

"First," my mother said, "he was pointing at the audience, not you. Second, you wanted to try one more time asking the Good Lord by going to church. Are you thinking to fool God? He said, 'Go to the Land of Nineveh, twice.' "You must go."

"All right, I'll go, Mam, where's the Sunday paper?" I asked. "Pappie said yesterday to look in the classified ads for a job. Maybe I'll find a possibility there."

I grabbed the Sunday paper from the table and took the classified ads section out.

I pointed to each ad and mumbled, "Secretary, English language necessary: Government...no; less pay; receptionist...no; boring; housekeeper in hotel... not my cup-a-tea. Wait, here's one... new hotel in Bali, has variety of job openings. Address, Hotel Jakarta Inter-Continental, Room 306, Harold Green, Human Relations." My finger traced the positions and stopped at Secretary to an Executive. I nodded in approval. *Tomorrow is Monday. Every interview starts on Monday.*

"Find one that attracts your attention?" my sister Tina asked. "You need to hurry before the whale swallows you." She grinned.

"Nothing better to do, Tina?" I retaliated. Tina didn't need to work, she was married.

The Jakarta Inter-Continental Hotel had opened two years earlier, managed by the American Inter-Continental Hotels chain. Every time I passed the hotel, I felt a strong desire to wander and explore. The grandeur overwhelmed me as it was the first hotel of its kind in Jakarta. Eight stories high, with an Olympic-sized swimming pool, and shopping arcade. It was a challenge to explore such an astounding place.

On Monday I went to the hotel. I took a deep breath and approached the Concierge.

"Where is the elevator to room 306?"

"That way, ma'am. Are you here for an interview with Mr. Green?" the concierge asked.

"Yes, that's right. Is he in?"

"I'll ring his office, ma'am, and announce your arrival," the Concierge answered. I nodded and continued walking to the elevator. It was a great feeling. *I need to announce your arrival, ma'am. Wow! As a 24-year old with a job interview, I have a reason to enter a hotel now. Remember my autograph hunting days? My mother forbade me to enter a hotel alone.*

The elevator door opened on the third floor and I walked to room 306, and knocked. A lady opened the door. She introduced herself as Fien (Pronounced Feen), Mr. Green's Secretary.

I told her I had come for an interview. She nodded and announced me while looking into the adjoining room.

"Mr. Green, your ten o'clock interview is here."

"All right, give her the application forms so she can fill them out. I will be there in a minute," came the answer.

"I brought my resume with me, Fien. Do I have to fill in the hotel's application form as well?"

"Yes," Fien replied, " this is a standard form for all Inter-Continental Hotels. What you have in your hand is your personal resume."

Mr. Green was a plumpish man with a friendly smile, salt and pepper hair, professional in his coat and tie. He carried a stack of folders under his right arm. I was fidgeting in my seat, rubbing my hands and scanning the room with my eyes. He looked at me and noticed my nervousness. He smiled. "A big room, isn't it? Take a seat."

While waiting for Mr. Green to finish studying my resume and application forms, I noted the modern secretarial desk, a hutch for books and two expensive lamps on each side of the desk. Behind the secretarial desk, a big window was adorned with artistic designed drapes and a million dollar view. Paintings on the walls, a sofa paired with a wood-carved coffee table, with magazines on top, completed this ensemble of luxury furniture.

He lifted his head, looked at me, and asked, "So, young lady, what job are you interested in?"

"Secretary to the Executive, sir."

"Which one, we have several."

"The top one."

"Oh, General Manager's Secretary?"

"Yes, that's the one."

I didn't know which Executive I should choose. It was a habit of mine to aim for the top position. Mr. Tan, our former teacher used to say, "Always aim for the moon. If you fail, you will land on the stars."

If Mr. Green felt amused, he didn't show it. He studied my resume, and then he faced me with a frown.

"Did you carry all that cash to Medan?" he asked.

"Yes, sir, I did." He looked at Fiona and mumbled "Incredible."

"If you've performed your duties as per your resume, I am sure you can do any job we offer," he said. "The General Manager's Secretary position isn't available." He glanced at Fien.

"What we can offer you is Supervisor to the Telephone Department. When you have shown your ability to Management, and get to know them better, then I suggest you request a transfer to a higher position. As a staff member of the hotel, your request for a transfer will be easier. This Telephone Supervisor's job is open. If you desire, you can begin your training in two weeks."

I breathed deeply. "Do I have to leave Jakarta and live in Bali, sir?"

"Yes, you do. We will provide training in this hotel, an orientation on what services we offer. Fien will update you on IDs and other necessary documents. You understand that we have received a lot of applications. I need a commitment." He got up from his seat and disappeared into the next room.

I was in a daze when I shared my interview with my parents.

"You need to move to Bali?" my mother asked. "Will they give you accommodations? How much money do you need to start there?"

"Oh, I am sure the representative will tell me when I am closer to my training. He said the Executive Secretary's position has been filled. I was attracted to the salary, the same as Mr. Grant's. Besides, we need the money."

My parents were silent. Tina mumbled, "You'll fly over the ocean. The whale will get to you if you don't land in the land of Nineveh."

I ignored Tina's remark.

As the days passed by, I became more and more restless and wasn't looking forward to next week's interview. The feeling of peace and calm perception was gone. Instead, I felt as if a big rock had landed on my shoulders. The burden I had to carry created a pressure on my chest.

"So, what are you going to do?" my mother asked.

"I don't know, Mam," I said.

Before returning to Fiona with my documents, I wandered around the lobby and shopping arcade of the hotel. A gentleman approached me and said,

"Esther, I thought it was you. What are you doing here?"

Steve was my stage acting partner. "I am job hunting, how about you?" I asked.

"Public Relations Department, at your service, ma'am." He bowed a little. "Are you serious with the job hunting?" he asked. "Were you interviewed by Green? He is the Representative of the hotel before Management secures a permanent General Manager. The Hotel is not ready yet, and might take another year to open."

"Well, I am not looking forward going to Bali."

Steve thought for a moment. "I can help you." He grabbed my arm, and said, "C'mon, follow me. I just remembered there was a job opening this morning relayed by Nora, the Assistant Human Relations Manager. It might still be available."

I met Nora, and everything happened quick as lightning. I filled in the Hotel's application, was directed to the second floor's Executive Office, introduced to an older looking man in his fifties called Mr. Schroeder, Resident Manager of the Hotel Jakarta Inter-Continental, and whoosh… I got the job.

My heels had wings, and I jumped and flew like a bird. I heard the birds chirping. No more heavy bricks on my shoulders. I threw my arms up and inhaled the air.

"What about Nineveh?" my sister asked when she entered my bedroom. "What about Nineveh? Have you arrived yet?" She liked popping my balloon.

"I don't have to cross the ocean, Tina. There will be no whale now. Out of here." I waved my sister out of my room. She disappeared.

I became Executive Secretary to the Resident Manager of the hotel, number two Executive after the General Manager. *Mr. Tan was right. I landed on the stars.*

Mr. Schroeder was a lonely man. He missed his daughter in Switzerland. He didn't believe in God. Understanding my background from the Council of Churches with no hotel experience, he offered to educate me with a tour of the Hotel.

"You've never visited a hotel before?" he asked.

"No, never, sir."

"All right, allow me to give you a tour. You need to know what we have to offer."

While waiting for the elevator to inspect the Supper Club on the eighth floor, he inquired how I had arrived at the hotel. I shared with him the quest for the land of Nineveh.

"As a Christian, you have no knowledge where Nineveh is?"

"No, sir, and now I am talking to a non-believer. I'll never find it," I said.

"On the contrary, my child, I know where Nineveh is." Mr. Schroeder said.

"Well, tell me, where is it?"

"You have arrived in Nineveh. The hotel is the city of temptation. A lot of sinful acts could happen here. The Bible told you this? Unbelievable."

Like the climax of a movie, the leading actress (me) gracefully slid into a heap on the floor. A non-believer showed me the way. What an irony!

Chapter 28: Herr Bauer, This is Living!

"Mr. Arifin is the Manager of the Drugstore," Mr. Schroeder informed me as we entered the store, our final destination of the hotel tour. The crystal bracelets, necklaces, rings, and high-heeled shoes from Europe and Hong Kong, took my breath away

"This is Esther, my Secretary, Mr. Arifin. I am leaving her here and she can purchase anything she desires. Send the bill," he said, pointing at himself… "All right?"

"Yes, sir, with pleasure."

The action caught me by surprise and I wondered whether this was a common gesture to new employees. Perhaps the Hotel had more updated rules in employee appreciation than the Council of Churches. I felt uncomfortable receiving gifts from strangers.

He turned toward the door and I followed him. "You don't have to do that, sir."

My boss looked at me, smiled, and answered, "But I *want* to do that, Esther. Take your time. You can return after lunch. Enjoy!" He left.

Arifin approached me, clapped his hands once and commented, "What can I do for you, Esther? I can tell you he had two secretaries before you, but none had privileges like you. You must be special."

I wasn't impressed, and I walked away.

"No, no, no, Esther. Don't do that." He caught up with me.

"Why not? There's nothing I want."

"If you ignore his request, you will hurt his feelings. You need to reciprocate by showing your appreciation. Other girls would love to be in your shoes. Let me show you what we offer."

A new education for the day began. "These are perfumes. Chanel from Gay Paree," Arifin said, imitating the French and pretending to tap his wrist. "Best in perfumes and more expensive." He opened the testers, and let me sniff them one by one. I tested all the expensive perfumes whose names I recognized from ads.

"Wow! Out of this world," I said.

"These are tester bottles, and it is free to try them. If you like, I will give you a new one to take home. Mr .Schroeder said he will pay for it. He has an account with us. Chanel or the Rose?" Arifin asked.

"Chanel," I said.

"All right, good choice. Chanel coming up."

"What is that?" I pointed at small bottles in a row on the shelf.

"Oh, those are Murine Eye Drops to help reduce red eyes."

"Is that expensive?"

"No, are you thinking of getting one for the family?"

"Yes, my mother cooks and sometimes develops red eyes. Two bottles, please."

"Two bottles." Arifin showed me before the two bottles disappeared into the bag.

It became easier to choose the next items, two beautiful imported bras with lace, a pink shade lipstick, and clear nail polish.

"Why don't you choose these...more sparkle to the beholder... bracelet, necklace, for instance?"

"Sure, they are alluring. Where would I go with that bracelet?"

He shrugged.

As the Resident Manager's Secretary, I enjoyed the privilege of eating in the dining room reserved for managerial staff members. Some came over and shook hands, introduced themselves. The shopping spree emerged as the main topic of the day.

"Make sure your boss only takes you to the Drugstore, Esther. All right?" Miss Nora, the Human Relations Assistant said.

I nudged Wati, the next door Secretary, " What does she mean by that?"

Wati smiled: "In this Hotel job, make sure you walk where people can see you, and nowhere else. Go home at the appointed time, and no overtime. Stay away from problems."

"What if he asks me to work overtime?"

"No, he won't, he will be occupiued…with other things…trust me." Wati waved my question away with her hand.

One afternoon Mr. Schroeder inquired, "Do they serve cakes in the dining room? I mean the ones made by the European Chefs?"

"I don't think so, sir, no dessert." He nodded and left.

A piece of cake on a gold-leaf plate was waiting for me on my desk. I loved the beautiful plate.

"This plate came from the Pandawa Restaurant, the Main Dining Room. The cake's name is Black Forest. Have you tried one?"

"No, sir, I know of the Black Forest, an area in Germany."

"Yes, the name came from there. Lots of dark chocolate. Try it."

I did.

"And…?" He asked.

"Wow, out of this world, sir." We both ended up laughing.

My journey to the world of delicacies continued. Black Forest cake, Lemon Meringue, Sacher Torte, and I devoured them all. Sometimes I took them home for the family.

As much as I enjoyed the glamor of the Hotel world, I was looking forward to more challenging duties. There were none. Wati was right. There was no overtime, as there was nothing significant to do. I would type a memo once or twice. I could say that Mr. Grant had much more work for me than Mr. Schroeder who had no appointments, no direct correspondence, and the General Manager never visited. He only showed up once to say hello and shake hands. Two months glided by.

"There she is, hush." I entered, and everyone pretended not to notice me as they continued consuming their meals in the Dining Room. They were avoiding eye contact.

I sat down beside Wati and inquired why the strange behavior.

"Oh, there are rumors going around. You may find out soon."

"Me, find out? Are you kidding? You are more well-informed. All right, are they talking about me? C'mon, speak up."

I stood up with my hands on my hips and scanned everyone. "Speak up, why so secretive? You have something to say, say it now. I am fed up with this hush-hush campaign."

Pak Amrun (pronounced Amroon), the Front Office Manager stood up. He cleared his throat and said, "It isn't you, Miss Esther. It is your boss. Management terminated his contract before the full four years. It was his personal request so he can be closer to his family."

I flopped back in my seat. "Do you know who will replace him?" I asked Pak Amrun.

"Yes, his name is Sigmund Bauer. I worked with him before he moved to Germany. He will return as the new Resident Manager. Quite a different personality, a no-nonsense man. He'll start on the first of next month."

"That's only two weeks away. What must I do?"

"Eat your lunch. I'll visit you a little later. The General Manager asked me to update and supply you with the Rules and Regulations and anything you may require. Your training with me will begin next week after your boss' departure."

Mr. Schroeder left without fond farewells by staff members. I wished him all the best with his family.

Pak Amrun kept his promise and provided me with a folder consisting of the names of Department Heads, Phone Numbers, Names of Managers of the Shops, the location of the Departments in the Hotel, their Job Descriptions, Schedule of Meetings, Rules and Regulations. I gaped at Pak Amrun.

"How come no one provided me with this information beforehand?"

"There was no need for the former boss, as he was not interested at all

Education time once more…memorizing names, numbers and everything else in the folder. I had nightmares. *What if I don't make it? Another job hunting in the air? But I've arrived at Nineveh. Was there a different Nineveh?*

As expected a week later, the door sprung open and there he was, a tall, good looking man in his thirties, my new boss.

"Sigmund Bauer." He gave me a firm hand-shake. My eyes flickered; I was intimidated by the energy springing out of him. "And your name is…?"

I stuttered, "Esther, sir."

He nodded, and without another word, he disappeared inside his own office. A few minutes later he emerged again with a question, "Where are the flowers?"

"What flowers?"

"Over there." He pointed at the end table behind me. " My secretary must have flowers. Connect me with the Executive Housekeeper."

I dialed Mrs. Rastetter's number.

"Ach ya, Frau Rastetter. Guten morgen. Bauer hier…. Canu I have flowers for my Secretary, please? *Ya, dass ist gut.* Every morning. *Danke."* Half an hour later a basket of flower arrangements was placed on the table behind me. What a difference flowers made. Rays of sunshine flooded my office…and poof…it became a garden. Hey, the birds chirped too. I joined them singing a happy tune..

The next day, Mr. Bauer ordered coffee.

"Yes, sir, I'll order it for you. Anything else besides coffee?"

"Order me some croissants."

"Kroa-what?" He looked at me and stopped reading his correspondence. With no comment, he turned around in his chair, picked up the telephone behind him, and dialed the number.

"Hello, Room Service. Bauer here. Could you send me some croissants and two coffee please?" *I felt so stupid, I should have just jotted it down and asked the Room Service myself. Aaarrggh! You will lose your job,* for sure.

"Are you expecting a guest? Why two coffee?" I asked.

"One is for you, and from this time on you can order anything you like from Room Service, and I will sign the bill. Order breakfast in the morning if you like. Oh, your favorite cakes are on the Room Service menu."

I stuttered again, "H…How could you tell I like the cakes?"

"News travels fast in the Hotel."

"One more thing. Let me know whenever you want to invite your family to the Pandawa Restaurant. You have the privilege of dining there too." My eyes became bigger and my mouth opened wider.

Back in my secretarial quarters, I looked around and reminisced over what had just happened. Apart from my salary which remained uncut plus medical benefits, private transportation, breakfast, my favorite cakes, and flowers every day, I could use the facilities of the Main Dining Room.

I raised up my arms and said, *"Hello, Nineveh! This is living!"*

Chapter 29: Blitzkrieg

My status had improved among the hotel staff and employees. This was because they respected my new boss. Activities increased, and I picked up fresh administrative duties every day.

The Hotel Staff recognized my benefits as an Executive Secretary had taken effect. I got the privileges commensurate to my rank, nothing unusual for the hotel. My life changed and it was a giant leap to my career. I never expected Nineveh to be a glamorous place. All the more I believe in the words "If God is For You…"

Mr. Amrun, the Front Office Manager, my greatest ally, advised me, "Try to be two strides ahead of your boss, Miss Esther, and no excuses."

His words were etched in my mind.

Every request I made to offices had the word 'priority' imprinted on the work order, even though the word was invisible. Everyone understood.

One clear day, Mr. Bauer entered and interrupted my adoration of the never-ending view from my window.

"Do you understand the word "blitzkrieg?" he asked me.

"Yes, sir, it means sudden attack in German; it was used during the World War II. Why?" I swung around and looked at him.

"You understand German?"

"Yes, I do, but I'm not as eloquent as you." I smiled. He noted my joke. I was being modest. Mr. Bauer was a linguist and spoke six languages meticulously.

"I will do a blitzkrieg, inspect the Hotel from top to bottom. It is confidential, understood?"

"Yes, sir. When will you do it? Any specific time and day?"

He shrugged. "If I tell you, it won't be a blitzkrieg. It is better you don't know," he said.

"What if anyone asks me where you are?"

"Tell them you don't know, and that's the truth. If they give you problems, ask them to consult me." *Wow! Consult him? That would be the day.* Everyone shuddered at the sound of his name, the no-nonsense Executive.

I wrote the request in shorthand on my agenda. I knew it was important. It was the first blitzkrieg for me, but I feared the hotel staff's reaction. Nobody liked a 'sudden attack.'

The next day, activity started as usual, and I dived into the correspondence pile in my inbox.

Nousri, the Warehouse Assistant entered requesting my boss' signature on some documents. He was a man in his thirties and wearing his usual white shirt and grey pants, his favorite outfit. He tilted his head and nodded toward the closed door. "Boss in?"

I put my finger to my lips, while nodding to the closed door.

"Kaboom!" World War III broke out. The door sprung open with a deafening bang and a stocky German Executive in his late forties entered. His face was red and he was panting. He was raving mad. His chest heaved up and down. He raised his arms and slammed his hands on my desk with another bang.

Nousri stood next to me, his jaw at half mast. I shifted away from my desk. We crossed our arms in front of our chests, looked at him in shock, and speculated what he would do next.

He leaned in my direction and yelled, "Next time, you tell me when he wants to have this... this... blitzkrieg, ya?" He spoke with a firm German accent. "I am not a child, and I have been in business for many years. I don't appreciate your treatink me like-e these. (That's the way he spoke.) Never do that again! You will tell me," he pointed his finger at me, then at himself.

The loudness of the banging and his voice made the staff members of the Executive Offices conscious of his presence. Then he waved his chubby finger in front of my face. Once again in a raised voice, he said, "Verstehen?"

He looked around and noticed the closed door to my boss' office. He stopped, turned around and slammed the door behind him.

"My God, what was that noise?" I could hear people talking to each other. Everyone stepped out of their offices to figure out where the noise originated and who the victim was.

I was still shaking when Nousri whispered, "Esther, I have to go now. Make sure your boss signs these papers. OK? Don't worry. That German guy will get it." He nodded toward the adjacent room of my boss' office and left.

I sat there, still shuddering. My heart pounded in my chest. I was staring out the glass window when the connecting door opened, and my boss entered my office.

He saw me sitting in my seat, frozen, thumping my fingers on my chest. He asked, "Are you all right?"

I jumped a little in my seat, looked at him, and stuttered, "D...did you?... pointing to my ears and him, then opened my hands, shrugged and said, " See..." I was stuttering and not making sense.

"Calm down, ya? Was that Mr. Kahler, from ...and he pointed... two doors down?" Mr. Bauer inquired.

I nodded.

"Who was here with you?"

"Nousri, from the warehouse. He has something for you to sign." I showed him the documents. My hands trembled.

He breathed deep and ground his teeth, paced my office floor and consulted his watch.

"Esther, why don't you take an early lunch?" He left.

It was a relief to dine early. Mr. Bauer was nice enough to let me go earlier to avoid the crowd. However, my peace was short-lived.

Mr. Amrun entered with a frown on his face showing concern. He regarded me as his protégé. "I called your office and nobody answered the phone. So, I guessed you may have taken your lunch early. Management will address his (Mr. Kahler's) bad attitude and temper."

"What are you talking about?" I pretended not to understand.

"News travels fast. Tough luck to him your boss had been listening to his outburst. He won't get away this time with his negative attitude. You are not working for Mr. Kahler. You were just doing your job. He will take care of that s.o.b. himself, and it won't be pretty." Mr. Amrun kept rambling to express his own displeasure.

"How do you know it was Mr. Kahler?"

"Who doesn't? We all know the bully. He always talks loud and his voice carries for miles around. He's hurt a lot of the hotel staff, in particular those who couldn't defend themselves."

The dining room filled up quickly and Mr. Kahler became the main topic of the day.

The hotel staff had been expecting a higher level executive to act and stop Mr. Kahler's behaviour and authoritarian attitude. If it wasn't for Nousri's presence, I thought for sure he would hit me.

After a lunch break, Mrs. Rastetter, the Executive Housekeeper, met me in front of my office. She was not smiling; her lips were tight and she was pacing until she saw me approaching.

While tapping her chest, she said, "Miss Esther, I want to talk to your boss and tell him he should do something about this bully. He made my girls at the Housekeeping Department cry. Someone should stop him. I am German, and I don't like his attitude. He shouldn't treat you that way. You were only doing your job, ya? "

"I will talk to him, Mrs. Rastetter. Thank you for your understanding. It was quite a scare for me. I will pass on your concern."

Mrs. Rastetter left and I sighed. What a day. My hand trembled when I used the key to unlock the door, and I looked left and right before entering to make sure no one had followed me. I flopped into my chair.

In the middle of typing, I heard the door rattle, and my instincts told me the bully had returned. I turned around and stared at Mr. Kane, the General Manager.

"Oh, it's you, Mr. Kane. You startled me."

He looked into my eyes, and asked, "Are you all right?"

I hesitated, and nodded, "Hmmm," as papers dropped to the floor. I was nervous and at a loss for words.

He raised his right hand and said, "Calm down," and he stepped into the office to look for Mr. Bauer, and then left.

My boss returned from lunch and I felt relieved.

"Anything going on while I was absent?"

I didn't answer him right away. After a moment of silence, I asked, "How long have you tolerated Mr. Kahler as a bully? The phone never stopped ringing. Callers demanded to get together and asked for a…" I stopped. "How should I put it…"

"Reprimand? Strong reprimand? Is that what everyone is expecting?"

I nodded. "If I may quote, everyone said, 'It's about time.' Mrs. Rastetter said so, and the General Manager was looking for you too. He came here."

Mr. Bauer thought for a moment and went straight to Mr. Kane's office. He returned after an hour's meeting, went straight to his office and closed the door. His private phone line kept blinking with phone calls.

A knock on the door and the shadow on the glass window told me the bully had returned. My boss' resence encouraged me to remain calm.

Mr. Kahler opened the door and cleared his throat. I could tell he was holding on to his composure and whatever he needed to do was difficult.

"Fraulein Esther, I'm sorry for what I did this morning. It was uncalled for and I apologize for my inappropriate behavior and verbal abuse. I promise it won't happen again." He stood straight and nodded like in the military, turned around, and closed the door gently behind him. I saw him outside my glass window wipe off his sweat.

The bully apoligized! How about that! I stood up and raised my arms – the bully apologized. I punched the air, pulled my right arm up and down, and said yes!

It was pure joy. I pretended to dance around a campfire lifting and stomping my feet, and created my own soundless victory cry. A squeak of a door opening made me realize Mr. Bauer was coming out of his office. I flopped in my chair and continued typing.

Mr. Kahler never bothered me again, and I enjoyed my peace, until the week after...

Chapter 30: Bali, Nineveh, I'm Home!

"There she is," shouted Wati as I entered the dining room. The scene with Mr. Kahler was long forgotten, as we didn't hear his harsh words anymore. Peace reigned once again in the Hotel. Rumors had it Mr. Kahler had received a strong reprimand from the highest level Executive to refrain from his arrogant attitude, or else!

"What have I done now?" I replied as I entered the dining room. I scanned the dining table searching for answers.

"Well, are you going? Are you leaving us?" Wati and other colleagues approached to learn more.

"Who is going, and why are you staring at me?" I asked in an irritated manner.

Everyone paused, "Oh no, she wasn't advised yet."

"What are you talking about? Can someone please speak up? I hate incomplete statements."

Mr. Amoen, the Front Office Manager, intercepted the conversations and noise. He held his hands high, "Everybody, it is obvious Esther hasn't received the news yet. Calm down, eat and return to your offices. All right?"

Mr. Amrun grabbed me by my arm and asked me to join him for lunch.

"What's going on?"

Before he could say anything, the Human Relations Manager, Mr. Daman, arrived and flopped into a chair next to Mr. Amrun. He said, "Miss Esther, I don't have your job review yet. Your boss, Mr. Bauer, didn't return it."

"Oh, my goodness, he will fire me. It's all Mr. Kahler's fault. He might think I lack the ability to manage difficult matters. Oh, my goodness." I rambled on and Mr. Daman interrupted.

"Miss Esther, it's a routine review. You have been here six months now. My assumption is that Mr. Bauer wasn't informed of this job evaluation report. He is new here, and in need of an update. Consult with him when you see him after lunch."

Shall I ask this afternoon? What if he says I'm not qualified to be his secretary? Oh my, what a mess. How do I tell my parents? I wished we had cooler air in the dining room. It felt hot. This was my best position ever. I've landed in Nineveh. What could go wrong?

Returning from the dining room, even the beautiful view from my window didn't distract me. The splashing of water in the swimming pool and the happy laughter of tourists remained muted. I walked in a stupor.

I avoided telephone calls. What for? I may not talk to them tomorrow. It was quiet when Mr. Bauer entered my office and noticed something was amiss.

He looked around and asked, "Did I miss something here? It is so quiet? What's wrong?"

I looked at him and answered, "Are you going to fire me today?"

"What? Why? Young lady, it's time to talk." He motioned to the door of his office. That's what I liked about my boss. He took care of problems right away. I followed him with the review form in my hand.

He closed the door and sat opposite me at his desk. He sighed and put his arms on the desk while facing me. "What made you think I would fire you?"

"Mr. Daman approached me today and wondered why you hadn't returned the Review form. I pointed at the paper on his desk. Mr. Bauer picked it up and read the contents. At one point he stopped, and exclaimed, "Huh? Council of Churches? What is this? It can't be."

"What's wrong with the Council of Churches?"

"Nothing's wrong. You didn't tell me what hotels you've worked in before.

182

There must be hotel experience, not only the Council whatever?" He pointed with his hand at the form.

"No sir, that's the only experience I have. You've never spoken about my work. I thought my work was unsatisfactory, which is the reason you didn't fill in the form."

He tilted his head back and chuckled. "I thought my predecessor had fulfilled his duties. You have performed well. That's why I thought you had had a lot of hotel experience in the past. Never in my wildest dreams did I expect your work history to be with the Council of Churches."

"You like my work? Can I stay? Why didn't you communicate with me?"

"You handled everything like a pro. Yes, ma'am, you can stay. Give me that darn paper. I'll sign it, and stop worrying. End of story." He signed the review form and returned it.

Thank you, Mr. Grant, for all your hard work to train me.

"Mr. Daman said I could get a raise after 3 months. It is 6 months now. Can you consider it?"

Mr. Bauer smiled and was amused by my straightforwardness.

"Right on the dot, follow the book," he said and thumped on the table with his fist. "I'll talk with Mr. Daman tomorrow. Can you arrange the meeting?"

"Yes, sir. Right away."

Phew, what a day. I would keep my job and get a raise. The sound of happy laughter reached my ears and the day regained its color. I took a few dance steps, and hummed…"*Oh what a beautiful feeling, everything's going my way…*"

The next day, bouncing and humming as I entered the dining room, I had an answer ready for my colleagues. They asked, "Are you staying or leaving?"

"For sure I can keep my job here in the hotel," I replied. "Are you happy now?"

Everyone looked flabbergasted. "She still doesn't know. Your boss is leaving. Are you aware of it? Come on, girl," Wati said.

Snapping of fingers... "Wake up. He has been going back and forth to the new hotel in Bali. Get it? That means one thing only. The IHC (Inter-Continental) has promoted him to be the General Manager of their new hotel. It has 600 rooms. Mystical paradise island. Swaying palm trees, white sandy beach, and the blue waters." Everyone chimed in and danced the hula. He will transfer to Bali."

"Oh no, Mr. Bauer should have told me, right?" I said with building disappointment. Everyone flopped into their seats and shook their heads. "Not always," Wati said.

I lost my appetite.

Blitzkrieg, that's what it was. Mr. Bauer was launching a blitzkrieg attack on me, his secretary. How unfair can he be? Oh dear, dear. One thing after another. When is this uncertainty going to end? I need peace.

The only person who would know about it was Mr. Daman, the Human Relations Manager. That's why he urged me to take care of the Job Review. I called his office.

"Mr. Daman, is it true what people here are asserting that my boss will transfer to Bali?"

"Miss Esther, rumors. If you want to confront him, wait until I am through with my meeting today. Understand?"

"Oh yes, Mr. Daman. Thanks for reminding me."

I felt as if I were sitting on a cushion of small nails. I was restless. *New boss, new interview. What if the new Executive doesn't like me? Again, I could lose my job.* I was talking to myself again, which was happening a lot this past few days. Arrrggh!

That afternoon before I left for the day, I knocked on my boss' door.

"Come in, ach ya, Esther, sit down, I have something to tell you."

Here it comes.

"I don't know how to explain this," he said.

"Let me make it easier for you, Mr. Bauer. You are launching a 'blitzkrieg' on me. Ya?" I was imitating him.

He looked surprised, and then he burst into laughter. "Blitzkrieg, on you? It will never happen. You know every step I make." He laughed again.

"Is 'blitzkrieg' a common term in the hotel world?" I asked. "Does everyone understand?"

"No, it's my personal term. 'Blitz' means flash or lightning. 'Krieg' means war. My term for inspection without warning. It wasn't a preferable choice as you have experienced yourself. The German colleagues understand that everything done without warning is a 'blitzkrieg'."

"You are leaving, right? Everyone in the dining room knows it. I was oblivious to what's happening. I received the news from other people. It's not fair."

He saw my eyes drop and fix on the desk. My boss sighed, and said, "I'm appointed as the caretaker of the new hotel in Bali. This is true. I have been going there every other week to monitor the building progress. The grand opening ceremony will be in July 1967. The hotel will send Invitations to local dignitaries. It is February now, and I have limited time. Nothing definite yet. I kept you in the dark as I have scouting to do. Getting acclimated with the hotel surroundings, its staff and executives."

"The Hotel already has an Executive Secretary. I applied for the position and got rejected. The interviewer, Mr. Green, offered me the position as Supervisor of the Telephone Department, and I refused." *I had to protect my position and working standard.*

Mr. Bauer laughed. "*You*, Supervisor of the Telephone Department? No, no, you can't be." He continued laughing. "You can do much better than that," he said, pointing at his forehead. "This is confidential, all right?"

I nodded.

"My plan is to have you continue working for me as my secretary in Bali. It is imperative for me to clear the path and make thorough preparations before I can transfer you there. Talk it over with your parents about moving to Bali. Now I have a meeting to attend." He left.

Wow, that's a pleasant "blitzkrieg."

God was watching to make sure I arrived in the real Nineveh. Thank you, Lord!

The sun looked brighter. Did I hear fanfares? Trumpets of Gabriel? Where did that music come from? I raised my hands up and screamed a muted sound, "*Nineveh, I'm home!*"

Chapter 31: A Miracle, Knock, and the Door...

"Wonderful news, people, I am promoted to Executive Secretary and will move to Bali." Silence from the family, and an empty gaze.

"What! No "hurrah?""

My family, seated at the dining table, stared at me as I walked into the room. Nobody had ever moved out of our parental house for any reason. My mother thought moving to Bali was out of the question. I had turned down the position last year.

My father was silent. I knew he liked to keep his children close to home. His young eagle had spread her wings, and she was ready to fly out to new adventures.

"Why?" I heard my sister Tina say. "Why Bali? You can carry on with your career here."

"Where can I find an opportunity that provides all the privileges? I can visit and dine in the hotel's plush dining rooms, swim in their giant pool with clear blue water, wander around their manicured landscaped grounds and will have assigned transportation. What about the beach? Can you point out one company that could afford to serve up all the conveniences I've seen in the movies only?"

"What about the ghosts? When you and Mammie returned from Bali a year ago, you told me ghost stories, and you can't swim. What's the big deal about the swimming pool?" My sister loved rubbing it in.

"Nobody swims on dry land, Tina, I can learn. As to the ghost stories, I have to deal with them. Can I suggest that they visit you?"

My sister stood up. She had a funny way of saying: *I love you sister, and please stay.*

"Esther has been our family's bread winner for several years," my mother said, "and she needs this job to help put food on our table."

"God commanded her to move out to Nineveh and she went. God will carry her through this spiritual mumbo jumbo."

"When are they expecting you?" my mother wished to know.

"Two months come July. My boss needs to make arrangements before I can follow him. Why do you ask?"

"I am considering your finances," my mother said. "You should have financial insurance when you're traveling to an unfamiliar area. I need to divide the household resources, as it is the only funds we have. Whatever you take out, I have to deduct it from the total amount. We need to consider the daily household expenses too. It will be a month before you receive your first salary. How about new dresses, a pair of new shoes won't hurt. Things will be different. It is like having a new home. Uncomfortable at first, but you'll get used to it."

I was her right hand, and she was going to release me. Must be tough on her too, I thought.

"Wow, that's very thorough, Mam."

"All right," my mother said, as she took out a piece of paper and a pencil. "Let's work out the estimates."

We came out with 25,000 Rupiah (Roupeeyah).

"If you can come up with this much additional income, we will get by. Otherwise, I will have to deduct this amount from your current salary. The amount will cover your expenses for the month before you receive your first salary. You cannot go to Bali empty handed. It is not much, I know. It will be tight," she said.

I felt bad whenever I had to withdraw funds that could lead to the family's financial hardship. But we have no other alternative, unless I could get additional part-time work.

Perhaps Mr. Amrun, the Front Office Manager, could lend a hand. He knew several business personalities in the hotel. They were always in need of administrative services. It might work out.

The next morning, I saw Mr. Amrun in his office.

"What can I do for you, Miss Esther? he asked.

I explained to him my requirement for extra income.

"Like a temporary personal assistant for these business groups, type letters for them or reports for their meetings, Mr. Amrun? I considered doing this after my regular hours."

"You will venture into a new territory, like Bali, Miss Esther?"

"You know?"

He nodded. "All right, I'll see what I can do. Does Mr. Bauer know you intent to work overtime? Working outside the regular hours requires his approval. He's the boss, you know."

"Mr. Bauer has given me his permission; however, I can only work in my office or in your office. Nowhere else. That was his strict order."

"I understand," he replied.

Every day I checked for a part-time job, to no avail. "Sorry, nothing yet."

I became restless. After two weeks of waiting, I confronted Mr. Amrun, "Is there nobody who requires a temporary assistant, or am I sabotaged in my effort?"

The Front Office Manager shook his head. "It is hard for me to point it out to you. Many men seek girls to work for them in their rooms. They will say

'I prefer privacy,' or 'it's a confidential business.' The truth is they camouflage their work with ...." He moved his fingers in a circle, "...other things. You get the idea?"

"You mean they want to have sex? And not work? Is that all they think about?"

"If you want to put it bluntly. Yes, and your boss knows. Therefore the strict rules."

"Oh, I see."

I hit my forehead with the palm of my hand, "stupid, stupid. This is a hotel where every sinful act can take place. How can I be so stupid? All right, stop the search."

"I'm sorry."

"It's not your fault, Mr. Amrun."

Back in my office, I noticed I was fatigued, sluggish and I coughed. I went to consult the hotel doctor right away. My fear of past childhood sickness returned.

"No doubt about it, you have bronchitis," the doctor said. "The air conditioner is too cold for you. I stressed my concern when I visited your office, remember? Ask the engineer to divert the flow to another direction, away from your neck and back. For the moment, you are to go straight home and take it easy. Here are pills, take them three times a day. I'll see you back on Monday."

The gavel struck the counter. Bam! Go home and rest. No work for you. I must admit I had lost the battle. I slumped in my seat.

Mr. Bauer entered and saw me staring out the window.

"You will find additional work, I am sure," he said, trying to comfort me.

"Who are you kidding, sir? I talked to Mr. Amrun this morning. The result was disappointing. I overlooked the sinful world we live in. You figured it out, but not me. Stupid."

"No, not stupid, just naïve," Mr. Bauer said.

"Now I cannot work overtime. The doctor said I have bronchitis and have to go home and rest. So, forget about working. If I don't work, how can I add to my income?"

"What can I do to ease your bronchitis?" Mr. Bauer changed the subject.

"Oh, the engineer needs to redirect the air current to another direction, away from my neck. That's all. I've already received medication from the doctor."

"Take care of yourself. Go home and rest. In about two weeks, the new Resident Manager, Jerald Werner, will arrive and I will transfer to Bali. I hope you will have fully recovered. You'll enjoy Bali, it's a wonderful place. Stop worrying, you'll be all right."

In other words...focus on the job at hand.

He left and closed the door to his office.

I said a short prayer: "Lord, I can work, and you know I can. However, I'm prevented from work because I'm sick. How can I earn additional money? I'll lay this prayer in your capable hands. Please help me. All things are possible through you. I don't know what to do anymore. In Jesus' name, amen."

I went home, desperate, and with a broken spirit.

Arriving home, I told my mother, "Forget about extra work, Mammie. To make matters worse, I've developed bronchitis. The doctor advised me to take it easy, and no extra work. I don't know what to do anymore." I stayed home for the rest of the week.

On Monday, I felt better, no more coughing. I returned to work. The air-conditioner had been adjusted. Good!

Around 10 a.m, I heard a knock on the door, and a gentleman in his forties carrying a briefcase entered.

"Good morning, my name is Ibrahim. Can I speak to Miss Esther please?"

"I am Esther. What can I do for you?" We shook hands.

Pak Ibrahim carried a leather briefcase and wore a blue short sleeved shirt. He sat down. "I am running out of time, so I will be brief. Did you work for the Council of Churches before? This is imperative for me to know."

"Can you tell me the purpose of your visit, sir?"

"I work for a company called 'BATA', are you familiar with the company?"

"Yes, they manufacture shoes, it is a well-known trade name."

"I work for them, and my boss wants to do a documentary movie on the company's success in Indonesia. BATA came from Europe. They need a narrator for their movie. I understand that you worked for the Council of Churches before and you are familiar with narrating their documentary movie."

"Yes, I am."

Pak Ibrahim looked more excited now he had found the actual person.

"The Indonesian National Movie Company showed my executives all the documentary movies ever produced that were narrated by men. They liked none of them. The manager of the movie company suggested watching the Council of Churches' movie as the last resort since it had the only female voice."

"My voice," I said.

"Yes. After 5 minutes, my bosses decided that they were determined to change their request to a female voice. Can you come with me and help finish the documentary movie, please?"

"Pak Ibrahim, I would love to help you. However, I can't work right now outside my regular hours. I can't do any translating work for you."

"The work is done. All we need is your voice."

I opened the door to my boss' office and consulted him.

"By all means, go. Make sure he brings you back," he said, loud enough for Mr. Ibrahim to hear. Always protective.

I turned to Pak Ibrahim who stood outside the door. He nodded.

After an hour of work, a BATA Executive wrote a check. What surprised me was the amount of the check... Rp. 25,000.- Coincidence? Due to the emergency of the matter, it slipped our minds to discuss the most important part of the work, which was compensation. How would they know I needed that exact amount?

Chapter 32: A Dream Came True, My Bungalow by the Sea

"Hey everybody, I'm leaving for Bali to work, "I shouted to my family. "We can write letters, and it is only an hour away by plane. C'mon, show me some encouragement here. Why so glum? I have my suitcases here, my umbrella for the rain, my beauty case. Waiting for the driver to take me to the airport." I said.

"Do you have everything? Did you pack the candles? They shut down the electricity at night," my mother reminded me. "We will say goodbye here at home."

My sister had tears in her eyes. My father gave me advice: "Always be alert and concentrate on what you're doing. Good luck." He placed his hands on my shoulders and gave them a gentle squeeze.

"Mam and I have been in Bali before, so it is a familiar place for us. Right, Mam?"

My mother nodded.

I tried to break the melancholic atmosphere. None of our family members had ever travelled for one day, let alone flying away to work. My trip to Bali meant not seeing each other for a long period of time.

"One more thing," I said. "The hotel in Bali will use regular courier service from Bali to Jakarta, and vice versa. I will use their services to send my salary. Mr. Bauer insisted on doing it this way, and the courier had been given strict instructions to deliver the package straight to you.

A car honked.

"My ride is here." I gave Mammie and Tina a hug, said goodbye to Pappie and my brothers. The driver helped carry a few pieces of my luggage to the car.

The day seemed cooler than the normal 75 degrees. 'Always summer, never winter,' I remembered my friends   joking in class. I turned back my head once more to see my family waving. I waved back. Sadness filled my heart and tears stung my eyes as I left the home and environment I had known for the past ten years.

I seemed to hear the hollow sound of a big wooden door closing behind me, like the big door at the convent. I was entering a new life. Doubt crept in. What if I felt lonely and had nobody to talk to? At home, there was always somebody, either my mother and father or my sister and brothers.

I sighed as the plane taxied on the runway and lifted.

I must have dozed off, waking when the plane touched down with a slight bump on the tarmac of Denpasar, the capital of Bali.

Beautifully carved sculptures greeted the passengers as we exited the plane and descended the stairs to the terminal. Umbrellas in colors of gold, red and green adorned the entry way to the terminal. *Well, Bali, let the show begin..*

A nice looking gentleman wearing colorful Balinese attire and holding a sign "Hotel Bali InterContinental Welcomes Miss Esther" approached the tourists' area.

I waved and he introduced himself as I Made Dharma (pronounced ee-mahday dharma, Balinese have three names), a representative of the Public Relations Department assigned to pick me up. I appreciated the gesture.

The air-conditioned car with license plate GM 1 was a welcome sight. It was my boss' car. The cool air caressed my face as I stepped inside.

"How long is the drive, Dharma?" I asked.

"30 minutes if we don't encounter heavy traffic, Miss."

I leaned against the car window as we started the drive to the hotel. I enjoyed observing the Balinese farmers plowing their terraced rice paddy fields. A small stream adorned both sides of the road, and banyan trees with their thick leaves provided shade for the vendors. It was a picturesque sight.

A slogan on a billboard read: "See Bali before you die."

I remembered the hotel itself when it was in its final stages, and the hubbub of construction till deep into the night. My mother chaperoned me. We stayed with my friends from the hotel's Engineering Department. That's how I came to visually encounter the grandeur of the Hotel.

Arriving from the big city, the road to the hotel seemed narrower, and no traffic was coming from the other direction. It was a two-way street with few cars.

Horse carts were still the main transportation. I noticed the quiet and the pitty pat sound of the horses' hooves on the asphalt. What a change from Jakarta!

In the back of my mind, I could still hear my sister saying, "What about the ghosts?" *Yes, what about them?* I can't believe there are ghosts on this island or the witch doctor's mumbo jumbo. Perhaps the locals want to scare foreigners from enjoying the island. The tourists might disturb their way of life.

I was a foreigner, a Christian visiting an island of the Hindus. We each have our own gods. The Hindu's god was a statue. It would be interesting to see how I integrated myself with the people and their beliefs.

"Dharma," I asked my companion who was quiet the whole way, "Is it true that Bali has spirits floating around? Are they bad spirits or good spirits?"

"Oh Miss, if you stay away from them, they won't disturb you." He laughed.

"How do I know where they could be?"

"You will know, Miss," Dharma said. "The spirits have a way of making themselves known. They may not appear in front of you, but you can recognize them from their smell. When the fragrance is good in flowers, it is a good spirit. You don't want the bad spirit close to you. They smell of death. You understand? " He put his fingers under his nose.

"Are you serious?" I asked.

"Yes, certain things have happened to staff members when they don't want to listen."

"Can you be more specific?"

"Take for instance one of the former engineers. This man was in his fifties, and he loved to tease young girls.

"He saw a young and attractive girl carrying flowers walk into a temple to pray. It was getting dark. He waited for this girl to re-appear at the doorway, as it was the only exit. After an hour, she didn't show up. He looked at his watch and questioned what a girl could do for an hour in the temple. Most Balinese took only ten minutes to pray. He went into the temple to check," Dharma said while continuing his drive.

Wow, he shouldn't have done that.

"He went to look for the girl in the temple, to no avail. The temple was deserted. She had vanished, but not through the temple's entrance. He would have noticed her. He searched for a back door, couldn't find one either. He realized he had encountered a supernatural being. He had seen an apparition. He made sure he stayed home after dark."

"It's creepy, Dharma. Is the town the only entertainment in this area?"

"Yes, Miss. The hotel will provide entertainment for the guests, but the employees visit the town of Denpasar."

"How about local entertainment?"

"The villages have a variety of folklore dances. No electricity, Miss. They use torches. Better watch the performances in the early evening, before it becomes pitch dark. The hotel shuts down the electricity at ten p.m. The current power plant has the capacity to provide only the hotel's needs."

"So we all sleep in the dark." I sighed.

I was happy my mother had packed candles for me. I made a note to purchase more.

"Thanks for the information, Dharma."

We drove until he stopped in front of the employees' club house.

"I will help you with your luggage and will show you your bungalow. It is the one facing the beach. You can see the sunrise from there. Once you are through unpacking, the boss wanted you to report to his office. Will two hours be sufficient, Miss?"

"Yes, that will do, Dharma, and thank you again."

My bungalow. How about that? It was a short distance from the sea. A rock wall protected the bungalow from the water during high tide. I could see the water mark. I opened the window and a cool breeze floated into the room.

My dream came true. I had always dreamed of living near the beach. I inhaled the fresh air and enjoyed the golden tint of sunshine through the leaves in the garden outside. The sound of the waves completed the sight that I have arrived on my paradise island. I couldn't imagine having my own bungalow so close to the beach? I could be the envy of my colleagues in Jakarta.

The bungalow had wooden designs on the porch wall. The size of the room was a few times larger than my room in Jakarta, and I wondered what to do to fill the space. Never in my life had I seen such space all to myself. It contained a queen size bed, ready made with white bedsheets, and a thin blanket. I sat on the bed, bouncing on the mattress.

I lay down for a few moments with my hands on my stomach and savored my new surroundings. A dresser drawer and a large armoire also adorned one side of the room, plus two chairs. Through the door at the end of the room was my bathroom. No hot running water, and no air-conditioning. I had a small utility room which I could convert into a kitchen in case I needed it. Through the back door I could see other bungalows spread out in the compound. A garden with plumerias separated our bungalows. What a beautiful sight. All mine.

Dharma was prompt in picking me up.

"Everything all right, Miss?"

"Yes, Dharma."

I nodded and gave him a big smile.

"The boss takes good care of you, Miss. You are lucky to have a boss like Mr. Bauer. We all met him last week when we had the grand opening of the hotel. He speaks Indonesian too."

"Have you told him the ghost stories?"

"Which one, Miss? There are a few. When you are settled you can ask the Assistant Executive Housekeeper. She is a Christian, just like you."

"How do you know I am a Christian?" I asked.

"There are no secrets in the hotel," we both said simultaneously, and laughed.

"Here we are, Miss. The entrance to the lobby is right there. Whenever you are done, you can call the transportation department and a car will be at your disposal." Dharma said.

He nodded and left.

I took a deep breath, and all I could say was "Wow! What service."

The entrance door opened automatically, and I entered the air-conditioned and luxurious lobby of the first Inter-Continental Hotel in Bali.

Chapter 33: Police vs. Witch Doctor

The sound of Gamelan music greeted me as I entered the hotel. It was different from the rowdy sound of rock n' roll. Gamelan sounded mystical. The use of glass walls made the lobby bright, with the sun shining through. The Drugstore was on the right side. Next to the Drugstore I could see the shops, Beauty Salon and Airline Offices.

A Spiral staircase of maple wood connected the lobby to the second floor in the far corner. Truly a first class hotel, and more luxurious than the hotel in Jakarta.. I walked straight to the concierge.

"You must be Miss Esther. I will take you to Mr. Bauer's office. He's expecting you." I read his name tag, Budi (Boo-dee).

"You are well-informed, Budi. I'll follow you."

We headed toward the elevator and I saw his hesitation to step in when the door opened. He gestured for me to take the first step. He followed suit.

"Good to have an elevator, right? You don't have to take the stairs," I said.

"We all have had to adjust to the elevator, Miss," was his answer. "We still feel awkward to see the door opening by itself. Some of us didn't dare step inside."

"It's high-tech, Budi, nothing else," I replied.

Mr. Bauer greeted me and shook my hand.

"Thank you, Budi, for bringing my secretary to my office."

He nodded and left.

"Did he take the elevator or go up the stairs?" Mr. Bauer asked.

"You noticed that too," I said.

"Well, it isn't surprising, as this hotel is the first one of its kind on the island. The locals are not used to high tech yet. We have limited electricity for now and we need to turn it off at 10 p.m. A second power plant will be the back-up, and it will operate in a few months. You realize you are now the prime secretary of this hotel and I would like to caution you to keep a low-profile. You understand what I mean?"

"No, but you will tell me, right?"

"You can eat in any of the restaurants. You have department head status. Whenever you invite a guest let me know, and I will tell the Maitre'd of the restaurant to look after you. Let us know in advance," Mr. Bauer commented.

"Don't worry, it will take time to build friendships, sir."

"You will find the Officers' Dining Room provided for all department heads.on the first floor," Mr. Bauer said. "Do you swim?"

"No, I don't, I would love to learn."

"Use the quiet hours when the guests are having dinner. Then you have the swimming pool to yourself. Anyway, whatever you do, do it in moderation. Your privileges can cause envy. Refrain from using the lobby as the entrance. Take a different entryway, the one from the swimming pool. Use good judgment. The employees need to get adjusted to seeing you around. In their eyes, you are a foreigner. A woman with a high-ranking position."

I nodded. "Yes, sir, I understand."

My desk was next to my boss' office, complete with a new IBM Selectric type-writer and telephone lines. The view from my office wasn't as spectacular as the General Manager's to the beach area, but I was content with it.

"This is the first time the Balinese will see an abundance of tourists arriving as guests of the hotel," Mr. Bauer said. "The locals prefer to live in peace. With the new hotel and a large number of foreigners, their way of life will change and they might feel disturbed. You are a foreigner. You came from a different island. Be aware that you will cause curiosity among the employees. They will ask questions."

I was living in a village on an island, primitive in many ways, different from the big city. Will they like having a 'foreigner' working among them? This island embraced Hinduism, and I was a Christian. It would be intriguing

"After all, we are in the year 1967," I commented.

"I understand," Mr. Bauer said. "Every beginning needs a lot of adjustments. And… watch for the coconut trunk call."

"What call?" I asked him with wide eyes. "Can you be more specific?"

"In the old days," Mr. Bauer explained, "people used the empty trunk of a coconut tree to relay messages to the other communities. It is speedier than a telex."

I nodded. "News travels fast. Is that all I need to know before I start my work tomorrow, sir?"

Mr. Bauer looked around and said, "Follow me," and I walked behind him through the corridor and he pointed to a message center on the wall, with cubicles for mail distribution.

"Whenever I need to send a memo or letter to the department heads, you can put the correspondence in here. Their names are printed on the cubicles. The concierge will pick them up and distribute them whenever he can."

"Can't I distribute the documents myself?" I asked.

My boss looked at me in disbelief. "Why do you want to do that? I can't believe this. You have the privilege of having assistance, and you want to play concierge?" He gave a short laugh and raised his right hand, saying 'Mama Mia.'"

"Well, you told me to start with a low-profile," I said, defending myself.

"Oh well, I guess you can do it, whatever works, as long as everyone receives their mail." He nodded and left.

I need to be sure, that's all.

I looked for Budi, the Concierge.

"Budi, where is the Housekeeping Department? I need to talk to the Assistant Housekeeper."

"Mrs. Henrietta? Let me show you now. Check-in time is within half an hour."

Off we strolled down the corridor behind the concierge station. Henrietta greeted us with her big friendly smile. Her eyes shone and she opened her arms to greet me. "So you are Mr. Bauer's new secretary."

"I already worked for him since last year at the hotel in Jakarta," I said.

"Tell me, what's new on this island?" I asked jokingly. I thanked Budi for his help when he left me with Henrietta.

"Everything is new. I have to get help from a witch doctor rather than going to the police to find my lost possessions," Henrietta blurted out.

"I heard the story on the way to the hotel," I said.

"Who told you the story?" Henrietta asked.

"I heard it through the coconut trunk call," I answered. We both laughed.

"That's what your boss calls it," she said.

"Wow, what time is it? I didn't realize it's already dinner time. Is it normal for you to work on Sundays?" I asked Henrietta.

"No. My husband is in Jakarta for a meeting. He travels frequently and I don't want to be alone. Better come to the office and work. Let's go to the dining room."

We walked together through the corridor. Henrietta gave me first-hand information on the offices and who the managers were. I loved going through the hotel, which reminded me of my stroll with Mr. Schraeder at the hotel in Jakarta..

"Who is the Executive Housekeeper here?" I asked.

"Mrs. Rastetter," was the answer.

"Oh, I know her from the hotel in Jakarta, too. Good to see familiar faces."

I loved the cool breeze floating through the corridor. As I passed several employees, I noticed few of them wore wrist watches.

"How come few people wear watches, Henrietta? Is there a church bell somewhere to tell the time?" I asked.

Henrietta laughed. "On a Hindu island? No such luxuries here. The locals prefer peace and quiet. The only Catholic church with a bell is in the town of Denpasar. Watch the sunrise from there," pointing toward the sea. "That's where the sun rises. Don't worry, you'll get used to it. On this paradise island, relax and be happy."

"Here we are," Henrietta said, and we entered the officers' dining room. It had nicely decorated round tables with crisp white linen tablecloths, and menus.

How about that? Wow! I raised my eyebrows. I can choose whatever I like to eat, similar to a restaurant. Nineveh, you never cease to amaze me.

We ordered our food and I insisted on hearing Henrietta's story.

"Three months ago," she started, "my husband, Ben, and I moved from Jakarta to our new house on the island. Since we will be staying here for a while, we decided to move our valuables as well. Ben told me that the local inhabitants are friendly people. "No thieves on the island, trust me," he said.

"I believed him. A long-term maid completed our household. My husband and I were happy to settle down, until one day. We arrived home to find our house door ajar. Our valuables were gone. We were burglarized and called the police.

"After a week passed by, the police didn't have any leads. Their investigating system was not as sophisticated as in the big city. My case had become an unsolved mystery.

"A staff member of our housekeeping department advised me to go see a witch doctor. She got her valuables back.

"As a Christian, I was shocked, but I had no other choice than to follow the advice. The longer I waited, the more difficult it would be to recover my possessions."

Henrietta continued, "Together with my Housekeeping staff and friend, we had to go through rice paddy fields and the wooded area on the mountain. My heart pounded. I was skeptical about whether this would be the appropriate way to find my valuables.

"Upon arrival at the witch doctor's house, he raised his right hand and gestured us to sit and be silent. We waited while he lit some incense and puffed on his long pipe. After a while, he inquired, 'Do you want me to turn this person crazy, ma'am?'"

"No," I said, "I want the thieves to return what belongs to me.

"The witch doctor then instructed me: 'Sit and wait on your back porch when the sun goes down. The first person to approach you and ask for mercy will be the guilty one.'" Henrietta paused.

"Don't stop now. Did you do as he instructed? Who was the culprit?" I asked. Curiosity drove me up the wall.

My new friend drew a deep breath as she was remembering. "I was so scared sitting all by myself on the back porch. I couldn't believe my eyes when I saw my long-time maid approaching me, crying for mercy. She even confessed to stealing my mother's necklace a few years ago. Following the advice of the witch doctor, I asked the police for assistance and tracked my possessions. The thieves returned my valuables without difficulties. They were more afraid to be made crazy by a witchdoctor."

Wow! *Unbelievable.*

Chapter 34: First Recruits

My first week of activities in Bali was exploring nature. I enjoyed the sunrise from the front of my bungalow. Its colors of gold, yellow and blue skies peered through the black and white clouds. I had learned that when the sunlight shone on the bottom of my armoire, it was six thirty in the morning. No need for a wrist watch to tell me the time. It became a matter of habit.

The cool breeze welcomed me while walking on the sandy beach to work. I splashed the sea with my feet and ran toward the water when it receded. I was alone on the sandy beach. Feeling free as a bird, I twirled around with my arms raised up and let the sun shine on my face.

When I was younger, my father took all of us to the sea, and we waded in the water for a couple of hours. Now I have the ocean in front of my bungalow and I don't tire watching the water rushing to the shore. I sat on my porch to savor the calming atmosphere, the cool breeze and the tranquility of the island. What more could I desire? This is heaven. I couldn't believe what has happened. God has blessed me in abundance. I remembered the words of wisdom a long time ago…

"I pray to God to give me all things I can enjoy,
God gave me life, so I can enjoy all things."
Quotation unknown

I cut across the swimming pool area, and washed the sand from my feet under running water from the tap.

The door next to the tap water area opened and Budi stepped out.

"Good morning, Miss. Nice walk?" Budi greeted me.

"Wonderful, Budi. Thanks."

It felt good carrying my shoes and strolling on the carpet with my bare feet, provided my boss didn't catch me. As I passed the middle hallway, I recognized the elevator had stopped with its familiar "ding" sound.

I heard a voice behind me, "Getting adjusted?" Mr. Bauer saw my bare feet. "You don't have to go to that extreme. It is all right to put your shoes on," he teased.

No use explaining. My boss had caught me by surprise.

I nodded. "Blitzkrieg this morning, sir?"

"Yes," he said, as he cleaned a tiny piece of debris from his suit.

"Let's go through the activities for today," he said as we arrived at the office. "We'll have our hands full," he added as he looked through the papers in his inbox. " I'll put you in charge of the new recruits while they work here as secretaries."

"Where are they from?" I asked.

"Surabaya."

"East Java. Big city girls Might be a challenge."

"Nice walk this morning?" Mr. Bauer asked.

"Yes, it's a shame to be indoors today."

"You will have lots of opportunities to enjoy nature, trust me," and off he rushed to his breakfast meeting.

I loved the thought of having new recruits. I would have colleagues, and hoped they could love this island and enjoy working here as much as I do. Some girls coming from the big cities had left because of the floating spirits on the island, and the lack of entertainment.

"It is too quiet for some city girls, Sis Esther," Nita, my assistant, commented. Nita called me "Sis," like a big sister, to show she respected me.

"Bali has no shopping mall, only two movie theaters, and no restaurants other than in the city of Denpasar," Nita said. "For the city girls, this hotel is too far away unless you have transportation. The lack of electricity isn't helping at all."

"You differ from the other girls. You aren't afraid and don't get intimidated easily like the British tourists in the hotel next door."

"Well, what about them? What made them scared?" I wanted to know more.

Nita continued her story. "Their reservations were for a one week stay. They found the place quaint and mystical, surrounded by lots of trees and shrubberies. The tourists loved the place and couldn't talk enough about it until they left the premises for no reason, my friend at the reservation desk said."

"What happened?" I asked.

"Neither husband nor wife shared the reason for their sudden departure. However, one of the taxi cab drivers probed for more information while taking them to the airport. The driver found out that the tourists had two daughters sharing a room. Every night the father checked on his daughters. They were fine for the first two days."

"And? What happened on the third day?" I asked.

"On the third night, the father as usual checked on his children," Nita said. "Instead of two girls, he saw three girls in bed. The next day they left. Everyone in that hotel is familiar with the story and it spread like wild fire. The former girl recruits were uncomfortable when they heard the story and left."

"Afraid of a story? I knew about it a year ago when I visited Bali for the first time. The hotel was in its final stages of being built. I wanted to verify the story.

"So the story goes around." I added.

"Yes it does."

After that occurrence, hotel reservations went down, except for tourists who were adventurers, and eager to meet ghosts. The hotel lost money.

"That's why we continued to interview new employees. As soon as they heard ghost stories, the girls changed their minds and left. Some locals are making bets to see how long you can hold out working here. I shared with my Balinese friends you are a Christian."

I asked my boss after lunch whether there was any truth in the story that had been floating around for over a year.

He shrugged. "It depends on the person you talk to, Esther. If that person is easily intimidated, he or she will believe."

"You never mentioned these incidents before you left the hotel in Jakarta."

"Would it make a difference to you?" he asked.

"You're right. It wouldn't."

My task to take care of the new recruits would be interesting. The hotel was peaceful and quiet, and I liked it that way, ghosts or no ghosts. Newcomers might not think the same way.

Seven p.m. after dinner, I was in my bungalow when I heard voices outside: "Here, this way. There's light from this window. Somebody is in there."

The next instant my door flew open and two girls came in panting and sat on my bed. They both looked at me with big eyes, hands on their chests, trying to calm down. I didn't have a clue who they were, and why they chose my bungalow.

I looked up from my desk, and I asked, "My goodness, who are you and what are you doing here at night?"

"You are a Christian," one said, pointing to my cross pendant necklace.

I answered, "Yes, I am, but what does it have anything to do with you? Can you at least tell me your names?".

"My name is Deena, and my friend is Margaret. We have an interview tomorrow at the hotel next door, the big one. We arrived a day early to explore the area. The cab driver shared with us this ghost story on the way to the hotel," Deena said. "We are staying at that particular hotel where it happened."

"Oh, you must be residing at the hotel next door, the small, quaint one with the mystical surroundings, incense, and mellow lighting," I said.

"Yes, we are Christians too and thought we could handle staying there for one night before the interview. The price is reasonable."

"For a haunted hotel? You can say that again," I said.

"The beach and the sound of the sea enticed us to take a stroll in the direction of the big hotel before retiring. As I was walking," Deena continued, "I felt someone tugging on my sweater. The more I tried to break loose, the more I was pulled back. I screamed and Margaret ran away. Finally, the sweater came loose, and we kept on running and saw your light. So, here we are."

"First of all, there was nobody pulling on your sweater," I said.

"There was somebody, I swear," Deena answered. "I felt the pull."

"Since you didn't stop to look, my guess is that your sweater got caught on the branch of one of the shrubberies that grow in abundance at that hotel. You should bring your flashlight next time you venture outside, if there is a next time.

"See?" I showed them my big flashlight. "It can serve as a lethal weapon too. "Better go back to your room now, before the hotel turns the lights off. Ten p.m. is the cut-off time here. One word of advice, when you have the interview tomorrow, make sure you think hard before you make a decision. Can you control your fear? I cannot afford both of you barging into my room every time you think a ghost is chasing you. All right? So, good night ladies, and I'll see you tomorrow. Maybe?"

Chapter 35: A Letter to Mammie

Hi there, Mammie,

The past four weeks have been fascinating. It is 1967, but in Bali, everything is underdeveloped and unaffected by modern forces. It is taking a while for the Balinese to adopt the InterContinental hotel and its high tech mechanical systems in their lives.

Take the elevator, for example, the Balinese staff waited for me to make the initial move getting inside. They believed only a spirit could open the doors without touching them.

Another time I heard a scream in the elevator and I automatically pressed the button to activate the door. The girl inside was frantic and in tears. She couldn't remember how to get out.

The front office employees needed to get used to the automatic door when tourists step on the welcome mat to enter. They jumped every time the door opened.

I should not be too surprised. Remember my experience a year before I came here? I was mesmerized with everything I saw at the hotel in Jakarta. I'd never ridden in an elevator before. Mr. Schroeder taught me. He also had to remind me every time we passed an automatic door, so I wouldn't jump when it swung my way.

The Balinese still believe in ghosts, and so highly respect the spirits that they refrain from wandering outdoors during evening hours.

Arman, the Concierge Supervisor, explained, "The morning hours are ours, Esther. The evening hours are theirs. Stay away from them. You won't like it when you cross paths. No local women stroll down the beach at night."

However, Mammie, as a person who had never worked and lived on an island like Bali, I discovered that the evening is so lovely and mesmerizing, especially when there is a full moon. We didn't walk like this when you and I were here a year ago. It is the best place to let your mind fly as free as a bird, and I can soar with the eagles too.

The sound of the sea rushing to the shore creates a calming atmosphere. The whisper of the swaying palms summons me to explore nature, from both a magical and serene perspective. I couldn't resist the temptation to stroll down the beach. I carried a lethal weapon with me, my big flashlight.

One evening as I walked down the beach, I saw a red light. At times it became brighter, and then it disappeared; there was no one in sight. I was afraid and my heart raced, wondering whether I should continue my walk. When I got adjusted to peering in the darkness, I saw fishermen smoking close to their boats. They also like to have a calming moment after a hard day's work. I had to laugh inside for my foolishness.

Girls in the office asked me why I carried a flashlight. They thought it was funny to visualize me strolling down the beach with a huge flashlight. I shared what you told me, "To protect myself from the spirits with two real legs. Ghosts float, understand?" They giggled at my description.

We still don't have electricity all the time. Mr. Bauer said in a few days the hotel will operate the second power plant for day usage only. It will turn off at 10 p.m. No problem for me, buy more candles. We had blackouts when we were small, so it is not a strange occurrence to sleep or walk in the dark.

During my second week in Bali, Nita my assistant, urged me to take part in a religious procession to cleanse the temples. I asked her whether we should be carrying a hose. She giggled and said, "We walk to the temples at the high priest's direction. The priests will perform their rituals and cleanse the temples from evil spirits and demons."

I asked her how the priests knew where to go? According to Nita, the high priest would be in a trance when the gods relayed where his followers should go. At every temple, they would perform a similar ritual and asked for their gods' instructions, enabling all of us to continue to the next temple. I wondered if I, as a Christian, should follow a spirit's directions?

As a foreigner, I could not approach the sacred area of the temple, so I cannot tell you what was happening in there.

Nita told me a great number of people will walk with me and I should be all right. It could be a short walk, depending on what the high priest receives. However, the procession could run until midnight. I can leave at any time as I'm not one of them, and I'm not bound by the rules.

Mr. Bauer listened intently to my request to participate. He asked me whether I would feel uncomfortable. "It could be quite different from your Christian belief," he said. I smiled and I assured him I would be fine.

Then he agreed. He said that it would be a good way to integrate with the locals and learn their culture. A car would be at my disposal should I become tired and want to return home at any time. I told him I'd never joined a Hindu religious procession before.

"It will be an interesting experience for you too," he said.

Nita dressed me up in their Balinese attire, Mam. It was a beautiful sarong woven in gold threads and colors of green and red. She gave me a sash and a top of hot pink to match. Oh, I shouldn't forget the flowers and gold leaves she provided for my hair. I felt like a Balinese princess.

Off we went at nine on Friday morning. I was the first foreigner to walk under the sun with them. After a few hours of walking, we had not visited the requisite number of temples. The locals had fun with me instead, telling Nita how white I was. Their own skin is tanned.

Nita gave me an annoyed look: they said I had white skin because I've never been under the sun. I smiled. I told Nita that it was nothing to be mad about. I was the first foreigner to walk under the sun with them.

After another two hours and still no words from the gods, Nita and the group discussed the situation. The high priest told them that this cleansing event would be a short one.

"It has never happened like this before," Nita said. "I wonder what has passed between the gods and the priests? You can go home if you wish, Sis Esther. We will follow shortly, I'm sure."

I left around four in the afternoon. I had fulfilled my first duty of blending with the locals. I was relieved and rested my aching feet at home. It was an interesting event, Mam.

The next morning, I saw the door to Nita's work room ajar, and I peeped in. She was asleep at the table with her head in her arms. When I tapped her on her shoulder, she awoke, startled.

"What's the matter, Nita? What happened? Didn't you go home?"

"Something strange happened, Sis Esther. Five minutes after you took off, the High Priest went into a trance and delivered the directives from the gods. We continued walking till deep into the night."

"My goodness, did the priest tell you what provoked the unforeseen change?" I asked.

"The gods were aware there was a stranger in our midst, a non-believer. So, after you left us, the gods came alive," Nita said.

"That's intriguing. You mean your gods knew I was a Christian?"

Why not? The group did, why not the gods, you might say, right Mammie?

"They must have, Sis," Nita said, "It was so strange and I got goosebumps when it happened. That's why I'm so tired this morning." I sent her home to rest.

You see Mammie, there is never a dull moment.

Remember the radio I used for learning English? Do you still keep it? I would love to hear music when I get up. Music can raise up my spirits to start the day and can help me tell the time, too.

Yesterday, the sky was overcast and I thought I was late for work. I dressed in a hurry and rushed to the hotel. Turning a corner from the shopping area, I almost had a head on collision with Mr. Bauer.

He looked surprised to see me in the lobby and asked what I was doing. "What else? I need to go to work and I'm already late," I responded.

He glanced at the lobby clock. It was 6.30 a.m. He teased me, "Do you have a changed schedule I need to be aware of? Since when do you start work at 6.30 in the morning?" He touched his watch. I could have sunk into the floor. It was so embarrassing.

Can you send the radio with the hotel courier, Mam? Also, please include the watch I forgot in the dresser drawer in my room. I thought I could get around by looking at the sunlight. Bedankt, Mam.

As usual, I am sending you half of my salary to help with the household expenses. Let's see how far the other half goes. Should you need more funds for medical purposes, please tell me. I know insulin is expensive.

The hotel will turn off its lights soon, so I'll stop now. Remind me next time to tell you about the dog.

Groetjes,

Esther

Chapter 36: The Dog

Nusran, the warehouse manager, stopped by my bungalow when he heard I had a prolonged flu. We sat together on the verandah savoring the view of the sunrise and shimmering blue waters.

"The locals need to adjust in accepting women of high-ranking positions," he said.

"You mean, women play second fiddle to men?" I asked. "This is 1967, Nusran —mind telling me why?" I asked. "Mrs. Rastetter occupies a high-ranking position, besides me. She is the Executive Housekeeper. Why is it appropriate for her, but not for me?"

"She is a foreigner holding a woman's job, housekeeping. The locals will accept foreigners coming from the west to occupy the high-ranking expatriate positions, male or female. In the eyes of the men, however, you have a position of authority that should be in the hands of a man."

"Do they want to be in a prime secretarial position?" I asked.

"No, they want the close relationship you have with your boss, the authority, and trust. I think the men envy your position."

"So, what's your recommendation? Mr. Bauer as general manager encouraged me to integrate with the Balinese and I joined your religious procession. Anything more I should do?"

Nusran was a good man and regarded highly for his understanding and considerable knowledge of white magic. He could detect anyone touched by evil spirits. When a person was ill, the locals often sought him for advice before consulting with the doctor.

Dr. Frances, our new lady hotel doctor, didn't believe in black magic or voodoo. As a foreigner, even I had a hard time understanding the Balinese concept of good vs. evil.

"Goodness gracious, you mean these people can use voodoo for whatever purpose?" I asked.

He nodded. "Remember Henrietta? She used it to get her possessions back.

"My advice to you, be careful with what you do or say. Get back to good health. The spirits could take over your subconscious mind when you are in a weak condition. That's why the baby next door became a victim. His parents didn't have the power to heal the baby's possessed body. Take care."

"Thanks." I said goodbye, and he left for work.

Nusran knew of the eerie dream I'd had a few nights ago. I had the flu, with a high fever, and it forced me to stay home. When I slept that night, in my subconscious mind, I saw a dwarf sitting on my bed. He had no eyes. Two deep dark holes stared at me. I recognized a dark force in my room, and I struggled to push him out.

The dark force sucked my strength away. I felt paralyzed. Whatever the force was, it was strong enough to lift me up like a ragged doll and throw me back on the bed. I couldn't utter a sound or move my limbs. My mind was clear, and I said a silent prayer. "Father, help me fight this evil being. If you are with me, who can be against me?"

A slight release of my right arm, a wriggle to get loose from its invisible grip, and a roll to the left facing the room wall next to the bed. I moved my right arm to draw a cross on the wall. Left to right, and top to bottom. In my mind, it was a cross. I was in a stupor.

After my cry for help, I could move a little more. I re-drew another cross larger than the first one. In my mind, I screamed, "Father Jesus, help me."

The dark force lifted my listless body once more and tossed me on the bed with a force that released me from its grip and control. I regained my strength and the movements of my limbs. My chest was heaving, as if I had arrived at the finish line of a long marathon. Beads of Cold sweat gathered on my forehead. My first battle with an evil force had resulted in total exhaustion.

I was conscious but kept my eyes closed, apprehensive of unexpected images which might appear. My posture was tense when I sat up and recited the Lord's Prayer. With the burden on my chest and shoulders lifted, I felt more relaxed. Peace returned to my room.

I opened my eyes and scanned my surroundings. Everything looked normal. Still shaking, I tried to comprehend what had happened. I wiped my damp forehead and face with the cotton blanket. Looking up I said, "Thank you, Father, for standing by me."

The next day Nusran came for a visit and I shared with him the eerie dream. He gave me his advice from his perspective. I was a target of envy.

The hotel doctor, as a Christian and a strong believer, laughed at me when she came by on her rounds. "You have a fever, and it could be you were hallucinating, or plain paranoid," she said.

"Doc, only because it hasn't happened to you, doesn't mean it will not happen." She waved her right hand and said, "Nonsense."

"Remember, Doc, you're the only female doctor on the island, and you occupy an enviable position," I said.

A few days later, a dog entered my life in a mysterious way.

"Nice dog you have, Esther. Did you purchase it?" my neighbor greeted me.

"What dog? I don't have a dog."

"Yes, you do, he has been sleeping on your doormat for the past three days. Every night, on the dot, at nine p.m."

The next morning as I left for work, my head was crammed with questions.

When I crossed the swimming pool area, I heard the Assistant Food and Beverage Manager, Parman, greet me, "Hey, I heard you got a dog."

"Did you see the dog?" I asked.

"Yes, every night returning from work when I pass your place," he answered. Parman and his wife Nani occupied a bungalow around the corner.

I hurried my steps and didn't bother to get entangled in a conversation. After my fight with an evil being, I needed a rest. What were these people talking about? My dog? Never seen one and never fed one, period. Arrggh!

I seldom got annoyed during the day. A beautiful morning always greeted me. How could I be angry?

"Good morning, Esther. I've heard you have a pet?" Mr. Bauer greeted me as I entered my office.

"Not you too? Who told you?" He shrugged and lifted his hands.

"Coconut trunk call," I said. "What else is new?"

"Well, tell me about the dog. Who gave it to you?"

"Sir," I pointed at my lips. "I…don't…have…a…dog. *Comprende?*" Mr. Bauer spoke six languages fluently. He knew I was annoyed when I used a Spanish word. I raised my right hand and shook my head. He gave a short laugh.

"I have to be careful today," he said. "My secretary is on the war path."

I turned and closed the door behind me. I knew why he said I was on the warpath. I got up late and didn't have a chance to put my long hair in a chignon as I always did.

Nusran came to see me during lunch hours. I was alone in the dining room.

"You got yourself a dog," he said. "That's a good way to protect yourself from evil spirits. Keeping a dog will be the best way to prevent the evil spirit from returning."

"This dog situation is driving me crazy, Nusran. I… don't… have… a … dog." "Yes, you do," he said, and left.

Before I retired for the evening, I glanced out at the veranda. The light was on. Silence all around and no people walking by. My bungalow was not in a high-traffic area, as it was an exclusive compound with rock walls all around.

I locked the door and read my book. After an hour, I turned off the light and went to sleep. I didn't see a dog until during the night...

I heard a sound like someone trying to barge into my room. Bang, bang, bang, the door trembled. I woke up with an uneasy feeling. I looked around and found nothing strange. It was dark except for the light shining through the window from the porch. *Had the evil spirit returned?*

I approached the door. Before I could peer through the drape, the door shook again, bang, bang, bang. I jumped and took a few steps back. After a few moments, I confronted my fear and looked through the drapes. Nobody outside. I looked left to right. Went to the side window and peered outside. Nothing. All was quiet. I looked at my watch, two a.m.

Once more I went to the door, and this time I forced myself to look down to the doormat. There he was, a big brown dog. He was scratching himself and thus creating the banging noise. I put my hand on my chest and sighed with relief. I climbed back into my bed.

The dog slept there for over a month after I had my scary dream. I didn't know its name or where it came from. He stationed himself on my doormat when I had already turned off my light; it departed in the wee morning hours.

He disappeared as mysteriously as he came into my life. No more scary dreams.

I had to tell my mother and wrote a letter.

Chapter 37: Once Upon a Christmas, A Miracle

Mr. Bauer opened his office door and gestured me in.

"What's going on?" I asked.

He sat behind his desk and paused before speaking. "I'm considering a Christmas celebration for the hotel," he said. "We're booked solid this season. It will be a nice gesture to provide additional entertainment besides our Supper Club. We can use the auditorium. What do you think?" He glanced at me and waited for my response.

"It's a marvelous idea, and I agree," I said.

"Excellent!" He clapped his hands. "I thought you would. I assign you to be the coordinator of the Christmas festivity."

My mouth dropped open. "Are you serious?" I asked. "I'll need help. Remember, this is a Hindu island. I don't know how many Christians work in the hotel. We may be only a handful."

"I have asked Management to support the festivities. Whatever you and your group need, let me know, and I'll make certain the department heads oblige. Put it on paper first. Discuss the plan with me before you present it to the employees."

Mr. Bauer's request caught me by surprise. After discussing the primary plan with him, I compiled a list of employees, to invite to the first planning meeting. Mr. Bauer followed up by dictating a memo to all department heads announcing the Christmas festivities. Employees interested in joining the celebration should report to the auditorium on Thursday at four p.m.

I mailed a message to Jakarta, asking my brothers to forward the Christmas Play called "The Star of Bethlehem", costume designs, and music sheets for the choir. I planned to recreate it for the festivities, our church had performed the play a year ago.

"What Christmas celebration?" Dr. Frances, the hotel doctor, asked. She was in her mid-thirties, and always wore her crisp white uniform and a stethoscope sticking out of the front pocket. She was of medium build, with curly black hair and she was a strong believer. I explained Mr. Bauer's idea of Christmas entertainment for the hotel.

All the executive assistants to our management team were there. Margaret, representing the Front Office, and Deena, Secretary of the Controller, both in their early twenties, were excited about the idea. They were active members of their church in Surabaya. They had gregarious personalities and were always ready to help. Jojo represented the office of the Resident Manager and Mellie, Food and Beverage. Both were quiet Catholic girls and kept their privacy. This was their first job outside their city of Surabaya. Arya was the new secretary to our Executive Assistant Manager.

Twenty people showed up at the auditorium. Not bad. I discussed my plan.

"The name of the Christmas Play is 'The Star of Bethlehem.' My brothers in Jakarta will send the script, music sheet and designs for costumes. Remember, this will be a simple play. Nothing fancy. We'll sing five songs and we'll be multi-tasking as actors. Mr. Bauer plans for us to use the auditorium.

"Shall we start now with a prayer? Doc, can you lead, please?"

Dr. Frances rose from her seat and stood beside me. She prayed for the Christmas celebration, the smoothness of the preparations and all the help we could get.

We discussed the tasks involved and began with making assignments. Dr. Frances would be the Choir Director. Jojo and Mellie could help sewing the costumes and Chris Han, Engineer could create a lighted cross for center stage.

"Give me a list of what you need, all right?" I said to the members.

"Oh, one more thing, Chris," I said. "We need the sound of church bells. Can you ask someone to ask the priest at the Denpasar Catholic Church to ring the bell longer? Somebody needs to make a tape."

"I'll do it," Chris said. "I'm sure the priest won't mind. Gosh, the only time the church rings the bell is at five o'clock in the morning." Chris looked at me while shaking his head.

"Christmas only comes once a year, Chris. Be a pal." I raised and lowered my eyebrows. "All right?"

Chris nodded.

"Good," I felt relieved.

I dropped into a chair beside Dr. Frances. She wanted everyone to call her Doc, explaining 'I earned it'. I had great respect for the doctor as she was sophisticated and more mature than the rest of us.

"Where did you learn to coordinate festivities like this?" she asked.

"My hometown church in Jakarta, Doc. I'm copying our church play. Christmas is no Christmas without a play. I have been helping them for years. How far can we go with the handful of people here? There will be challenges." I rose and glanced at the group.

"OK, now the actors. Who will try his or her talent on stage?" Silence. They looked at each other and then stared at the floor.

"All right," I said. "It seems I have to select the actors. Simon, you will be the lead actor. You are conversant with the story of the three kings going to Bethlehem?"

Simon nodded.

"The three kings can be men or women. You'll be wearing robes anyway, and we'll cover your faces with whiskers."

Giggles and laughter. This would be the first Nativity Play the hotel had ever organized. Their excitement was like a fresh breeze passing through a hot day.

"You can always get in touch with me for questions. We'll meet again next week Thursday, same time. If you know of others who would like to join, please bring them along. Remember, we have only four months to prepare. Doc, can you close with a prayer, please?"

We all stood up and bowed our heads.

I went to the Coffee Shop for dinner before going home. Doc waved at me, and we sat together. The waiters waved and smiled as I entered.

"I didn't realize it was a huge project," Doc Frances said. "I hope more people will come forward."

"Don't hold your breath, Doc. Only a miracle can make it happen."

The next Thursday, Mr. Bauer returned from his lunch with a frown. I watched him pace the floor. He thumped his leg with a rolled piece of paper and blurted out. "Esther," he gestured to his office with his right hand. I followed him. I had a bad feeling.

He drew a deep breath. "I am at a loss," he said, cursing under his breath.

"It's hard for me to say this…Management rescinds support for the Christmas celebration. There, I said it." He threw the paper on his desk.

My jaw dropped; and I gave him a long stare of disbelief. I felt all alone on an island, watching a boat floating away and people waving goodbye.

"What caused the sudden change of heart?" I asked.

"It began as an innocent gesture to please the guests, ya?" Mr. Bauer said.

"Entertainment. It had become a big issue, with the other religions feeling left out. Why only the Christians? Why not the other religions in Bali?

Would Management support us too? I had to separate Management from the celebration. The employees can continue on their own if they want. I apologize, Esther. If you want to abandon the idea, I'll understand."

How shall I break the news to an upbeat group? We all expected challenges, but not so soon, and least of all from Management.

I got up and returned to my desk. I was shocked.

There's a package for you from Jakarta," Nita said. "It's on your desk."

I looked at the package, picked it up and patted it with my fingers. I had the Christmas celebration in my hands.

"What are you going to do now?" Nita asked. "It's not fair of Management."

Instead of a failure, I saw the hope of Christmas. "Let's see what the group thinks this afternoon, Nita."

I breathed deeply and spoke above the commotion. I was standing between the front row seats and the stage. "Ease up, everyone. Get yourself a seat, anywhere. I need to have a vote." I clasped my hands in front of my chest. "This afternoon Mr. Bauer told me that Management had to rescind their support because non-Christian groups felt they were 'left out'. We can do it on our own or we can abandon the Christmas idea."

Before anyone responded, the door opened, and Simon, the lead actor for our Nativity play, entered and stood beside me.

"I have bad news. My wife forbids me from joining the play." Simon's wife was Muslim." Our department received the memo from Management. I cannot argue with my wife every time I need to rehearse. To preserve peace in my household, I have to withdraw. I am so sorry." Simon left.

Everyone stared at each other and remained silent.

First Management, now Simon. Who's next?

"Let's pray," Margaret suggested. Doc Frances stood beside me and we prayed.

After the meeting, Jojo's glance fell on the package I'd brought with me. "What's in the brown envelope?" she asked.

I held up the package I'd received that day from my brothers. I showed them the music sheets, costume designs, and scripts for the play.

Doc Frances said, "We can move forward. Give me the music sheets, please?"

I handed them over to her. She hummed the tune while moving her hand up and down with the beat. "I can do this," she said. "Simple music arrangements."

She distributed the copies to the choir members. "All right, line up," she said, and started with "Silent Night."

The simple song cast a spell on everyone. Doc was right. The beat, the tune, and the voices formed a great harmony and carried well through the auditorium.

"Well?" Doc said. "Shall we move on with our plans?"

"Yes, you shall," Mrs. Rastetter, the Executive Housekeeper, who had just entered the auditorium said with gusto. Her smile and beaming face showed her enthusiasm. She was German, in her mid-forties and beautiful. Tall and slim with her hair in a chignon, she wore an ensemble of fashionable well-coordinated dress.

She had caught the doctor's comment.

"Yes, you shall, Doctor," she repeated." As long as I have worked in the hotel, I have never seen a Christmas play. It's a wonderful idea."

She smiled at me. "You need robes as costumes, ya? Someone can cut the patterns and my girls can help sew them. We have clean unused bedsheets you can use for your robes. Cut the patterns, and deliver them to my department. I am not Management. '*Naturlich*' (A German word, meaning of course), I can help." She winked, and with her thumbs up left the auditorium.

"Everyone clear on this?" I asked. "Mellie and Jojo are to cut the bedsheets and make the patterns. The Housekeeping girls will help sew them together. We needed help and we got it, people. Wonderful news. Get the bedsheets from Mrs. Rastetter."

Bang! The door to the auditorium slammed against the wall. This time a husky gentleman, slightly bald-headed, Mr. Salhan, Laundry Department Manager, came in with his right arm raised. "Mrs. Rastetter is right, the Christmas celebration is a wonderful idea," he said. "My department will help, too. I have colors of the rainbow for you. Bring the ready-made costumes to my department and we will help by dyeing the robes with colors of your choice." He left as noisily as he entered. His parting words, "I am not Management," still lingered in the hallway.

My assistant Nita ran into the auditorium. "You need girls to greet the guests. We can wear our colorful attire and welcome them as they arrive. We'll present all female guests with a necklace made of flowers. They will look gorgeous."

"Whoa, hold it there, Nita. You're Hindu. I couldn't keep Simon for the play because of his wife's belief. I'm not looking forward to facing a Hindu priest."

"You won't. This is my choice; not Management's nor my priest's. My friends wish to support the celebration too," Nita said.

"Your friends? How many are there?"

"I have gathered ten girls, and I can get more if you need them."

"What? This is incredible. Nita, can you put an announcement on the employees' bulletin board by the cafeteria, that we're searching for an actor?"

"Will do." Nita flashed her sweet smile and left the auditorium.

"All right, people. Let's move on. We can't disappoint our audience now."

The spontaneous outpouring support touched me. It came straight from the heart. A calm and peaceful feeling enveloped me, the same feeling I encountered when I had to deliver Rp 82 million to the Batak Church in North Sumatra.

"When God takes you to it, He will carry you through it," I seemed to hear Reverend Lee's voice whisper in my ear. Reverend Lee was my high school Bible teacher.

The kitchen door to the auditorium opened. "I assume you require food and beverage for the festivities too, Estah." It was Heinz, the Pastry Chef. "What are you going to serve the guests, Estah? Ice water only? Will you let us help?"

"You could make the world's best mocha cake for me, Heinz, any time. But for this occasion, I wish I could place the order, Heinz. Sorry, no Management support, remember?" and I shook my head.

We agreed that the Christmas play was the core of the festivities. No one had ever taken responsibility for performing a Christmas play. This was the first and one-of-a-kind Nativity Play for the hotel and the community. "Let's pray for the lead actor's substitute. We still have three months to rehearse. Should no one volunteer, we can decide whether to move forward with the festivities or to cancel. We'll wait two weeks until Thursday, four p.m."

Two weeks later, Thursday afternoon, in the auditorium. Doc Frances and I were sitting and reviewing our notes. Doc Frances leaned over and whispered, "Do you think we'll get a candidate for the lead actor today?" I crossed my fingers. "We still have time, Doc," and glanced at my watch.

Margaret pointed to the clock, 3.45 p.m. "Are you certain you want to continue? We need to decide in fifteen minutes whether we sail or sink."

Everyone continued to keep themselves busy and kept looking at the clock.

Then…a gentle knock on the door. "Sshh! Did you hear that?" I said, putting my finger to my lips. There it was again, a gentle knock. I glanced at my watch…3.55.

Nobody moved, as if frozen to the floor. The knob turned slowly and all eyes were glued to the door. A head showed in the door opening.. "Are you still in need of an actor? I want to play."

In my mind the church bell chimed four times. It was a sign.

Syamsuddin, nicknamed Udin (Oudeen), from Room Service entered.

I should jump up and down with delight that someone *did* appear.

"You?" everyone said in unison.

"A Muslim, and you want to play a Christian role?" Deena asked.

"Why not? The ad on the bulletin board didn't mention you required a Christian."

Udin was right. Anyone could.

The next few weeks we all pitched in to train Udin. Doc Frances explained the story of Christmas, and we also explained the star played an important role. It had led the Three Kings to Bethlehem to see the baby Jesus.

Christmas Day, 5.30 p.m.

The actors glowed with excitement, ready to present their performance of a lifetime. Mrs. Rastetter arrived full of smiles and two thumbs up. So did Mr. Salhan. He rubbed his hands together, fascinated with the outcome of the robes' colors.

The auditorium was artistically decorated with Christmas decorations purchased from Singapore.

The city dignitaries and religious representatives were all in attendance. They were looking forward to the performance.

Nita and her retinue of Balinese beauties stood by the entrance ready with the flowers. Other visitors entered the auditorium. The audience expressed their oohs and aahs when the Christmas tree lit up.

The recorded church bells chimed and silenced the noise. The regular lights were dimmed and lights on the cross shone. The choir arrived carrying candles in their hands and singing the mystical and beautiful "Silent Night." It was perfect.

After various dignitaries gave their speeches, the play began. As amateurs, Udin and the actors worked hard. We ignored the stumblings on the script. I heard the audience's laughter. We moved on. Udin, the Muslim, saved Christmas. He was our hero. Without him, we would have lost our Nativity Play.

We bowed when the play ended and the curtain came down. As I descended from the stage, I overheard one of the Balinese attendants say, "Who is this baby Jesus?"

The auditorium doors opened. Waiters carrying trays of snacks and soft drinks entered to serve the guests. Heinz stood behind the kitchen door on the stage, with a big grin. He gave me thumbs up. I thought, Mr. Bauer must have had a change of heart.

Christmas was over.

"You're early," I greeted Mr. Bauer in the office.

"Yes, I wanted to catch you before my breakfast meeting. The Christmas presentation was superb, ya. Compliments galore. The choir was perfect and the guests loved 'The Little Drummer Boy.' Both foreign and local guests embraced Christmas."

"Thank you for sharing the audience appreciation," I said. "It means a lot to us."

Mr. Bauer held his hand out. "Now I can justify signing the bill for the food and beverage," he said. "C'mon, give me the bill. I'll sign it."

"What bill? I don't have a bill. I thought you had a change of heart, and that you approved it anyway."

"Huh? If you and I didn't order the food and beverage, who did?"

I shrugged.

It remained an unsolved mystery. It must be the miracle of Christmas.

Chapter 38: Busy Sundays

Deena

Sunday morning. We were spoiled with beautiful weather most of the time. My colleagues and I had planned on spending the day in the mountains and shopping in the village of Ubud for Balinese world-renowned woodcarvings.

We would have a chance to visit the best woodcarver in the world, Pak Ida Bagus Tilem. He was Mr. Bauer's friend, and had often enjoyed our restaurants and amenities. Pak Tilem was a very courteous man, in his fifties, curly dark hair and a constant smiling face. His shop was huge and looked like a museum with a variety of woodcarvings, from small birds to a humongous eagle with spread wings. I was looking forward to our trip today.

The trip would take us also to a unique restaurant on a hill overlooking a canyon, stream and rolling green rice-paddy fields. On the other side of the canyon and stream, a group of flutists playing traditional Balinese music would entertain the visitors while enjoying their French cuisine. The restaurant was called the House of Flutes. I let my imagination fly and hit the gong as we entered the restaurant announcing our arrival. Instead…

Bang! The back door flew open against the cupboard of my small kitchen area. Deena's housekeeper, Hanna, stumbled into my bungalow barefoot. Disheveled and with tousled hair, she was a horrendous sight. With eyes wide open, and arms waving to get my attention, Hanna yelled, "Sis, you've got to come with me. Hurry!"

Deena was the only secretary who could afford a personal housekeeper, who cooked and cleaned the bungalow which Deena shared with Margaret and Hanna. The hotel help wasn't sufficient for her. Hanna also washed and ironed her clothes.

"Sis Esther, hurry, you need to come with me." She kept tugging at my sleeves.

"Whoa, relax. What's the matter?" I stopped combing my hair. "A car will pick me up in fifteen minutes to go to church. Not now, Hanna."

"My missy wants to kill herself. Please help!" She grabbed me by my arm.

I stared at her. "Excuse me? Does she want to take the easy way out? Your missy has already caused me many headaches," I said. "No matter what I advise Deena, she doesn't listen."

I never thought for one moment that Deena would commit suicide. She bluffed often. Her bark was louder than her bite. I've known my colleagues for over two years. We walked together, ate, laughed and exchanged stories. Often enough we discussed reincarnation, which is a Hindu belief. If you're good you might become a princess. Otherwise, the best you could become was a pig. We laughed and joked often.

How could I know if this threat of suicide was real?

I had cautioned her to stay away from the men in the hotel. Now Deena was involved with a man who had a girlfriend, a local girl, and she faced anger from the locals. Margaret was her best friend. Where was she?

I wriggled free from Hanna's grip. "Your missy has been ignoring people's feelings and my boss' instructions. Has her boyfriend dumped her? Good riddance, fewer headaches for me." I continued combing my hair.

"No, no, this is not helping," Hanna cried. "You are her friend. She needs you." She walked in circles, hands holding her tousled head. "C'mon, Sis."

"Friend?" I raised my eyebrows. "Friends listen to friends. Your missy doesn't listen to anyone."

Hanna grabbed my arm again and half pushed me to the door. I had no choice but to leave my bungalow with her.

"Is she serious? What is she doing anyway?" I asked on the way to Deena's bungalow.

"She was sharpening a knife."

"How can she be so stupid? When did he dump her?"

"Last night. She came home late and was so angry, she woke up Margaret." Hanna said. Margaret attempted several times to calm her down, to no avail. She scattered her things on the floor and kept everyone awake through the night. This morning, she planned to kill herself.

Hanna panted and walked faster. "C'mon. Hurry."

At their bungalow, Deena was sharpening her knife. She didn't look up.

"What do you think you're doing?" I asked.

"I'm sharpening my knife to kill myself."

"Why? Dead is dead, sharp knife or no sharp knife. Makes you look stupid, too." I tried to reason. *My goodness, what am I supposed to do?* I put my hands on my hips and pointed my finger at Deena.

"Do you think this guy will mourn you? Let me tell you what will happen. He will celebrate your death. He will be relieved that you have cleared the path for him to wed his girl. Do you think he will remember you and say 'thank you?' Do you know what people will read on your tombstone? 'Here lies a stupid girl who killed herself for loving a jerk. How does that sound, huh? Are you listening?"

"No, I'm not listening and mind your own business." She was pointing the knife at me. I tried to grab the knife away from her. It made her more violent.

"Well, all right. Be careful with that knife." *Lord, what now?*

Talking made no difference to her. I put my left arm across my chest, with my right arm pointing to my forehead. "Let's see, I have to make your death worthwhile for the tourists.

"In Bali, there will be a cremation. As you know, they believe in celebrating death as the beginning of a new life. If you are good, you will be reborn a princess. But you're killing yourself, so you might be reborn a pig. Since you are not Balinese, you might become half pig, half human. Which part would you like to be? Head or tail, huh? You need to consider the consequences. It will be more work for me, as I need to create a flyer for the tourists. You can't die without fanfare. We must profit from your demise. There's another thing that's scarier."

Deena continued to sharpen her knife. She looked funny with half her hair done up in curlers. She was standing about five feet away from me, and glanced in my direction. Margaret was sitting on the bed. She covered her mouth with her hand and tried not to scream.

"What?" Deena asked.

"Let's suppose you don't die right away? Your knife hits the nerve in your face? Nobody will want to look at you and you will never get a boyfriend. Wow! What a useless sacrifice."

I looked at my watch. "I'll be late for church. Let's do this."

"What?" Deena said.

"*You*, you still want to kill yourself?"

Hanna stood ten feet from Deena. She was waving her arms and shaking her head frantically.

"Hanna, give me a Bible." She took a Bible from the dresser drawer and handed it to me. *Deena believed in the Bible. I think she's scared every time I mention 'Bible.'*

"As far as I know, Deena, you are still a Christian. Right?"

"Right. So what?" She answered.

"Well, here is the Bible and I want you to put your hand here on the Bible and repeat after me."

"What do you want to say?"

"It is not what *I* say, it is what I want *you* to say. You tell the Lord that you are doing this of your own accord. That Esther has nothing to do with this. She has tried her best to revert your mind from stupid to wise, to no avail. And it's not Esther's fault you have been acting stupid. Oh, one more thing. Tell the Lord what you want to be, in case you are reborn half pig, half human, head or tail, remember? OK, all right, let's do this quick. I'm late for church. You know

I get transportation every Sunday at 10 a.m."

Silence.

"When is the car coming to pick you up?"

"In ten minutes," I said.

Deena paused, looked at me, and said, "All right, I'll go with you."

Somewhere, in my mind, I heard a song 'I got a wonderful feeling, everything's going my way'.

The pregnant woman

On a different Sunday morning, I went to check on pending work for Mr. Bauer, who was leaving for Singapore the next day. I needed to type up his meeting notes. At most, I expected to spend less than an hour in the office. My colleagues and I were planning to have lunch in Denpasar and afterward watch a movie.

There may not be many places for entertainment, but we could always depend on movies, good lunches, and shopping. In the evening, we would take a tour of the hotel and watch a cultural dance called the Monkey Dance. A hundred men and women would join and perform this dance that simulated the love affair of Rama and Sita. A wonderful dance under the torch light, as there was no electricity in the villages yet.

As I entered, I saw Budi, the concierge, glancing into Mr. Bauer's office.

"Do you need something, Budi? My boss is not in."

Budi turned around as if stung by a bee and stared at me.

"It's me Budi, not a ghost. Can I help you with something?"

"I was looking for you, Miss. A pregnant woman needs an ambulance to deliver her to the hospital. She's in pain, and her baby is due. Her husband is below the pay grade. The transportation manager has denied his request for an ambulance." Budi kept rambling.

"All right, I understand, slow down," I said. "Only the doctor can instruct the transportation manager to release the ambulance. So why are you here?"

"The doctor's not here. Nobody wants to give the approval. Perhaps you can help."

"Budi, I'll have the doctor on my back. Let me see what I can do. I can't give direct orders. Understand?"

Budi nodded and returned to his Concierge station.

As Budi said, nobody wanted the responsibility. The transportation manager refused to release the ambulance. "Could Miss Esther call the doctor's office? The doctor's assistant can release the ambulance. A short note or call to the transportation department would do."

My quest for a signature began. Sukri, the doctor's assistant didn't dare give the approval. The doctor was at the hospital in Denpasar.

Every departmental manager responsible (Transportation, Assistant Doctor and the Assistant Manager) preferred to follow the rules. This poor woman was in pain. She couldn't afford a taxi. *Somehow this occasion reminded me of Joseph and Mary trying to find a place to sleep. All the hotels rejected them and there was no place to give birth to the baby Jesus.*

What am I doing here in my office? I asked myself. I was to do Mr. Bauer's job, not take care of a pregnant woman. Mr. Bauer himself might not share my compassionate meddling in another department's problems. However, my heart couldn't leave this woman unattended. I didn't even know her. But...as a woman, I felt for her.

I called the transportation manager again. "Surya, can you deliver a baby?"

"No, miss. I am not a doctor."

"Thank you, Surya."

I called the doctor's office. "Sukri, can you deliver a baby?"

"Not on my own, miss. Only the doctor can."

"Thank you, Sukri."

I dialed the Assistant Manager's office. "Is there anybody in your office who can deliver a baby?"

"No, miss. Nobody."

"Thanks, everyone."

I dialed the transportation manager's number again. As calmly as possible, I said, "Well, Surya, you need to release the ambulance, otherwise someone will have to deliver the baby here, and it won't be pretty. What will happen if something goes wrong with the mother only because *you* denied the help she needs."

"Can you authorize the release, Miss?"

"Yes, Surya, I can. Send the note to my office for me to sign. Ask the driver to take the pregnant woman to the hospital *now*." *What other choice did I have?*

"What are you doing here?" Mr. Bauer asked. "I thought you had plans to watch a movie with the girls."

"I thought so too, sir."

Mr. Bauer listened as I told him what happened when I tried to find someone to authorize the release of the ambulance. "Someone else besides the doctor needs to be a back-up," I said.

"So what happened to the woman?" Mr. Bauer asked.

"She's in the hospital. I gave the authorization, sir."

Mr. Bauer chuckled, raised his hand and said, "What would have happened if you had not been here?"

The telephone rang, and I picked it up.

"Mr. Bauer's office. Yes, Budi, what's going on…really?…Huh!, Oh great news. Thanks for telling me."

"We have good news?" Mr. Bauer asked. "What now?"

"Budi told me he received news from his friend. His wife delivered twins, and they were all happy it went well."

"All right," Mr. Bauer answered. "Authorization justified."

The Catholic Priest

It was dark when Doctor Frances and I returned from our dinner in town. We heard the frantic call when we were close to the entrance of the hotel.

"Doctor Frances, Doc, wait a moment." We both heard someone quietly calling.

"I'm here, please wait." We walked faster as we didn't see anyone, except for a black figure coming toward us. The doctor had always been a strong believer, but this time she had a shocked expression on her face.

I turned around. If it was an evil force, I wanted to be prepared. I saw the flash of something white.

"Relax, Doc," I said, tapping her on the shoulder. "It's a priest. I saw his white collar."

"Huh?" she said, and turned around to face the dark figure. He was a catholic priest wearing his black robe. He was waving his right arm, and was panting.

"You called me?" The Doctor asked.

"Yes," the priest said, "I wonder whether you can help me. I have a friend in the van and he is sick with Leukemia."

"Leukemia?" the doctor asked. "What stage?"

"Four," he said.

"What do you expect me to do? The hotel is not equipped to handle serious situations like this one. Take him to the hospital in town, so he can get better treatment. Better still, find his doctor."

"I couldn't find his doctor tonight, Doc. They are all at the Governor's ball."

"Oh, for crying out loud." Doc Frances went with him to the van, and she felt the pulse of the other priest.

She frowned. "There is nothing I can do to help your colleague. He is screaming in pain. I don't have the medication for him. Please take him to the hospital as fast as you can. The doctor in charge will be able to stabilize him. I'm so sorry."

Doc and I continued to enter the hotel.

I noticed she was still shocked at the sudden appearance of the priest, so I suggested we have a cup of tea in the Coffee Shop. She relaxed a bit. "Gosh, he really scared me with his sudden appearance," she said.

"Yes, I noticed," I said.

"Wow, Leukemia, stage four. There's nothing more I or anyone on this island can do. He needs to be transported to Singapore. I wish I could help him more." She covered her face with her hands, and sighed. As a doctor, she probably had experienced many situations when she felt helpless and hopeless.

The tea helped calm her down, and we called it a night.

"Church, tomorrow?" I asked.

"Yes, sure." She said.

Bang, bang, bang. Someone was banging on my door. "Esther, open the door."

I peered through the drapes. It was Jojo and Mellie.

I opened the door and asked, "What's happening. Where's the fire?"

"Don't make fun," Jojo said. "We need your help."

"It's Sunday, and I'm late for church already. Can we do it after church?"

"No," Jojo and Mellie said simultaneously. "We can drop you at the church later and pick you up again. But this is priority. We need you to go with us to the hospital."

The priest. It must be, who else could it be?

"All right, you two. It's the catholic priest, who has leukemia. Right?" I opened my eyes wide, and looked at both of them.

"How do you know that?" Mellie asked. So, I told them what had happened last night. "Nobody on this island can help him. He is in pain and needs to be transported to Singapore, girls. If you need transportation, you can come with me and I will drop you off at the catholic church. You can then approach a Catholic priest to help with prayer. You can join him, and that's the best I can do. Agreed?"

"No, we want you to go with us and pray for him."

"Are you serious? Don't you think a catholic priest will be more suitable for this task?"

"No, we want you, because God listens to you," Jojo said.

"What, this is unbelievable," I said. "God listens to everyone. The question is, do you listen to Him?"

"Oh, c'mon, we're losing time." They grabbed me, Jojo on my left, and Mellie on my right. I could hear Deena screaming, "Are you kidnapping her?" Deena's bungalow was behind mine, and she heard the noise from her window as we passed.

"Oh, shut up," Jojo and Mellie answered. "She'll be back soon."

It wasn't difficult to find the ailing priest. We could hear him screaming; the hospital attendants were at a loss. Shaking of heads and male nurses answering phones.

Jojo and Mellie returned to where I was standing, and said, "We do it here. They won't let us come any closer."

"Why, what's happening there?"

"The priest is in pain and they tried to subdued him. They are afraid to let us alone with him. So, Esther, you pray."

What must I say?

We bowed our heads and I said a simple prayer, "Father, please release him from his pain that he may be transported to Singapore for better treatment," and then silence, before I could even say "Amen."

We opened our eyes, and Jojo and Mellie ran inside. I saw them talking and then they returned to me.

"He is asleep and seems to be all right. I told you, God listens to you."

It was the strangest occurrence for me, as I've never prayed for a catholic priest before. It was a simple prayer.

The next day, I asked Jojo and Mellie what happened to the priest.

"He was transported to Singapore for treatment, and then he will be released from his duties to return to the Netherlands."

I never knew his name, but I knew I had done a good deed.

Chapter 39: When Muhammad Doesn't Come to the Mountain

What a day! Deena realized her dumb moves. She couldn't explain how she could come to suicide. We giggled together a lot on this.

"No more stupid actions, Deena?" I asked.

Yes, Deena, how could you be so stupid, huh?" Jojo, Mellie, Margaret said in a chorus. This was a bonding I would look back on with fondness. We had shared happiness and sadness together, dealt with personal issues, like one big family. Sometimes we included Dr. Frances.

During vacation time, we all separated and returned to our hometowns. During weekends, we always found a project to do and places to explore. Bali was a great place to be, and wonderful weather to enjoy.

I was in a stressful situation myself, and nobody could help me.

I'd developed a skin disease on my right foot, due to wading in the sea. Starting with itchiness, it became red and warm to the touch. Dr. Frances recommended ointments, pills and shots, to no avail. There was no dermatologist in town either. The only way to get a cure was to fly off the island and visit a dermatologist in Jakarta.

"Explain to your boss, and ask him for permission," Margaret said. "He'll help you."

"I can't disturb him with small details like this. He has enough problems of his own, working to get approval for an international airport in Bali."

I launched a prayer before retiring. "God, if I can't leave for Jakarta to call on a doctor, can you send the doctor to Bali, please?" What else could I do?

My colleagues met me during lunch hour. "Well, did you ask the doctor again?"

"No," I said. "I asked the Almighty Doctor to send the doctor."

"Oh my God," Deena and my colleagues said. "You're too much."

"Does anyone have a suggestion?" I looked around…only heads shaking….

"Esther, you speak Dutch, ya?" Mr. Bauer asked as I returned to the office.

"Yes, sir. Not much, but I can conduct a simple conversation. What's up?"

"A Pharmaceutical VIP will land this evening. He met a Dutch girl, on the way." Mr. Bauer asked me to help entertain the girl friend, while he entertained the VIP.

"Dinner at 7.30 p.m, OK with you?" Mr. Bauer asked "I'll send the car to pick you up."

I nodded. "Fine, Mr. Bauer."

It was a wonderful dinner. I chose escargot. My boss glanced at the meal in front of me.

He remembered the time when he introduced escargot to me during my first month's exposure to the exotic gourmet of the hotel. I loved escargot. "How do you know escargot?" Mr. Bauer asked.

"Oh, my mom cooked it often, Mr. Bauer. We call them snails. *A snail is a snail, whether it's called escargot or by any other name, it would still be a snail.*"

Mr. Bauer couldn't stop coughing while he looked around the restaurant to make sure nobody had heard what I said.

Balinese music accompanied the cultural performances on the Bali Agung stage, while we enjoyed a full moon above and a cool evening breeze. What else could anyone ask for? I was a blessed bystander. Life couldn't be better. Other people had to pay, while my entertainment was free of charge.

The guests were ecstatic. They expressed their delight by agreeing to meet again tomorrow, Sunday, for breakfast. Mr. Bauer shook my hand as we parted for the night.

"Good job," he said. Thumbs up. "See you tomorrow morning at 8.30 a.m. at the Baruna Pavilion."

"I cannot stay long, sir. I need to go to church."

He nodded and we left.

On this tropical island, beautiful mornings greeted us most of the time. Arriving at the Baruna Pavilion, I didn't see either Mr. Bauer or his guests. I asked the waiter, "Did you see Mr. Bauer and his guests?"

"No, ma'am, I haven't seen him this morning." My high expectations for another big event was questionable.

I went straight to my office and found Mr. Bauer looking out the window. He was deep in thought. *Oh, oh, didn't look good.*

"Good morning, is breakfast off?" I said, greeting him.

He turned around. "Ach ya, Esther, you wouldn't believe what has happened. Everything went well last night, ya? After we left them, they insisted on cruising down the highway. Of all places, why did they have to cruise down the highway? They crashed under the famous banyan tree."

"Oh no! That's the hang out place of the spirits. Tourists don't pay heed to warnings from the locals. Are they all right?"

"The girl came out all right, and she left for Singapore this morning. The man was worse off. He has to wait until his company doctor arrives tomorrow. There's nothing we can do except wait." Mr. Bauer raised his hands in despair.

I left and went to church.

During lunch in Denpasar, my friends and I talked about the creepy corner down the highway. I mentioned to my friends that one day I was riding home in a horse cart, and the horse turned to the side of the road approaching the banyan tree.

The driver had to coax him and said, 'My Prince, where are you going, your highness? Please return to the main road.' It was a while before the horse followed his instruction. The driver said, 'Thank you, your highness. We're running along now.' As foreigners, we can't ignore their beliefs," I said. "It gave me the creeps."

The hotel staff was in panic mode when I entered the hotel on Monday morning. I asked the Front Desk what had happened. My boss' guest insisted on leaving Bali using his private plane and ignoring the local doctor's request to wait for him. *He had no desire to face the music or appear as a headline in a local newspaper.*

It all happened in the wee morning hours, and Mr. Bauer was caught by surprise by his guest's strange behavior. Dr. Ho, the VIP's Company doctor, was in Mr. Bauer's office when I stepped into mine.

When the doctor came out, he looked at me and said, "I feel bad about all this, and your boss has extended me and my wife a complimentary three days' stay including all amenities."

"Well, doctor, there is a lot you can enjoy during your stay. Swimming pool, gourmet food, trip to the mountainside. Shop for world famous woodcarvings and remember to watch their cultural performances in the evening. They are mystical. You should try. And if there is anything else I can do to make your stay more enjoyable, please let me know." I said. Those were *standard words to make guests feel more comfortable.*

He scratched his head, walked a few steps and returned. "Yes, there is something you can do for me," he said. "There must be something *I* can do. Do you perhaps know whether there is anybody who is suffering from a skin disease, preferably over 30 days?"

I looked up, mesmerized. *The only person I knew was me, and it had been over one month.*

I lifted my hand. "Are you serious? Why skin disease?" I asked.

"*You?*" he asked, ignoring my question. "Come to my room at 2 p.m. Let me look at it. Don't worry, my wife will be there. I hope I can take care of your problem." He gave me his room number and left.

After lunch I went straight to his room, keeping it quiet from my colleagues. *What if it didn't work?* His wife opened the door and let me in. She was a pretty lady, graceful, and had a friendly smile. The doctor told me that the pharmaceutical company had come out with a new ointment for skin diseases. He was on his way to a promotional trip when his boss sent for him. The doctor intended to at least help someone with the new ointment.

I showed him my right foot. It was swollen and the affected skin was thick and the color had turned purple, showing advanced stage. The doctor said, "It is infected."

He showed me how to scrub the ointment on the affected area. No soap, as it could aggravate the itchiness, and gave me two tubes. He put his rubber gloves on, and showed me how to rub it on.

"Do you know a doctor in Jakarta to get more supplies? You need a prescription." He wrote it for me. *I made sure the prescription went out with the next mail.*

"Always wear a pair of shoes on the beach, young lady," he said. "There are lots of unknown critters in the water."

My skin cleared up after one week.

"What a bummer," said Deena. "A doctor came to town, but he was not a skin doctor. So, what now, Esther? Do you need another prayer?"

"No," I said. My colleagues approached me. I lifted my long pants, and showed them my healed foot.

"O, my God, how did you do that?" they asked me.

"When Muhammad doesn't come to the mountain…" I said.

They all responded: "…the mountain will come to Muhammad."

"Don't underestimate the power of prayer," I said.

Chapter 40: 1969 The Dark Year

"According to Chinese belief, the number 69 is a figure that will remain 69 no matter how you arrange it. Lopsided or upside down, it would still be 69," my mother said in her message. "I checked with a palm reader in town about you and the torments you experienced this year. He told me whatever happened to you had to happen. But, don't worry, it will pass."

First my grief over my boyfriend of a year and a half. He fell in love with another woman. Then his lies started. It was unpleasant as we worked for the same hotel. Like a beautiful vase, it was broken to smithereens. No matter how I tried to put it back together, I would always see the cracks. I ended the relationship. I cried at night until, I promised not to cry anymore.

Another relationship presented itself. A tourist arrived and looked me up. My name was given to him by an acquaintance who sat beside him on the plane.

The days became brighter, the flowers more colorful, and my heart felt lighter and sang with joy to engage in a new relationship. My friends supported me and encouraged the meetings. Five days later, the island's mystical environment worked its magic on this American Navy Pilot, James Scofield, and he proposed marriage.

Mr. Bauer cautioned me, using the word rebound. "Be careful," he said. "make sure he is the right one." Mr. Bauer suggested employment for James, my fiance at the hotel with the full benefits of a foreign expatriate.

It was to be the Balinese wedding of the year, with gourmet food and cultural performances fit for a princess. Mr. Bauer would see to it and promised to make it happen. "You deserve it," he said.

What could go wrong with this relationship of honey and roses?

Yet, it turned out to be a marriage not written in the stars. After spending a few hours at the American Embassy in Jakarta, he returned a changed man. We discussed my 'excess baggage' as the bread winner of my family. He felt awful about taking me away from them. It was an ill-fated relationship. He was 26 years old and needed his parents' blessings before he could go ahead with the wedding.

I said goodbye to him at the airport in Jakarta, and he promised to write.

"I'll return in three months, don't you worry," he said.

My instinct told me once he stepped on the plane, I would never see him again.

I cancelled all wedding arrangements in Jakarta, my wedding dress, the church, the caterings. I was more embarrassed for my parents, who had lost face. That was the worst, and I felt crushed watching them suffer.

Perhaps my luck would change. Perhaps for once I could be happy, a normal human being in love, getting married and building a family with my husband. Could there be a man who would like me for me? Why was I denied this happiness?

I returned to the island subdued. This break-up was more painful than the first. I tried to put on a good face and carry out my daily duties. Mr. Bauer worried.

"No more provocative laughter in the day's schedule?" He said.

Silence.

I ignored the joke.

I'd hurt my parents and brought shame to the family. They felt humiliated, so did I. Walking down the beach at night, listening to the calming waters, didn't help much. The distress was pressing heavily on my chest. Twice in a year, back to back heartbreak, and I became ill. My old childhood illness, tuberculosis, had returned. Dr. Frances and the X-ray confirmed it.

"Leave this island. Take a break and find new friendships. Get good treatment," she said when she broke the news.

The doctor forgot that once I left the hotel, there wouldn't be any treatment, as I wouldn't have a job. It would be a long while before I could get back on my feet. What would happen to my family?

Dr. Frances needed to report the case to Mr. Bauer. I was running out of options. All I felt was disappointment, and sadness.

In the comfort of my room, my inner voice returned and asked me to 'clean your cabinet.'

"Why? It is eight p.m. and I have no intention to do any cleaning." The pain I felt was like a beating from a rattan stick on my back.

I did everything you asked me to do, Lord? Why me?

'Clean your cupboard.' The inner voice again urged me. I obeyed. Out fell a booklet called "Our Daily Bread." I read the page that fell open in my hands.

"As much as I have suffered on the cross, so you must suffer.

But do not be afraid, my eyes are upon you."

I burst into tears but felt peaceful that HE understood and could identify with my grief and pain.

Deena, Margaret, and Arya entered my bungalow and found me sitting on the floor, in tears. They thought I'd had a breakdown. I showed them the booklet and the words.

"Are you feeling sorry for yourself?" Deena asked.

"Yes, and no. Yes, because I'm tired of fighting. No, not for myself, but for my parents. They must be disappointed and feel bad for me. I should have known better. How could I be so stupid?"

My friends felt hopeless, and so did I.

They stayed for a while and left to retire for the evening, making sure I wouldn't do anything stupid. I assured them, "Don't worry, I have no desire to be reborn a pig." We all laughed.

Before I turned off the light, I sat in my corner sanctuary and read the Bible. It fell open, and it said,

"I send my son from the West, to meet my daughter from the East and I'm planting a tree." The verse I didn't recall. Perhaps those were the words He wanted me to read.

Pak Tan's voice whispered in my ear, "Remember, it will not happen overnight. Be patient."

I took a deep breath, and turned off the light.

Mr. Bauer's door was closed when I arrived the next morning. I asked Nita who was inside.

"The doctor," Nita said. "They have been there for a while."

I nodded and started my daily duties, until the door to Mr. Bauer's office opened.

Both the doctor and Mr. Bauer had frowns on their faces.

The same familiar feeling of peace embraced me. Whatever happened, I was prepared, and I knew God was standing by.

Mr. Bauer invited me into his office.

"Esther, this is difficult for all of us, and I am sorry it happened to you. Blame it on the magic of the island. I will write a letter to his parents telling them I don't appreciate the conduct of their son. Since your father couldn't write this letter, I'll write it on his behalf."

He stopped when he saw tears trickling down my cheeks. I was touched. It felt good that someone cared.

I wiped away my tears, and answered, "Thank you, sir."

"I also had a meeting with the doctor, and she updated me on your situation. I am aware of the rules, but this is what I will do after a further session with the doctor.

"She doesn't want to lose a friend. I don't want to lose a good secretary. Sure, it's easy to find another one, but someone who can love this island? Sending you home to Jakarta won't do any good. So I thought it's much better if you remain here, and continue your work. Your work schedule will allow you to take a break after lunch. Stay home till 4 p.m. and return for work till 7 p.m. No evening out with friends until you complete your treatment. I have to promise the doctor. Are we in agreement here?"

I was in a daze. A turbulent storm had loomed on the horizon, and God calmed it. I was glad my family would be spared from more bad news.

"Is there anything else Esther needs to know, Doctor?" Mr. Bauer asked.

"She needs to drink her one glass of milk every morning. No excuses." *I hate milk. Dr. Frances knew it well.*

"I'll make sure Room Service brings her milk every morning. Cakes too?" He was teasing me. "Whatever we have discussed here, will *remain* here. Agreed?" Mr. Bauer asked.

The doctor nodded and left. I started my treatment the next day.

Within a month, I felt much better. Mr. Bauer was right. It was much better to work so I could get my mind off the painful thoughts. The doctor made sure I got my supply of multi vitamin shots... *ouch, so painful...* and anti-biotic pills plus the milk and the needed rest.

Then, one event changed my life.

Chapter 41: Australia

Since the hotel was new, Mr. Bauer proposed to organize a Regional meeting in Bali. The Australian Regional Manager was impressed with my English and asked me where I got my education. When I explained I'd never been overseas, he recommended I should visit Australia and undergo training to learn more about the hotel business.

"It will do you good. It will open a broader horizon for you," he said. It couldn't have presented itself at a more conducive time.

Mr. Bauer jumped at the marvelous idea. "Leave this place for a while and get to know new things in new surroundings, meet new people, ya?" he said.

"Are you sure you don't want to get rid of me after all?" I teased.

A few months later, I was on the plane to Melbourne, Australia, to undergo a six months' training at the Hotel Southern Cross. It was quite an experience, and, a cultural shock. Arriving from a protected environment, I needed to adjust to the liberated way Australians handled booze and women. I had to get acquainted with the way they speak English. Hilarious.

To the Australians it was an innocent toga party. As invitee, it was a shocking revelation as to what people could do with their togas to enhance the merriment, whether or not they wore anything under their togas.

"C'mon, I'll take you home," I heard a man say. He was standing beside me and saw my eyes getting wider and wider as the toga merriment progressed. "You don't belong here," he said. I was thankful he rescued me. Since that event I preferred to stroll around the hotel, or walk down the strip mall during my days off. After a while, I became lonely, and longed to return home to Bali.

One hilarious experience I had was with the language. I encountered some chefs from the hotel, but I didn't see the Executive Chef.

"Goodaey, maete! How a'ya? Where's the Chef?" I tried to at least sound like an Australian. The reply gave me a shock.

"Auw Estah, he is gouing to the 'ospital todoiay!"

"What? How does he know that he is going to die?"

"Naw, naw, Estah. He cudn't gou yesterdaoiy, not tomorrouw, so he's going toodoiay.!

Then it dawned on me that the Chef went to the hospital today. Darn English pronunciation!

Six months passed by and my training was extended for two more months so I could get acquainted with other Inter-Continental Hotels in the area. I got the trip of a life time visiting the Philippines, Hong Kong, Bangkok and Singapore before returning to my paradise island.

I appreciated the experience gained, however, I would never leave the country unless I had someone with whom to share my travels. Life was different on the other side of the fence. I was alone. For eight months it was all right, knowing I could return to my island of paradise.

I needed support, financially and spiritually, therefore Mr. Grant didn't want me to leave for the United States alone. He knew how vulnerable I could be. .

My new title was Sales Manager. If being an Executive Secretary had its challenges, Sales Manager was a new stratosphere for a woman. More challenges, especially when it involved traveling overseas. That happened often due to my strong English. I represented the hotel at the Pacific Area Travel Association.

Envy brewed envy, and after a year in the position, I decided it was time to move on.

Mr. Bauer transferred to the Manila Inter-Continental and I returned to my hometown, Jakarta. Saying goodbye to my paradise island was tough. I had built up great friendships on the island. Nita cried. My other friends promised to meet again in Jakarta.

After two weeks off in my hometown, I started a new job as Executive Secretary to the Second Vice President of Chase Manhattan Bank, Corporate Head Office.

I learned a different business, and often longed to return to my former environment. Since my salary level was already high when I applied for the position, after two years the Bank couldn't raise my salary anymore. I had hit the ceiling, the highest level.

Then came another miracle. Everything happens for a reason…

My brother and his fiancée came for a visit and they discussed marriage with my parents. Both agreed that after four years, they could get married. My father was quiet as he knew he didn't have the funds to support a wedding. I was listening to their plans, and out of the blue, I asked his fiancée, "When are you planning to get married?"

"My mom suggested by June 30th of this year." I glanced at my mother and saw her raise her eyebrows. My father remained silent. It was January. Five more months? *It was too soon. I felt sorry for them.*

"Sure, why don't you prepare for the wedding?" I blurted out. "I'm sure we can accommodate your wedding. All right? Tell your mother, we go for it."

Off they went to share the good news with her mother.

My mother looked at me, "How are we going to come up with the funds? Do you know how much the cost might be? Why are you making promises you can't keep?" My mother kept on mumbling and shaking her head.

"We'll find some way, Mammie. Otherwise they'll have to wait another four years. I feel sorry for them. Let's go to church tomorrow, we may get the answer."

"Excuse me, wait," I heard someone call. One of the church members approached me. He asked me whether I could help his daughter find a job at the Bank. When I asked him whether his daughter could speak English, he smiled, and said, "Well, that's where you come in. You can teach her better English."

I was promoted to Supervisor of the Credit Department, and had a staff of eight. We were in need of a typist to help the credit staff, and Julia came onboard.

A few weeks later I found a package on my desk, and it turned out to be a request for a loan, from Julia's father, whom I called Sam. I brought the request to my team. "No rush, find out whether we can accommodate the loan. Let me know."

Two weeks passed by and one of the credit staff members said, "Esther, we can do this loan."

"Everyone in agreement?" I asked. Everyone nodded. "Great, let's do it."

We were busy. The loan request was difficult, more documents were needed to support the request. Two months passed by before the loan was approved. Sam was full of smiles.

I was still struggling to find the funds for my brother's wedding. It was the end of April. My parents became jittery. "You shouldn't have promised them. What if we can't come up with the funds?" My mother said.

Three weeks later Sam came to our house. We sat on the porch and my mother joined the conversation.

"My investors were happy to get this loan. They tried many times, only your bank was able to fulfill their request…" and he rambled on. "As a token of appreciation," he said, "they want you to have this. Thank you for your hard work." He handed me a package, and left.

I opened the package and it was money. Wow! In time for the wedding. I handed over the money to my mother. "I don't want to know the total amount, it is meant for my brother's wedding," I said.

Seeing smiling faces and the happiness of the bridegroom and bride were enough for me. My parents never doubted my power of prayer again, as they were to experience another miracle.

The biggest ever…

Chapter 42: The Miracle of a Lifetime – Esther Met Phil

My brother's wedding was a success, and I went to work for the Dow Chemical Representative office with a step up in wages. Our office suite was on the 17th floor of a Japanese subsidized business building on the main drag of the Embassy and hotel row. Gorgeous views from every window to the sprawling city of Jakarta.

I was the Country Manager's Secretary, and assisted in setting up their office. I received my training in Singapore and Hong Kong.

We were enjoying peaceful years, until the worst riots of all times erupted, due to an insignificant incident in the city of Bandung, a few hours away by car from Jakarta.

I showed up in the office with no bosses around. At nine a.m., my phone rang. The Regional Manager, based in Singapore, instructed me and the entire staff to vacate the premises.

"Look out the window," Mr. Phil Meeks said. "The building is being besieged, and I want everybody out."

Looking out the window I saw a mob approaching our building.

"Everybody out and lock the doors, please," I called out. "Hurry, everyone, out. The building is being besieged!" We all dashed out the back door and headed straight into the elevator.

"Girls, you go straight home. I hope we can all get out of the building. Stay home and we'll return on Monday."

My bosses found out about the impending riot and left Jakarta the previous night. They were watching television from their hotel in Singapore. That's why they had a full view of the rioters approaching. It was all over the news. Right at the time our elevator closed, I heard the "ding" sound of the other elevator, and voices shouting, "Check the offices." Vandalism and looting. That was my first thought. The elevator slid downwards without stopping at any other floor. So far so good.

I made certain everyone had moved away from the premises before I stepped into my waiting car. Too late, the mob surrounded us, and my car was being rocked up and down with force. They planned on turning the car over and igniting the gas tank, with Jody the driver and me trapped inside.

"Oh my God, Jody, I hear they damaged Japanese cars, but this is Holden, Australian made. They mistook our car for a Japanese one. Can we reach the leader of the mob to say they are vandalizing the wrong car? I don't want to die here, do you?""

Jody said, "You are right, Miss. Let me try." He rolled the window half-way down and yelled, "This is a Holden, not a Toyota. Look, are you blind?" and he pointed to the front that bore its name. The leader motioned everyone to step back, while he checked. He nodded and verified it was Australian made. He made a circular motion with his hand and signaled the mob to leave the car. Phew! What a Day! *When would this ever stop?*

I wiped my forehead, and realized we were free to leave the premises unharmed. I looked up and said, "Thank you, Lord for saving our lives... again."

Even though we were in the 1970's, riots still erupted from insignificant misunderstandings. I kept my faith to go to America.

1976 was to be my dream trip year, to include Europe. First to Bangkok in February for a week, then to Europe in April. I calculated it would take at least ten weeks to cover the countries in Europe I had dreamed of visiting. I had accumulated 6 weeks vacation, plus one month leave without pay.

My biological clock kept ticking, and I had saved for my old age. Thirty-three years old and no boyfriend in sight? The path of certainty was spinsterhood.

"Shall I take the offer of my cousin to go to Europe, Mammie? It might take a lot of money," I asked my mother.

"If not now, then when?" asked my mother said. "You are not getting any younger, and it's your money. By all means, go."

I had worked on the airline schedule and I determined April 18, 1976 to be the date of departure to Europe.

As host of the Olympics, Russia had opened their doors to visa offices pertaining to immigration requests, smoother visa applications and approvals, travel within Moscow, at no extra charge.

Aeroflot was the Russian Airline that could accommodate my flight from Jakarta to London, and return to Jakarta from Vienna. I planned to stay for two weeks and see Scotland with my other cousin Kim who lived in England. I purchased a three-month Eurailpass for extensive travel by train throughout Europe. The plan for my dream trip was unfolding. I would meet Tom, my aunt's son, in Vienna, Austria. I sent a letter to both Kim in England, and Tom to inform them of my impending visit.

April 15, 1976, three days before my departure, I had a premonition. I was to get married after a short encounter with a man I'd never met. I alerted my mother.

She asked, "Anybody I know?"

"No."

"Are you desperate?" she mumbled.

"No, Mammie, I'm not desperate. There's nothing you or I can do. It will happen."

I made three copies of my birth certificate, as it was in three languages, Dutch, Indonesian and English.

"Return with a husband, Esther?" Mr. Goodchild, my boss, asked.

"I'll do my best, sir. From Russia with love. Remember the James Bond movie?"

At this moment, Dow had a change in leadership. My new boss was the Regional Manager for South Asia, as Dow had secured a big contract with the Indonesian Petro-Chemical Company. He gave me a letter of introduction, in case I needed help during my trip.

Springtime in Moscow was freezing cold for me. We arrived at dawn and the bus would not come until 9 a.m. to take us from the airport to the hotel.

"Where can I have my breakfast?" I expected a little more courtesy from the airline staff or anybody else in this matter.

Breakfast was "get out of this door, turn left, and two doors down, again to the left. You'll find a cafeteria there. Here is a voucher, *in Russian*, to get your food." Sounded more like I belonged in the military. I took my time eating my cold breakfast of a cold egg and biscuits. Luke warm tea. Survival was the motto for me. I only stayed one night.

The hotel staff told us to stay in our rooms until summoned for lunch, dinner or to go on a tour. Every floor had a guard who collected the keys of everyone when we left the rooms for whatever purpose. There was no running hot water. I felt sure they watched our every move.

At 2 p.m. I got a call to assemble in the lobby for a tour around the city. I made sure I joined their free tour. It was a once in a life time view of Moscow. I could see the buildings I'd only seen in pictures.

More tourists entered the bus, and I recognized an American accent. I looked up when he passed my seat. His camera case bore his name, Phil Hauser, Redlands, CA.

If I get lost, I will run to this man, as Gerry Ford, his President, will look for him if he gets lost. The tour went well with no incidents.

Moscow was a great city, if only we could enjoy more of their artistical designs. No such luck.

The next morning we were herded at 5 a.m. to catch the plane at 10 a.m. The feeling that I was about to meet that special person was strong, but at the airport I had no clue who the person could be. People were swarming all over.

After retrieving my baggage, I searched for a push cart. I couldn't find one, until I saw the American from Redlands walking towards me with one.

I felt sure he wouldn't mind if I put my bags in his push cart (*remember, suitcases had no rollers then*). To attract his attention, I blocked his way. He had to stop. What else could he do? I looked up and with a smile asked, "Do you mind if I put my bags there?"

He looked at me, and for the first time acknowledged me as speaking English, and replied, "Be my guest."

The Russian Immigration allowed no mingling among tourists who had a visa and those who didn't. They processed me first because I had one.

Their visa was a document folded in two. When I entered Moscow, they ripped one part. They took the other part when departing. No one would ever know I had been to Moscow. Scary thought. I asked the officer to stamp my passport as a "souvenir."

The terminal was huge. I got organized, making sure I had everything I came in with. My beauty case was missing.

An hour later I saw the American enter the terminal. I stood up and with a big smile waved at him.

"Yoo hoo, I'm here." I waved at him.

He looked at me and held my beauty case high, "Is this yours?" he asked.

"Yes," I replied. We sat together.

"Phil Hauser," he said and we shook hands.

"Esther Kurniawan."

"Let's have breakfast. I've got a voucher," Phil said.

During breakfast we found out we were going to the same destination, London. We also agreed that the Russians had to improve the quality of their breakfast if they wanted to host the Olympics.

Time to board. Phil said, "Sit with me in the back."

"Why in the back?" I asked.

"You are riding an Illyushin airplane. In order for the plane to fly and lift off the ground, the front part should be lighter. After it's off the ground, then you can spread out and sit wherever you want. Sit in the back with me anyway."

I was mentally and physically exhausted with preparation, overtime work to have everything finished before departure, so I appreciated someone taking charge.

"All right," and I sat beside him.

The plane lifted off and soon we were 30,000 feet in the air, between Mosow and London, between the Heaven up above and the Earth down below..

Phil took off his seat belt and tried to continue reading his 'Kissinger' book.

"Oh no, buster. You asked me to sit with you and you want to read a book?"

But before I could ask him a question, out of the blue I heard a deep voice say, **"He's going to be your husband."**

I jumped from my seat and looked around, thinking someone was playing a trick on me. Nobody could match that voice. It was so clear, loaded with dignity. I looked at Phil reading his book, and asked him a stupid question, "Excuse me, how old are you?"...realizing I was 34 years old, and Phil looked like a student just graduated from college.

I looked up at the ceiling and said, "If he says 27 years old, I'll have to pass, Lord."

Phil looked up and said, "I am 31, why do you ask?"

"Oh, it's all right then. It is O.K.," I replied.

"What's all right? What's O.K.?" Phil asked again.

You'll be my husband. That's what. I'll betcha you will run down the aisle, and ask the stewardess to open the door so you can jump out of the plane without a parachute.

"Everything will be just... fine," I said calmly. I looked up at the ceiling again: *"OK, now what Father, he will be my husband...when?...in a week, a month or a year perhaps?*

That deep voice returned, "He is going to follow you all over Europe."

A feeling of peace came over me. The same feeling I have been familiar with over the years. The big heavy burden fell off my shoulders as I understood that my premonition had become a reality.

We learned to know each other better. Phil came from Redlands, CA, and his father Joel Hauser was a famous rockhound. He went to Redlands High School, and continued to UCLA where he graduated. His family had been devout Christians, and Phil was the number three son. Joel and Barbara Hauser had four sons.

Arriving in London, Phil took charge through Immigration and picked up the baggage; he shook hands with my cousin Kim. She extended a warm invitation to Phil to stay at her townhouse in Brentwood, Essex.

Scotland countryside was beautiful. Green meadows and lakes, hills and majestic castles reminded us of the era of King Arthur and Robin Hood. After a whirlwind trip through beautiful and cold Scotland by bus, with Phil following us by train, we returned to my cousin's house, where Phil proposed to take me home to the United States.

We married on May 12, 1976, three weeks after we met, in the tiny town of Brentwood, Essex, England. This time I made sure I got the blessings from my parents. We were celebrities of the little town.

However, God didn't stop there. "When HE leads you to it, HE will carry you through it."

"We need to get you an entry visa to the States," Phil said. The American Embassies in London, Amsterdam and Paris suggested I return to Jakarta, and apply from my home country. We would lose time and money. We tried one more time in Switzerland, a neutral country.

"Let's try there,." I said. "Apply first, then we'll continue our trip around Europe."

The American Consul was a young man in his thirties. He was new to his post in the Consular Section, and he had no experience with inter-racial marriages. He admitted it and apologized, but he was very helpful.

"The gentleman is covered with his passport, Ma'am, but I need to ask important documents from you to accompany the visa application. He gave me a list and assured me that "even though I would love to help you by using the diplomatic pouch, there is no way these documents can return on time before your departure to Jakarta, Indonesia, Mrs. Hauser." I liked the sound of *Mrs. Hauser*.

With the help of the Dow Chemical Office Staff I sent a telex to my boss, requesting the documents. I was scheduled to depart to Jakarta on June 30, 1976.

I said a short prayer for God to help me. "When God is for you, who can be against you?" God had arranged for this wedding to take place, and He will make sure I get the documents on time. My boss had changed, remember? He was of higher authority now.

There was nothing more we could do but wait, so we went on a trip to Spain, met my cousin Tom and he showed us Vienna, the castle of schonbrun, and on to Chamonix. We also took a river cruise down the River Rhine.

Upon our return, I called the Bern Office, and the Consul came on the phone.

"Mrs. Hauser, yes I remember. He paused as if he thought for a moment, and I heard shuffling of papers in the background. "Just a moment," he said. Footsteps fading away, a door closing, and a few minutes later, a door opened, faster footsteps, and, "I can't believe it. They are here," he said. "Come back in three days, I'll have them ready for you."

I told Phil, "You'd better believe it. God is watching. As a woman of 34 years old, I can marry anyone without my parents' consent. However, since I had hurt them so much in 1969, I will have a church wedding in Jakarta for their sake. I don't want people to talk behind our backs. I owed it to them." It was a wedding already blessed by the Lord Almighty.

I received my entry visa in Jakarta within three days after I submitted the package in July.

The quest for a bridal gown continued from one disappointment to another, as many salons rejected the order. "What? Two weeks to get married? Not possible, ma'am. We need at least three months." From the most expensive to the simplest salon, all shook their heads. July was still the favorite month for weddings, and they were booked solid.

As a last resort, my sister-in-law said, "Sis, let's try my seamstress. She could do it for you if I asked her."

"All right, let's go," I said. "No harm in trying."

"I like you a lot, but I can't do this in two weeks," was Sheila's answer to my sister-in-law. Oh well! We tried.

As I walked out of the salon, I glanced at a picture by the exit, on a decorated table.

"Sheila, who is this man? Wait, let me tell you. His name is Richard. His father was the principal of a school near China Town."

Sheila's eyes were big when she looked at me. "You know my husband?" she asked.

"Yes, he sat behind me in sixth grade." Bingo, I got my wedding dress.

The quest for a bridal cake met with similar challenges. Not enough time. As a last resort, I asked my sister to meet with her baking teacher. "I'm sure she can bake a wedding cake for me," I said.

"Sure, she could. However, she died three years ago." We both sighed.

"Who died?" Phil asked. He arrived on July 10, 1976, from Bangkok to join me in the preparation.

"My sister's baking teacher. I'm asking her for help to find a baker for our wedding cake," I said.

"Actually, her son was the best Master Chef," Tina said. "He got his degree from Germany and he lives there now. What a pity." We both sighed.

"Let's look for her daughter, Tina," I said. "Certainly the daughter can follow in her mother's footsteps. All I need is a simple wedding cake."

"Good idea," my sister said, and she left.

What if she couldn't find her? What other alternative did I have?

Tina returned an hour later. "You wouldn't believe who I found there," she said.

"Who? The daughter? Can she bake the cake for me?"

"The son was there, the Master Chef. He had a week's vacation, and decided to return home. He is happy to bake the cake for you."

Halleluyah! Instead of a simple wedding cake, I got a beautiful and delicious three-tiered wedding cake baked by a Master Chef. He returned to Germany the day after our church wedding on July 17, 1976.

God had walked us through all the tiny details.

"I will send my son from the West to meet my daughter from the East... and I'm planting a tree..." The tree he planted had now become a strong tree.

On July 23, 1976, I flew with my soul mate Phil to the United States of America.

The hollow sound of a big wooden door closed in the background of my mind, and a new era unfolded for Mrs. Esther Kurniawan-Hauser.

To be Continued...

Epilogue

In Chapter 39, 'When Muhammad doesn't come to the mountain,' I shared my serious skin problems. I prayed for a doctor, as I couldn't return to Jakarta to visit a dermatologist.

One remark from a writer caught my attention. "Why not just pray for a cure?" Perhaps much better than praying for a doctor?"

I had to sit and mull over this remark for a while, as I always do when I need to improve the contents of my writing. Was it a challenge to my faith, or was it a mockery to the Lord? Or, perhaps, what's the purpose of the story?

A bright light turned on in my mind. The simple question became the answer to the whole story of faith and miracles. Perhaps that's the reason why God bestowed on me my miracles, because I believed without asking questions. I followed, like a child holding her Father's hands. I let Him lead.

God was there fifty years ago, and God had answered the current question fifty years ago. I didn't know my story would trigger a question like "Why not just pray for a cure?" But God did. He knew that fifty years in the future, someone would ask that question. So He provided my story with the answer.

When the doctor came to the island, he didn't know about my skin problems. He wanted to give back by helping someone, anyone, and he found me.

In his hand, he brought a cure. An ointment that he wanted to test for potency. What better way than trying it on a person who really needed that help? I became a tool for the doctor to help many other people with skin problems.

We didn't know that a question "Why not just pray for a cure?" would emerge. God did.

This simple question has become the answer to the whole story. God existed then, and still exists in the present.

"Why not just pray for a cure?" I asked God for a doctor; He gave me a doctor *with* a cure.

About the Author

Esther Kurniawan-Hauser was born and raised in Jakarta, Indonesia. Her passion for languages came through her parents, who spoke Dutch, Indonesian and English. She earned a B.A. in English from the Christian University of Indonesia in Jakarta.

Her strong knowledge of the language allowed her to work with top management of several international companies as their Executive Secretary. She had enjoyed working for an Inter-Continental Hotel in Bali, received training in all aspects of banking while at the Chase Manhattan Bank, and received an award for helping open the Dow Chemical Representative's office in Jakarta as their Regional Manager's Secretary.

While vacationing in Europe, she met her soul mate, Phil Hauser, in Moscow. They married three weeks later in England. After traveling throughout Europe, they settled in Los Angeles.

Esther started a new career in real estate and loans while raising their three sons, and became a Real Estate broker and loan specialist of her own company. She loves reading and pursues the fascinating craft of writing. She is currently writing her second book.

www.againstthewindbooks.com

Made in the USA
San Bernardino, CA
22 May 2019